## PRAISE FOR *CYBERSECURITY FOR BUSINESS*

Cybersecurity is national security. The only way to effectively protect ourselves is through a collective defense model. *Cybersecurity for Business* describes the roles and responsibilities individuals across an organization must take in this new age to work together to protect their enterprise and in so doing contribute to our nation's defense.

**Gen (Ret) Keith Alexander, former head of US Cyber Command. Co-CEO, IronNet Cybersecurity, Inc.**

In a literary landscape awash with lifeless and tiresome cybersecurity "how-to" books, *Cybersecurity for Business* is a bonfire of wisdom for leaders who desire to be part of the executive decision-making team in their organization. Co-authored by an extraordinary group of global leaders and luminaries, with topics as diverse as "managing" your board of directors, developing key interorganizational relationships, and aligning business goals to cybersecurity, among others, this book will find a home on the desk of leaders and managers across the cybersecurity community.

**Mark Weatherford, former Deputy Undersecretary for Cybersecurity at the US Department of Homeland Security and Chief Security Officer at AlertEnterprise**

*Cybersecurity for Business* is one of the few books that recognizes that cybersecurity is not just a technology issue—it's a strategy issue and a leadership issue. Here you'll find excellent and timely guidance that will help leaders around the company and around the world do their part to succeed in an environment of cyber risk.

**Daniel Dobrygowski, Head of Governance and Trust, World Economic Forum**

This ISA book on cybersecurity risk management hits the mark and enables organizations to contextualize cyber risk to financial, operational and business outcomes. These core principles align to the heightened expectations across the regulatory (SEC), investor, risk management and boardroom communities.

**Chris Hetner, Former Senior Cybersecurity Advisor to the SEC Chair and Special Advisor for Cyber Risk to the NACD**

Leadership and management of cyber risk continues to evolve. Beyond just C-Suites and IT departments, this book brings the total organization—HR, PR, Finance, Legal Compliance, Marketing, etc.—into sharp focus. Cybersecurity is a team sport that must address leadership, management, and the culture of security throughout the entire business enterprise. *Cybersecurity for Business* sets the principles and de facto standard for modern cyber risk management.

**Harry D. Raduege, Jr. Lieutenant General, USAF (Ret). Chief Executive Officer, National Cybersecurity Center**

*Cybersecurity for Business* tracks the principles we recommend our colleges and universities follow to enhance their own cyber risk resilience. As such, it's an excellent book for graduate and undergraduate courses in cyber, and its use will help create a more coherent, secure and sustainable digital environment.

**Henry Stoever, President and CEO, Association of Governing Boards (US Colleges and Universities)**

The aspect of *Cybersecurity for Business* that compelled me to adopt it as my textbook for Columbia's Enterprise Cyber Threats and Defenses course, K5301, is the holistic approach taken to defense of complex networks. As demonstrated by the impact of Hurricane Katrina on New Orleans, disaligned localized defenses cannot withstand systematic attacks on complex multi-part networks. Even a single point of failure in an otherwise robust entity "perimeter" renders the entire entity vulnerable. Because there is no security thru obscurity, the only sustainable cyber defense is one architected top-down.

**Corey Hirsch, CISO, Teledyne**

*Cybersecurity for Business* outlines a model any business should consider to align its technical systems with proper management to strengthen its cyber resilience. Besides serving as a guide to better manage cyberattacks this book provides confirmation of our security program and the approach we've taken. Additionally, it reinforces concepts we routinely share with partners, customers, and other stakeholders across our ecosystems. What I like most is that it offers practical advice with a robust list of references for readers to dive even deeper into the various topics.

Jon Brickey, Senior Vice President, Cybersecurity Evangelist, Mastercard

Despite the deluge of cyberattack headlines, too often boards of directors remain focused on how they should be preparing for the next inevitable breach, rather than thinking proactively about their cybersecurity oversight responsibilities. *Cybersecurity for Business* is an invaluable guide for directors and executives at organizations of all sizes to better understand the business, legal, and technical dimensions of cybersecurity risk management, and how to optimize corporate governance to meet the challenges posed by multifaceted cyber threats. I consider it required reading for everyone interested in safeguarding their critical systems, supply chains, employees, and customers.

Professor Scott J. Shackelford, JD, PhD, Chair, Indiana University Cybersecurity Risk Management Program

Larry Clinton's *Cybersecurity for Business* is the first comprehensive, practical, strategic and tactical guide to this rapidly evolving and constantly challenging subject that fits the bill of both business and academia. Indeed, it is exactly what I have been looking for as someone who both advises boards and management on strategic cyber risk management and governance and as a cyber-professor teaching a course on "Cyber Leadership, Risk Oversight and Resilience" at NYU where it will become my core textbook for future semesters. This is an outstanding contribution because it is written by people with true and tried direct experience on the front lines—indeed on the bleeding edge—of this ever-evolving threat and opportunity matrix and incorporates some of the groundbreaking risk governance work that Larry and the Internet Security Alliance have been doing for years with the NACD, the World Economic Forum and a number of leading industry associations around the world. And, finally, it goes beyond other publications by looking at the bigger

systemic cyber-picture including the role of culture, economics, governance and how all the strategic and tactical dots interconnect. Kudos to Larry and his team—they really made it happen!
Andrea Bonime-Blanc, Founder and CEO, GEC Risk Advisory

Regardless of industry—whether it is agriculture, aviation or health care—organizations are all increasingly susceptible to cyberattacks, and businesses need to adapt accordingly. *Cybersecurity for Business* provides the tools for business and IT leaders alike to successfully navigate through this new reality.
Richard Rocca, CISO, Bunge

I had the pleasure to spend some time today with this wonderful book and I must say that it is rare for a new volume to provide such excellent guidance on cyber for the working manager and practitioner. I particularly loved chapters 2 and 9, and I hope board members and executives everywhere invest the time to absorb this book's fine contents.
Ed Amoroso, Former CISO, AT&T

As an early advocate of enterprise risk management, I have seen the significant business value from better quantifying and integrating strategic, operational, and financial risks. Cybersecurity cannot be managed effectively as a silo given its critical business and risk interdependencies. This practical book will help any organization break down that silo and address cybersecurity as a strategic, enterprise risk issue.
James C. Lam, President, James Lam & Associates; Chair of the Board, Recology; Chair of the Audit Committee, RiskLens; Author, *Implementing Enterprise Risk Management*

Today all businesses, large and small, will eventually find themselves the target of sophisticated cyberattacks. Companies need to account for and adapt to this reality, especially as we all rely more on technology and data to drive our businesses. *Cybersecurity for Business* provides specific guidance for directors down to the front lines of IT, that, if followed, can place a company in a far better position to be armed and prepared for the inevitable cyberattack.
Kevin Mandia, CEO, Mandiant

*Cybersecurity for Business* is one of those rare practical books for businesses that can help large, medium and small companies manage the ongoing and unavoidable cyber risks now facing all industries. The threats facing manufacturers and all firms compound by the day, so learning these lessons now is crucial.

**Jay Timmons, President and CEO, National Association of Manufacturers**

Utilities have been hit hard by hackers during the past few years, creating a need to balance risk with the demands of the new economics of the digital world. I cannot recommend *Cybersecurity for Business* enough. It helps organizations evaluate security for an enterprise wide perspective consistent with the economics required to maintain effective service.

**Ryan Boulais, Chief Information Security Officer, The AES Corporation**

*Cybersecurity for Business* takes the complicated and ever-changing world of data security and technology and offers a remarkably cogent collection of guidance from industry experts. The result is a practical and wide-ranging text and a powerful tool for keeping businesses safe.

**Preet Bharara, former US Attorney for the Southern District of New York, Distinguished Scholar in Residence at NYU School of Law, CNN Senior Legal Analyst, author of the NYT best-selling *Doing Justice*, and host of *Stay Tuned with Preet***

# Cybersecurity for Business

*Organization-Wide Strategies to Ensure Cyber Risk is Not Just an IT Issue*

Larry Clinton

KoganPage

First published in Great Britain and the United States in 2022 by Kogan Page Limited

Apart from any fair dealing for the purposes of research or private study, or criticism or review, as permitted under the Copyright, Designs and Patents Act 1988, this publication may only be reproduced, stored or transmitted, in any form or by any means, with the prior permission in writing of the publishers, or in the case of reprographic reproduction in accordance with the terms and licenses issued by the CLA. Enquiries concerning reproduction outside these terms should be sent to the publishers at the undermentioned addresses:

| | | |
|---|---|---|
| 2nd Floor, 45 Gee Street | 8 W 38th Street, Suite 902 | 4737/23 Ansari Road |
| London | New York, NY 10018 | Daryaganj |
| EC1V 3RS | USA | New Delhi 110002 |
| United Kingdom | | India |

www.koganpage.com

Kogan Page books are printed on paper from sustainable forests.

© Larry Clinton, 2022

The right of Larry Clinton to be identified as the author of this work has been asserted by him in accordance with the Copyright, Designs and Patents Act 1988.
Carter Zhou would like to indicate that the views he expresses in this book are personal and based on research carried out during his tenure as a Research Associate at the ISA.

**ISBNs**

Hardback    978 1 3986 0638 8
Paperback   978 1 3986 0614 2
Ebook       978 1 3986 0639 5

**British Library Cataloguing-in-Publication Data**

A CIP record for this book is available from the British Library.

**Library of Congress Control Number**

2022931798

Typeset by Integra Software Services, Pondicherry
Print production managed by Jellyfish
Printed and bound by CPI Group (UK) Ltd, Croydon CR0 4YY

# CONTENTS

# Foreword: Guidance through the Gray

PETER GLEASON, PRESIDENT AND CEO, NATIONAL ASSOCIATION
OF CORPORATE DIRECTORS

When it comes to ambiguity and risk, few leaders are better acquainted with the challenge of providing sound advice than the directors of companies across the globe. As members of organizations like NACD and the Internet Security Alliance (ISA) seek guidance on how to oversee the threat of cyber-attacks and govern their organizations accordingly, they are having to reckon with an increasing range of shades of gray—in how to respond, whom to alert, and what can be done to secure against this existential risk.

In a December 2020 blog post Elizabeth Braw, a visiting fellow at the American Enterprise Institute, pointed to North Korean state-sponsored hackers' theft of data from one of the companies involved in Project Warp Speed as committing "grayzone" warfare. A quick search of the term reveals some disagreement among foreign policy and security researchers on how to define this term, but one thing's for certain: cyberattacks are one of many, and possibly the best, tools in the grayzone for wreaking havoc on enterprises operating in the traditionally borderless world of the internet. In a world where, for instance, life-saving vaccines and critical supply chains are developed collaboratively and across borders in the cloud, bad actors of all types have the power to cause significant harm to people and enterprises.

Meanwhile, despite efforts to secure sensitive data and respond to the regulations of varying nation-states, trust is waning internationally in institutions like national governments and corporations that are tasked with data and network security. According to a Pew Research survey conducted in June 2019 of people living in the United States, 66% noted that the risks outweigh the benefits of sharing data with government. The same cohort reported even greater mistrust of corporations. 81% of those surveyed said that the risks of allowing companies to collect their data outweighed the possible benefits.

Business, government, and society are no doubt at a crossroads. According to the World Economic Forum's 2020 Global Risk Report, in one direction is the economic and human promise of the fourth industrial revolution and all that the associated technologies can bring to bear. In the other direction is increased geopolitical tensions caused by grayzone tactics, the possibility of a fragmented internet brought about by reactions of embattled nation-states, and resultant stifled innovation where great promise once existed. The Forum's 2021 report found that geopolitical fragmentation has indeed led to an increase on cyberattacks. If our institutions continue to operate out of lockstep with accepted governance principles, cyberattacks may continue to grow in breadth and severity.

The partnership between NACD and ISA to develop a global set of cyber-security principles nudges along on the right path the institutions overseeing this ever-changing risk. This book takes these principles, discussed in greater depth in chapter 2, and extends them to the management level. It provides guidance on specific processes that current and aspiring corporate executives should enact in their specific domains, all in order to fulfill their boards' expectations for sound management of the complicated, ever-growing challenge of enterprise cyber risks.

Please dig into the principles discussed in this volume and prepare to apply them and advocate for them in your boardrooms and beyond. The principles aim to make cyber-governance more affordable, streamlined, transparent, and accountable for companies, vendors, and other stakeholders to operationalize. There's time left yet to define, in black-and-white terms, the way forward through the gray.

Onward.

# PREFACE

This book is essentially a companion document for corporate managers enabling them to better understand and align their activities with the growing expectations of boards of directors as they work to manage their organization's cyber risks.

Starting in 2014, and continuing through the date of publication and beyond, organizations representing corporate directors from around the world have been engaged in programs to better understand and articulate the role of the board in overseeing cyber risk. These efforts have resulted in a series of cyber risk handbooks created by these organizations in partnership with Internet Security Alliance (ISA). The current volume has been written by the board of directors of the ISA.

The handbooks are now available on four continents in five different languages. While each of the handbooks was uniquely adapted to the specific needs, culture, and structure of the various regions represented, they all endorsee the same core principles for boards to conduct their oversight responsibilities regarding cyber risk.

As will be discussed on greater detail in Chapter 2, these handbooks are available in five languages and have been endorsed by a wide range of directors, organizations, and governments on four continents. Moreover, the effectiveness of the principles outlined in these handbooks have been independently attested to by PWC in their Global Information Security Survey. As such, these principles are increasingly becoming the standard expectation for business executives to meet as they seek to manage the growing cyber risks organizations face.

This book takes the principles which boards are using to oversee cyber risk and retarget them down to the executive level. This book begins with reconceptualizing the nature of the cyber threat. While the traditional focus on cyber threats has been to focus, almost exclusively on technical operations, this book demonstrates that cyber risk is increasingly being thought of as a strategic business issue. Although technical operations remain an important consideration in managing cyber risk, the economic aspects of cybersecurity are increasingly becoming critical element of understanding how organizations are engaging in digital transformation.

We then proceed to describe how corporations are evolving dynamic new structures to create multi-dimensional cyber risk teams that enable an enterprise-wide, as opposed to an IT-centric, approach to cybersecurity. Based on this evolving board appreciation of cyber risk from a business perspective and corporate structural reforms we proceed to describe how cyber risk assessments are—and need to—evolve, enabling cyber risk to be understood in an empirical and economic basis.

Consistent with this emerging enterprise-wide appreciation of cyber risk management, we then discuss how cyber risk now needs to become a factor in a wide range of corporate roles and functions. This includes the role of technical operations, but also includes a description of how functions as broad as human resources, legal, supply chain, audit, M and A, external communications and crisis management now must include a cyber risk analysis. We conclude by discussing how the relationships between these previously disparate functions now need to develop to facilitate the enterprise-wide model of cyber risk management which boards are coming to expect.

# ABOUT THE AUTHORS

**Internet Security Alliance** provides thought leadership in cybersecurity and works with the US government to advocate for public policy that will advance the interests of cybersecurity.

**Larry Clinton** is President and CEO of the Internet Security Alliance. He advises industry and government on cyber policy and regularly appears in the media to provide an expert opinion. He has briefed NATO, the Organization of American States (OAS), G-20, and the US Congress. He has twice been named to the NACD 'Directorship 100' list of the most influential individuals in corporate governance.

# 01

# Cybersecurity is (Not) an IT Issue

BY LARRY CLINTON, PRESIDENT AND CEO, INTERNET SECURITY ALLIANCE,
AND CARTER ZHENG, ISA RESEARCH ASSOCIATE

## Five Key Ideas to Take Away from This Chapter

1 Organizations have made little progress in addressing cyber risk in large part because they have viewed the issue with an excessively narrow focus as just a technical/operational issue.

2 To compete in the modern economy, enterprises must engage in digital transformation.

3 Digital transformation can generate a substantial increase in growth and profitability but can also vastly increase risk.

4 Foundational technical security measures are necessary, but alone are not sufficient to address cyber threats. Cybersecurity must be an enterprise-wide risk management issue.

5 Organizations cannot completely secure themselves, but they can manage their cyber risk with appropriate understanding, structure, investment, and risk-management methods.

## Introduction

One of the most incontrovertible facts in the field of cybersecurity is that the attack community is winning the battle for cyberspace—and winning by a large and growing margin.

In February 2020, the Executive Director of the World Economic Forum's Cybersecurity Center, Troels Oerting, addressed the G-20's Digital Economy Working Group in Riyadh, Saudi Arabia and reported that cybercrime in the previous year had cost the world's economy $2 trillion. The WEF estimated that the losses will increase to $6 trillion in three years.[1]

The G-20 is a group of the world's largest economies. Although the cybercrime nation does not have a GDP, the damages from cybercrime as a whole rank equivalently to the GDP of the top 10 G-20 countries—just ahead of the United Kingdom.[2]

There are a number of reasons why cybercrime is such an enormous and growing problem, but none is more fundamental than the fact that the cybersecurity issue is wildly misunderstood. Most governments, enterprises, and individuals think of cybersecurity as a technical or IT problem. That is a misnomer. Cybersecurity is an enterprise-wide risk management issue. Obviously, technology is an important part of that issue, but it is not the only part of the issue—perhaps not even the most important part.

According to the *Cyber Risk Oversight Handbook* published by the National Association of Corporate Directors (NACD):

> Historically, many companies and organizations categorized information security as a technical or operational issue to be handled by the information technology (IT) department. This misunderstanding was fed by siloed operating structures that left functions and business units within the organization feeling disconnected from responsibility for the security of their own data. Instead, this critical responsibility was handed off to IT, a department that in most organizations is strapped for resources and budget authority. Furthermore, deferring responsibility to IT inhibited critical analysis of—and communication about—security issues, and hampered the adoption of effective, organization-wide security strategies.[3]

Consequently, the vast majority of initiatives designed to address cybersecurity concerns are technical and operational, and the individuals selected to manage the problem are almost always IT specialists.

The result of this historic pattern was revealed in a recent study by EY, one of the Big-4 audit firms:

> 77% of organizations are still operating with only limited cybersecurity and resilience [against cyber threats], while 87% of organizations warn they do not yet have sufficient budget to provide the levels of cybersecurity and resilience they want.[4]

## Why we are not Making Progress in Securing Cyberspace

While this traditional, largely tactical approach to cybersecurity needs to be part of a comprehensive cyber risk management program, it is insufficient to create a resilient organization. The reality is that cybersecurity is not just an IT issue. It needs to be understood as a strategic, enterprise risk, not just as an IT risk.

There are multiple different types of risks that poor cybersecurity can generate: loss of data, corruption of data, blackmail, damage to the organization's reputation as well as legal and compliance risks. The responsibility for managing these cyber-related risks extends throughout the organization. For example, many studies have shown that half, or more, of cyber breaches are caused by human failure—the realm of the HR department—not technical breakdowns. The defining characteristic of the internet is a broad interconnection between vendors, partners, customers, etc. These relationships are typically defined by contracts or service agreements, which means it is the legal department—perhaps in tandem with a separate vendor management team—who may be the nexus of the cybersecurity issue. When (not if) cyber breaches occur, most enterprises are rightly concerned with the reputational impacts of the breach. So, managing the cybersecurity risk at this stage is largely a function of the communications/PR department.

Unfortunately, relationships between the cybersecurity function and other critical elements of the business are often fraught with misunderstanding and mistrust. A 2020 survey by EY found that, in most organizations, there was a systemic failure in communication between the cybersecurity function and the business units. For example, EY found that in 74% of organizations the relationship between the cybersecurity function and marketing department was characterized as—at best—neutral to mistrustful or non-existent. Nearly half of HR departments characterized their relationship with the cybersecurity function the same way, as did R and D departments and finance departments.[5]

In short, cybersecurity is everyone's responsibility. But, as the old saying goes: to a hammer, everything looks like a nail. If an organization views cybersecurity as essentially a technical issue and vests cyber risk management solely with the IT departments, it is going to get primarily IT solutions that are unlikely to be sufficient to address their full cyber risk.

As another old saying goes: if you ask the wrong questions, you get the wrong answers. To better assure that an organization is asking the right questions about cybersecurity, the organization's leaders need to understand that cybersecurity is not going to be handled by the IT guys. Cybersecurity needs to be understood and managed comprehensively as an integral element of the organization's business and mission.

ESI ThoughtLab completed a study of over a thousand companies in early 2020, concluding that to reduce risk probabilities Chief Information Security Officers (CISOs) must go well beyond compliance with technical frameworks.[6] Cybersecurity leaders need to integrate these technical frameworks into their business goals, strategies, and individual risk profiles.

## Digital Transformation Makes Cybersecurity a Business Issue

One of the most important questions enterprises face in the 21st century is how they can balance the economic imperative for digital transformation with the substantial cybersecurity risks that come with such transformation.

Melissa Hathaway, the Chief Cybersecurity Advisor for both President George W Bush and President Obama, noted that:

> Corporations have embraced, adopted and embedded information and communication technology into their network environments and infrastructures and realized phenomenal business and economic growth through improved services increased productivity and reduced costs… Yet this digital transformation underpinned by affordable communications and cheap devices has introduced new risks.[7]

The NACD Cyber Risk Handbook points out that in the past 25 years, the nature of corporate asset value has changed significantly, shifting away from the physical and toward the virtual.[8] This rapid digitization of corporate assets has resulted in a corresponding transformation of strategies and business models—as well as the digitization of corporate risk. Organizations are taking advantage of entirely new ways to connect with customers and suppliers, engage with employees and improve the efficiency and effectiveness of internal processes.

---

NOT ALL DATA IS OF THE SAME VALUE—PROTECT THE *CROWN JEWELS*

Corporations can now amass both enormous amounts of data and an enormous number of data types, and virtually all of this data is at risk. However, when companies assess cybersecurity risks, it is erroneous to assume all assets are created equal and therefore need to be protected in the same way. Each company has a distinct set of crown jewel data (the data most critical to the organization's mission) to protect. For instance, the customer data associated with credit card information is of greater value than the invoice numbers that companies generate in-house. Companies do not have endless resources to protect all data at any cost, and yet most deploy one-size-fits-all cybersecurity strategies.[9] In Chapter 4 we will discuss how a modern, sophisticated cyber risk assessment can differentiate between these different types of data and assign appropriate, cost-effective security measures.

For several years it has been fashionable to talk of disruptive technologies that generate innovative and productive business models. Enterprises have been quick to build the benefits of the digital age into their business plans, such as expanding markets globally, reducing operating costs, establishing new strategic partnerships, or enhancing the worker experience by enabling business through mobile and remote locations.

However, organizations have been far slower to appreciate the downside of the digital revolution. The unhappy reality is that while digital transformation stimulates growth and profitability, it can often undermine security. This can put personal consumer data, proprietary intellectual property, corporate reputation, and even critical services vital to collective national security at risk. For example, many technologies, such as mobile communications, cloud computing, and "smart" devices, can yield significant cost savings and business efficiencies, but they can also create major security concerns if implemented haphazardly.

One recent study found that 83% of directors said they would support management undertaking potentially disruptive innovation projects if they have the potential to increase long-term value, even if they create additional risks.[10] A region-wide example of this is in Latin America, where there has been widespread adoption of mobile communication platforms (particularly in financial services), in an effort to boost urgently needed economic development.[11] However, this quick adoption has led the sector to experience major breaches, as much of the technology being implemented does not have the proper security controls in place.

Studies by the Organization of American States (OAS) among others have shown that cybersecurity now ranks at the top of the list of risks to Latin American markets, with Brazil, Argentina, and Mexico ranking as 3rd, 8th, and 10th place respectively in global rankings of the country of origin for cyber-attacks.[12] Ransomware alone has increased in Latin America by as much as 131% since 2016.

Similarly, trends in business practices stimulated by digitalization such as BYOD (bring your own device), 24/7 access to information, the growth of sophisticated Big Data analytics, and the use of long, international supply chains may be so cost-effective that they are functionally required for a business to remain competitive. However, these practices, if not properly integrated into the entirety of the business model, can also dramatically weaken the security of the organization. We will discuss these threats in detail in Chapter 8.

## The New Frontier: Artificial Intelligence (AI) and Attacks that Learn

One of the most promising business enablers now being realized is the integration of Artificial Intelligence (AI) into business processes. Organizations in virtually all industry sectors are looking for—and implementing—these enhanced technologies to create new efficiencies and promote profit and growth. However, at the same time, AI-enabled attacks have the potential to vastly increase cyber risk. With its ability to learn and adapt, AI will transform cybercrime by allowing assailants to execute more personalized and insidious attacks. This quickly changing cyber environment is creating an ever more dynamic threat picture demanding a multi-dimensional full enterprise approach to cybersecurity.

AI attacks are unique in that when they penetrate a system, they obtain information on the defense system and evolve to counter accordingly. These attempts do not always work on the first try, but because of the knowledge they gain, they are often fruitful in succeeding attempts.[13]

A McKinsey report suggests that by 2030, AI could generate $13 trillion for the global economy per year, which means that the profit margin for cybercrime will also grow exponentially.[14]

The World Economic Forum's recent report assessing AI as the latest weapon to be used in cybercrime noted that:

> Cybercriminals are adept at adopting any techniques or innovations that give
> them an edge over cybersecurity defenses. Early case studies and research
> indicates where defenders are already seeing the earliest impact: defending
> against 'strong' AI—where criminals use systems that operate, think and act as

humans—and against 'weak' or 'narrow' AI—where systems are modelled on human behavior to execute specific tasks. Given its potential uses, AI is expected to drive systemic changes in the cybersecurity landscape and will create key challenges in cybersecurity in the near future.[15]

Although there is a trend of heightened awareness of AI risks among corporate executives, few leaders have had enough working knowledge to associate AI risks with the full scope of societal, economic, and organizational risks they pose. As a result, executives often trust the company's risk-mitigation capabilities and appoint IT specialists to do that.[16] This one-dimensional view of AI is likely to prove counter-productive given the broad impacts these newer technologies will have on an overall organization. Companies with a better awareness of cyber-risk are more likely to adopt some form of the multi-dimensional risk management structures (as discussed in Chapter 3) that can broaden the perspective of the necessary balance between growth and risk. This will lead to a more sustainable, AI-enabled, business model.

Leading executives will recognize that cybersecurity is an integral element in the critical and often highly challenging transformations that their companies are undertaking to grow and compete in the digital age. The EY 2020 survey found that:

> Board members view technology disruption as the greatest strategic opportunity for organizations and are seizing this opportunity by undergoing a technological transformation. This requires the CISO, the board, the C-suite and the business units to work together even more closely so they can embed cybersecurity at a much earlier stage of new business initiatives creating a culture of security by design.[17]

This means that key questions regarding digital transformation are no longer limited to how technological innovation can enable business processes, but rather how to balance major digital transformations with effective management of the inherent cyber risk that can compromise the enterprise's long-term strategic interests.

Proper management of this difficult (and often frictional) balance begins with understanding that cyber risk is not limited to narrow technical domains but stretches throughout the enterprise and directly impacts key business outcomes. Management teams need to acknowledge the tension between the need for strategic innovation—increasingly fueled by digital transformation—and the imperatives of preserving security and trust. This broader, strategic, element clearly needs to involve the IT experts, but almost certainly outstrips their expertise in areas that must be considered in order to develop a coherent and sustainable business model in the digital age.

With sophisticated management and adequate resources, it is possible for organizations to defend themselves while staying competitive and maintaining profitability. However, successful cybersecurity cannot simply be bolted on at the end of business processes. It needs to be woven into an organization's key systems, processes and culture from end to end—and when done successfully it can help build competitive advantage.

Richard Clarke and Robert Knake observed in their recent book *The Fifth Domain* that:

> Corporations can now achieve a fairly high level of cybersecurity if they spend enough, deploy state of the art IT and cyber solutions and adopt the right policies and procedures.[18]

The key is determining what are the right policies and solutions and assessing the cost of these mechanisms within the context of a specific entity's business plan.

---

IT'S NOT JUST ABOUT SPENDING

Many companies falsely assume that the more they spend on cybersecurity, the better position they are in. In reality it can actually be counter-productive to increase budget on every aspect of cybersecurity within the organization just to improve the maturity level.[19] Similarly, companies typically decide cybersecurity budgeting based on benchmarking with their peers to assess how much is needed to close specific gaps, rather than evaluating the effectiveness of their programs.[20] Instead, companies should embrace a modernized risk-based approach (as we will detail in Chapter 4) that quantifies cyber risks into empirical measurements just as approachable as financial and regulatory risks.

---

## Why Balancing Business Growth, Profitability and Cybersecurity is Difficult

Cybersecurity cannot be considered in a vacuum. Organizations must strike the appropriate balance between protecting the security of the organization and mitigating downside losses while continuing to ensure profitability and growth in a competitive environment.

Leading companies view cyber risks in the same way they do other critical risks—in terms of a risk-reward trade-off. However, this approach is challenging for two reasons. First, the complexity of cyber threats has grown dramatically and continues to evolve. Corporations now face increasingly sophisticated threats that outstrip traditional defenses, and threat actors have become more diverse; including not only cybercriminals but also ideologically motivated hacktivists and nation-states. At the same time, the competitive need to deploy new and emerging technologies in order to lower costs, improve customer service, and drive innovation is stronger than ever. As we have illustrated, adopting these technological innovations and capabilities may offer strong returns but can also increase cyber risk. Properly deployed, they could increase security, but only at a cost. Management must find methods to determine what is the appropriate cost in relation to the organization's risk appetites determined by the business plan. Traditional, IT-centric cyber risk assessment methods were inadequate to this task. However, as will be detailed subsequently, new methods are being developed that are far better suited to integrating cyber risk assessment with the organization's mission, and doing so on an empirical basis.

Cybersecurity discussions can no longer be treated as disembodied appendage issues that can be tacked on to the end of a board meeting as an extension of the IT report. In the digital age, there is virtually no substantial business decision that does not have a cybersecurity component. If the enterprise is considering a merger or acquisition, they will be jamming together two or more highly complex information systems. The chances for opening massive new vulnerabilities exposing intellectual property or consumer data is substantial. If the company is innovating a new product that is only cost effective through use of long international supply chains, then the cybersecurity practices not just of the core businesses but of the partners along the supply line—extending to the second and third tiers of the chain—need to be considered. If the bright, new millennial and gen-z workforces are to be recruited and retained, human resources may stress the need to develop better policies for BYOD (bring your own device). New Internet of Things (IoT), and other cutting-edge products may need to have cybersecurity built in at the R&D stage and carried through fabrication, manufacture and even marketing.

## The COVID-19 Pandemic: Cyber-Enabled Business and Increased Risk

The worldwide COVID-19 pandemic which started in late 2019 created the largest and fastest transformation to how work is done in history. It also further complicated the cyber risk situation.[21] Prior to the pandemic roughly 20% of the US workforce worked occasionally from home, and virtually overnight 80% switched to online platforms as a necessary step to maintain viability.[22]

PwC's *Digital Trust Insights Pulse Survey*—essentially an after-action report on the first responses to the COVID-19 pandemic—found that:

> The digital economy propped up the whole economy when businesses shuttered workplaces during the coronavirus outbreak.[23]

A much larger survey taken by ESI ThoughtLab confirmed the PwC findings:

> Even before COVID-19 hit, firms saw malware phishing and password reuse as the largest risks. But the crisis has upped the stakes. As consumers rely more on remote working—often on less secure devices and connections.[24]

The mounting use of technology, another byproduct of COVID-19, also took its toll. A CrowdStrike study revealed that 56% of people were now working from home due to the virus, with 60% using their personal devices for work.[25] Cyber intrusions were already up in Q1 of 2020 (with twice as many attacks occurring as in all of 2019), and the report anticipated that attacks would significantly rise throughout 2020. The FBI reported that cyber-attacks—many using COVID-19 as a lure—were up by nearly 200% within weeks of the virus hitting the US.[26]

The pandemic—coming on top of the existing technological and business model changes—has ushered in an entirely new approach to cybersecurity. In the wake of the pandemic, PwC reported that 98% of Chief Security Officers are changing their cybersecurity strategies.[27]

## The Cybersecurity Problem is Serious and Getting Worse Fast

The statistics from the World Economic Forum on the extent of cyber-crime cited at the beginning of this chapter are among those on the high end,[28] with some projections predicting that the financial impact of cyber-crime could rise to as much as $10.5 trillion a year by 2025.[29]

To be fair, calculating the precise economic impact of cybercrime is extremely difficult because we are probably not aware of most cyber-attacks until well after they occur—if at all. It is extremely difficult to calculate the actual economic impact of stolen (usually digitally copied) intellectual property, and even when enterprises discover attacks they are often not reported publicly.

However, even more modest estimates suggest stunning economic costs from cyber-attacks. Figure 1.1 illustrates how costs from cybercrime estimated by the WEF compare with revenues of the world's top industrial nations. More modest estimates suggest annual revenues from cybercrime are comparable to nations such as Sweden, Poland and Belgium.[30] Even with the more modest estimates, the revenues cyber-criminal entities generate are comparable to a major industrial nation.

Calculating the financial impact of successful cyber-attacks is just one aspect of cybersecurity costs. There has been all manner of costs from cyber-attacks that, while substantial, cannot easily be calculated in dollars and cents. For example, all 17 US Intelligence Agencies have confirmed that the Russians successfully attempted to use cyber means to compromise the 2016 US Presidential election.[31] The cost of these attacks—even discounting the possible impact on the election outcome—in terms of undermining American democracy and faith in the democratic process is literally incalculable. In 2015, the US Office of Personnel Management was successfully attacked, potentially compromising high value intelligence and putting US intelligence officers' lives at risk.[32] Germany and other countries have reported similar incursions.[33] The Chinese government have reputedly attempted to hack

FIGURE 1.1  Cybercrime costs vs. nation-state revenues

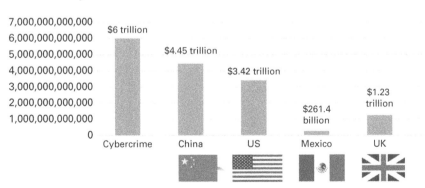

into US medical databases in an attempt to steal or possibly corrupt intellectual property associated with research creating a cure for COVID-19.[34]

Crowd Strike's 2020 Global Threat analysis reported:

> A dark turn in cybercrime preying on schools, municipal departments, and our other chronically underfunded and overburdened public institutions… disruption in 2019 was plagued by sustained operations targeting the underpinnings of our society… sowing widespread disruption and discord among individuals, institutions and even whole countries and populations all in the pursuit of political and economic gain.[35]

And the prospect of rogue terrorist groups eventually being able to wreck damage on critical infrastructure as sophisticated cyber weapons become increasingly user-friendly continues to grow.

In early 2021 the United States government became aware that the Russian government had penetrated multiple US government agencies—including the Department of Homeland Security—and that attack had gone on for months without even being noticed. Moreover, this attack was not on a unique entity like many previous high-profile hacks. In this case, the attackers compromised the SolarWinds Orion software used by literally thousands of government and industry entities. SolarWinds was a different style of attack—an attack on the system itself—not just a particular target. It is generally understood that the attack itself, even though it is now known to have occurred, could potentially continue for years, and similarly, its long-term impact is at this stage literally incalculable.[36]

## Technical Vulnerabilities are a Problem—but not the Only Problem

Given the enormous potential harm from cyber-attacks, the steady growth of the problem over several years, and with tens of billions of dollars spent to address the issue, it is surprising that there has not been more progress in abating cybercrime. One likely reason for this lack of progress may be that the issue has generally been considered through an excessively narrow and limited lens—essentially as a technical operational issue.

The history of cybersecurity to this point is defined by its overwhelming focus on the vulnerabilities in operational technology. Obviously technical vulnerabilities in the system are an important element of the cybersecurity problem—but they are not the only element of the problem.

It is self-evident that our cyber systems are technically vulnerable. In fact, the entire system—or more precisely the system of systems we call the internet—is vulnerable. Indeed, the internet was built to be vulnerable. The internet was built as an open system. It was not designed with security in mind.

President Obama's Chief Cybersecurity Advisor Michael Daniel often remarked that in his position he had the opportunity to meet some of the individuals who actually wrote the core protocols that the internet is based on.[37] One of the things Mr. Daniel reported learning in these conversations was that the originators had pretty modest intentions in creating the internet. They were just trying to create a system enabling scientists to pass some research data back and forth. They weren't trying to design a system that the whole world would run on—but that is what we have now done. In the 21st century virtually everything is now digitally-based—vulnerabilities and all.

Not only is the internet vulnerable at its core, but as the system continues to evolve, we are making it increasingly technically vulnerable. Virtually no one writes code completely from scratch. The common technique is to build on the (vulnerable) protocols already in place. As the systems evolve both the attack surface and the vulnerabilities continue to grow. For example, a single technology provider reported to the *Wall Street Journal* in 2020 that in one year it needed to apply 150 million patches to just one of its newer systems.[38] That is just one system and one company.

The patch model was institutionalized by Microsoft in 2003 with the establishment of Patch Tuesday, when the company regularly reports on new patches they are releasing to address vulnerabilities in their products—sometimes dozens of patches, sometimes hundreds. Other vendors also release patches, although with less regularity or transparency. Some experts have noted that Patch Tuesday is inevitably followed by "Vulnerable Wednesday", when malicious actors, newly aware of vulnerabilities, attack the vulnerable systems.

Many portions of our cyber systems have vulnerabilities with no patches. For example, a study by *Risk IQ* found that some of the internet's most popular websites are running on systems that may be especially vulnerable to compromise. The company found that about 25% of the 10,000 biggest domains relied on at least one component with a vulnerability scored as "high" or "critical" on the Common Vulnerability Scoring System:

> While some of these instances will have patches or other mitigating controls to prevent the identified vulnerabilities and exposures from being exploited, many will not.[39]

The term patch itself may be misleading. Patches are not like Band-Aids that can be quickly slapped on a vulnerability to secure the device. Patches can have impacts on other elements of an integrated information system and thus need to be tested for unexpected impacts, that can even disable other critical applications. As such, the gold standard for implementing a patch is 30 days.[40] The result is that most organizations are simply unable to promptly update their systems in response to the newly revealed vulnerabilities.

But the fact that a system is vulnerable does not mean it is necessarily going to be attacked. Much of our physical critical infrastructure is extremely vulnerable and yet rarely attacked. Our water systems are extremely vulnerable to being compromised with many types of toxic chemicals that could cause substantial harm to the population. Our food system is almost as vulnerable, similarly our expansive ground transport infrastructure is extremely vulnerable. Yet, we rarely hear of attacks on these systems despite their vulnerabilities.

Our cyber systems, on the other hand, are literally under constant attack. In 2020, one ISP reported that it received an average of 80 billion malicious scans every day. EY's 2019 Cybersecurity Survey reported on one single attack that exposed 773 million records.[41] Microsoft has reported that they discover 77,000 instances of malicious code every month.[42] In 2019, ransomware attacks increased 41% compared to the 4th quarter of 2018. It is estimated that a business will fall victim to a ransomware attack every 14 seconds. One reason for the increase is the appearance of Ransomware-as-a-Service. Ransomware kits can now be purchased for as little as $175 and require little or no technical skill to deploy.[43]

## Why Cyber Infrastructure is Attacked—Follow the Money

Examining technical vulnerabilities and their exploitation, as important as that is, only reveals *how* cyber-attacks occur. To comprehensively address the issue, we also need to know *why* cyber-attacks occur.

The *why* of cyber-attacks is almost always economic. Most typically, the economic motive is purely financial, but even in non-financial attacks (e.g., nation-state theft of national intelligence data) there is a profit and loss equation the attacker is using when deciding if and how to launch the attack. Rarely are systems attacked just because they are technically vulnerable.

Understanding this economic equation is critical to properly confronting the attacker and securing your system.

To understand why cybercrime is such a vibrant business, it is helpful to look at the cost for entry into the cybercrime business compared to the profit margins.

Cyber-attack methods are comparatively cheap and easy to acquire. There is a robust market for them on the dark web. You can outsource a Distributed Denial of Service, or DDoS attack, for about $300.[44] Shodan, a publicly available search engine developed to locate digitally connected devices, can easily be used to find unpatched systems.[45] You can purchase access to corporate mailboxes for about $500 dollars.[46] You can get false credentials for social media platforms like Twitter and Instagram for about $100. You can create a dummy retail website for $24.43. If you want to go high-end, you can have a dummy banking website created for $67.91.[47] Of course, you may need training on how to operate such a criminal website. A tutorial on how to conduct email attacks costs $25, complete with a template on how to conduct the attack—$3 extra.[48]

Of course, this is the low-end retail cybercrime. There is also a big league for cyber criminals and it too is growing. Many of the high-end attackers are nation-states (North Korea regularly robs banks) or criminals who are affiliated with nation states (often former military) for the country who go into business for themselves and contract out their services to a client or client state.[49]

## The Economics of Cybersecurity is Upside Down

One of the greatest challenges for enterprises in assessing their cyber risk in economic terms is that the economics of cybersecurity are often not what we assume they are. The economic incentives are a much greater element of creating an effective cyber defense than is realized.

In their classic book *The Economics of Information Security*, Anderson and Moore pointed out that:

> Security failure is caused as least as often by bad economic incentives as by bad technological design. Economists have long known that liability should be assigned to the entity that can manage risk. Yet everywhere we look we see online risk allocated poorly… people who connect their machines to risky places do not bear full consequences of their actions.[50]

With little more than causal reflection, the Anderson and Moore observation rings true. We all know, for example, that if someone uses the same password—say 123456, which is the most popular password in America—and goes to sketchy websites, they're probably going to get their credit card hacked. Let's say a hacker runs up $100,000 in false claims on their card. What does our victim owe? Fifty bucks, at most.[51]

The banks pick up the rest. Although we also know that the banks don't really pick up the rest. They charge it back to the rest of us in higher fees and interest rates. What this acutely means is that in the digital economy, we "good cyber citizens" are subsidizing the sloppy cyber risk takers.

In another instance of misplaced incentives, people will often ask: why don't the IT vendors simply make their products more secure? The assumption is that surely the relational consumer will gravitate toward purchasing the more secure item.

The reason most companies don't focus on making more secure products is there is very little market for secure products. Consumers have generally not demonstrated that they truly value (are willing to pay for) enhanced security. Security ranks low in comparison to other consumer interests in purchasing digital devices. Price, speed and size are generally bigger drivers for consumer behavior. This attitude is also carried over to corporate and government spending on products.

As Anderson and Moore's study reported: "Developers are generally not compensated for creating secure products."[52] Rather than building security into systems on the front end, the market for technological innovation—spurred by competition in broader market economics—is to focus on getting to market quickly and fix security problems later with updates and patches. In fact, the information technology market—by rewarding vendors getting to market quickly over developing secure products—actually incentivizes developing vulnerable products.[53]

Another surprising example of how digital economics fail to operate as expected is shown through well-publicized cyber breaches such as the Target data breach and the Sony hack. It has been widely hypothesized that rational shareholders will force management to pay a heavy price for allowing these attacks to occur. However, the data doesn't bear that out. The accompanying chart shows the results of a number of prominent cyber-attacks on stock prices. In instances where cyber breaches result in bad publicity (and that is not universally the case; many breaches receive little notice) there is typically a short-term negative impact on stock prices. However, what longer-term data shows is that very often not only does the stock not take a sustained

FIGURE 1.2    Stock prices rebound after major breaches

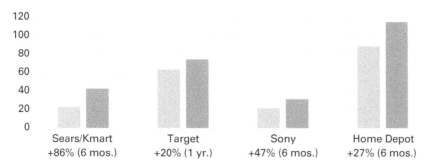

hit, but often it increases significantly shortly following the attack, perhaps because the market sees the company's fundamentals as good and the bad publicity as a *buy* opportunity.

The point is not that cyber breaches are good for stock prices. The point is that many of the assumptions we make about economics in the digital age are simply not born out by the facts. Therefore, organizations need to examine cyber threats and their expected economic impacts carefully, systematically and empirically as will be discussed in Chapter 4.

The digital age has changed many things, including conceptions about privacy, the fundamentals of national defense in an era of asymmetric war, and certainly economics. The role of economics in developing a competent and resilient cybersecurity program needs to be carefully and systematically assessed based on economic realities, not assumptions that need to be developed.

## The Economic Balance in Cyberspace Favors the Attackers

The economic balance between the attackers and defenders in cyberspace favors the attackers. They have low costs and high profit margins. They also have and a great business model because they can use the same methods repeatedly on a world-wide set of targets. Their capital reserves are outstanding since, in addition to their massive profit margins, many cyber attackers are actual nation states or state-affiliated. As a result, the business model for cyber criminals is becoming increasingly sophisticated, which will only make the prospect of curbing cybercrime as difficult organizationally as it has already become technically.

THE EVOLUTION OF THE CYBERCRIME STOCK MARKET

Fueled by the massive profits of cyber criminals, the cybercrime market is constantly evolving. For example, in addition to ransomware attacks becoming increasingly sophisticated, the models for operating them are transforming. We now see the emergence of Ransomware-as-a-Service (RaaS).In this model, RaaS operators who have no technical expertise can commission malware tools with payment-on-commission for the successful ransom. This innovation may lead to a new financing mechanism for cybercrime. Cyber criminals have discussed in open forums proposals to create a venture capital organization— essentially a stock market for cybercrime—where interested parties can finance the development of malware tools and frameworks without ever writing a line of code.[54]

On the defenders' side, we are protecting an inherently vulnerable system, one that is getting technically weaker all the time. We are almost always playing catch-up, as the attackers have first mover advantage and there is virtually no help from law enforcement. We successfully prosecute maybe 1% of cyber criminals.[55] As a result, the 2018 *McAfee Cyber Crime Report* concluded:

> Cybercrime is relentless, undiminished, and unlikely to stop. It is just too easy and too rewarding, and the chances of being caught and punished are perceived as being too low.[56]

## Good Cyber Hygiene is not Enough

Flush with terrific profit margins, the high-end cyber criminals turn out to be extremely competent businesspeople, and like any good businessperson they reinvest in the business. Everyone serious about cyber systems knows that there have always been vulnerabilities, but the criminals—who have their own R&D departments—have actually uncovered all-new vulnerabilities in the core system we didn't originally know about. Moreover, attackers are innovators and collaborators; constantly generating new attack methods and increasingly personalizing attacks. This includes creating designer malware for high-end targets.

> While criminals are relatively predictable in their tendency to always chose the path of least resistance… in 2019…we observed not just a continuation but an escalation of attack sophistication. Ransomware demands grew larger. Tactics became more cutthroat. Established criminal organizations expanded operations. In short, the greedy got greedier and the rich got richer.[57]

A good deal of literature has been written about the need for organizations to practice good cyber hygiene, and certainly adhering to the basics of good cybersecurity is the foundation for any competent program. However, good cyber hygiene is not enough. Moreover, what good cyber hygiene means is rarely defined, but it is generally accepted to mean having some allegiance to a standard set of good practices, such as those defined in the National Institute of Standards and Technology' Cybersecurity Framework (NIST CSF).

It is often said that following these frameworks will help combat most cyber-attacks—and that is essentially correct. Moreover, following these basics of cybersecurity is generally a necessary element for defending against more sophisticated attacks sometimes referred to as APT, or Advanced Persistent Threats.

However, in an environment where attack methods continue to evolve, just following the basics is often not enough to reach the needed level of security. The ESI study confirmed the inadequacy of simply following NIST or other similar frameworks when it concluded that:

> Many firms use NIST as a framework for risk mitigation and have made considerable progress. But they are behind on response and recovery…While NIST provides a solid foundation for cyber security planning, communication and regulatory compliance, it is not enough to ensure the effectiveness of cyber security programs. A minority, only 64 of the 151 companies (42%) classified as leaders in NIST compliance are also advanced in cyber security effectiveness. These numbers confirm what many CISOs already know: firms need to go beyond NIST and other frameworks to secure their enterprises from escalating cyber-attacks.[58]

One of the defining characteristics of these more sophisticated APT attacks is that they can penetrate virtually all of a company's perimeter defense systems, such as firewalls or intrusion-detection systems, and even access cloud-based data where companies are not directly managing security. Intruders look at multiple avenues to exploit all layers of security vulnerabilities until they achieve their goals. The reality is that if a sophisticated attacker targets a company's systems, they will almost certainly breach them.

The National Counterintelligence and Security Center's National Counterintelligence Strategy of the United States for 2020–2022 states:

> Our foreign adversaries are capable of conducting cyber espionage and technical operations against U.S. interests around the world and they continue to develop new and more effective capabilities in these areas. Readily available and advanced cyber and technical surveillance tools offer threat actors a relatively low-cost, efficient, deniable, and high yield means of accomplishing their goals. The development of next generation technologies such as the Internet of Things, fifth generation (5G) cellular communications technology, quantum computing, and artificial intelligence will continue to present new opportunities for foreign intelligence entities to collect intelligence and conduct cyber operations against the United States and its allies.[59]

In the face of sophisticated attackers, organizations relying too much on simply providing the basics of security will find themselves outgunned. The McAfee 2018 Cyber Crime report summed it up this way:

> Cybercriminals at the high-end are as technologically sophisticated as the most advanced IT companies and like them have moved quickly to adopt cloud, computing artificial intelligence and encryption.[60]

The key issue again is the economics. If the target is rich enough, attackers will persistently deploy ever-increasing attack methods. Good cyber hygiene, as laudable as that may be, will generally not prove sufficient to protect the system.

Modern enterprises need to be aware that these sorts of APT-style attacks—that were once common only in financial services and defense sectors—are now used in virtually all economic sectors. In fact, these types of multi-dimensional attack methods have become so common in the attack community that the term APT is now colloquially redefined as an "Average Persistent Threat." The continuing evolution of cyber-attack methods combined with their inverted economics underlines the need for entities to assess risk uniquely with regard to their own system's risks and business plans, accounting for economic value as much as technical proficiency. Sketching out methods for conducting such an analysis will be the focus of the balance of this book.

## Security vs. Compliance

Compliance with cybersecurity regimes is a fact of life. Many organizations will face the need to document that they adhere to a prescribed set of requirements, which may come in the form of regulatory mandates, contractual agreements, or corporate policy. In Chapter 6 we will discuss the legal obligations involved in meeting compliance regimes, and in Chapter 7 we will detail the essentials of the modern audit process that is required for compliance. Being able to meet compliance regimes, often defined via a checklist of requirements, is obviously valuable at least to maintain operations. However, it is important to understand that there is a major difference between compliance with a checklist of security requirements and actual security.

The compliance model has numerous flaws when applied to cybersecurity. At its most fundamental level, the traditional compliance model—as illustrated for example through traditional financial compliance—is misdirected when it comes to cybersecurity. Financial compliance is essentially a pass/fail proposition. Financial audits will typically ask if you disclosed as required, performed as required, and did so in a prescribed timely fashion—or not. You are either in compliance or you are not. Security is not a pass-fail proposition. An entity is not either secure or insecure. Security is a continuum. Total security, especially regarding cyber systems with their inherently weak structures and advanced threats, is not possible. While check-box compliance framework fails to address the dynamics of cyber risks, it is often a costly, tedious, and burdensome process. A study shows a typical cyber incident responder at a federal agency needs 40 hours to go through compliance paperwork before the 5-minute reparation work.[61]

Compliance also tends to be a backward-looking function. An auditor assesses if an entity has complied. Cybersecurity is a forward-looking risk management issue. Competent defense entails assessing future and developing risks and determining the level of threat as it applies to that unique entity. Cybersecurity needs to be assessed on a forward-looking risk management maturity model, judged not against a disembodied unitary pass/fail checklist.

Finally, there is the issue that the multiple checklists and heat maps that have become so common have not been proven to actually enhance security. In his classic book *How to Measure Anything in Cyber Security*, Douglas Hubbard provides a detailed review of the literature on the use of ordinal scales used in nearly 80% of organizations to assess and communicate risks, concluding: "there is not a single study that the use of such methods actually helps reduce risk."[62]

This again underlines the need for enterprises to not simply rely on adherence to a predetermined checklist but to do a more sophisticated cyber risk assessment. An adequate risk assessment will include an examination of the economic value a potential attack would net the attacker and calibrate cyber defenses with that in mind. Organizations need to determine what level of security is appropriate for them (their risk appetite) and what steps they must take to assure that level of security.

## The Punitive Model of Compelling Reasonable Security

The massive economic imbalance between attackers and defenders also calls into question the blithe assertion of some commentators and politicians that the reasons corporate cyber systems are regularly and successfully attacked is a general lack of care or accountability on the part of selfish and uncaring corporations.

Just how hard it is to adequately protect even the best-defended cyber systems is illustrated by a passage from a 2015 Annual Report issued by the Pentagon. This official report stated:

> The military's computer networks can be compromised by low to middling skilled attacks. Military systems do not have a sufficiently robust security posture to repel sustained attacks. The development of advanced cyber techniques makes it likely that a determined adversary can acquire a foothold in most DOD systems and be in a position to degrade DOD missions when and if they choose.[63]

This acknowledgment begs the question: if the best funded, and most sophisticated cyber defense system in the history of the world is subject to low to mid-level attack—when and if the attacker chooses—what level of security is reasonable for discount retailers like Target, movie producers like Sony, or any private entity?

There is, no doubt, a percentage of ignorant or uncaring or even corrupt system operators in business (and probably government too) who, due to selfishness or incompetence, do not invest appropriately in cybersecurity. However, the essence of the cybersecurity problem is not lack of care or accountability, it's the economy of the system.

Even when economics would seem to be of a lesser concern, such as in national defense, we still see the same sorts of effects. For example, a 2019 report from the Department of Defense's Inspector General found that:

The US Department of Defense (DoD) purchased and used millions of dollars' worth of electronics last year (2018) containing 'known cybersecurity vulnerabilities' that make them particularly susceptible to Chinese government espionage... At least $32.8 million in COTS (Commercial Off the Shelf) purchases made by the US Army and Air Force during the 2018 fiscal year were singled out for concern. The products include software, cameras, and networking equipment red-flagged by the Department of Homeland Security (DHS) and the Joint Chiefs of Staff Intelligence Directorate, as well as computers that have been banned for use by State Department employees since 2006.[64]

The essence of the cybersecurity problem is that we have an inherently vulnerable system housing incredibly valuable data. Attempting to design a cybersecurity policy without conscientiously factoring in economics is as misguided as attempting to design economic policy without conscientiously factoring in technology. Yet that is what most industry and governments have done for two decades. Fortunately, new models are emerging to assist management and boards in better understanding and assessing their cyber risk. The use of more sophisticated methods will enable organizations to better calibrate effective cyber strategies in empirical economic terms.

## What's an Organization to do About Cybersecurity?

Organizations cannot solve their cybersecurity issues. The goal for an organization should be to manage their cyber risk to an acceptable level consistent with their unique business plan.

Coming to the realization that the cybersecurity problem is an enterprise-wide problem rooted not simply in technical/operational factors—but the result of wildly out of sync economic incentives—is the first step toward building a resilient system. To address this issue organizations need to take a systemic approach. A variety of specific organizational models will be discussed in Chapter 3, but a good place to start is for enterprises to adapt their current Enterprise Risk Management programs and update them for cybersecurity.

Recent guidance from the National Institute on Standards and Technology (NIST) calls for cybersecurity to be more fully integrated into an organization's Enterprise Risk Management (ERM):

At its core, managing cybersecurity risk is balancing the benefit of applying information and technology against the potential impact and likelihood of the consequences of that application deployed at the system, organization, or enterprise level. An enterprise that avoids all cybersecurity risk might stifle innovation or efficiencies to the point where little value would be produced. Conversely, an enterprise that applies technology without regard to cybersecurity risk might fall victim to undesirable consequences. Effectively balancing the benefits of technology with the potential consequences of a threat event will result in effective cybersecurity risk management that supports a comprehensive ERM approach.[65]

There is emerging evidence that properly developed cyber risk management programs can be cost effective.

In the wake of the COVID-19 pandemic, PwC found:

Boards and C-suite executives who in the past may have wondered about the return on investment for all the cybersecurity personnel, solutions and architectures don't anymore. The value of their cybersecurity expenditures ... became clear during the crisis.[66]

ESI, which conducted an even larger survey during the crisis were able to prove more precise calibrations of cybersecurity ROI. They found that on average, organizations saw an overall ROI of 191% from their cybersecurity investments. For every dollar spent was almost a $2 return. In particular, ESI found that ROI averages 283% for investments in people, 164% for investments in process 135% for investments in tech—about half the ROI for investments in people.[67]

While these numbers are impressive it's important to note that this same study found that about one third of companies have a negative ROI for spending on cybersecurity.

So, the data tells us it is not spending on cybersecurity that is cost effective, it is wise spending on cybersecurity that is cost effective. There is also no one-size-fits-all standard of what constitutes a wise cybersecurity investment. That is determined by a careful assessment of the unique risks an entity faces, its risk appetite and the effectiveness and costs of the risk mitigation or transfer mechanisms available to the organization. Fortunately, there are emerging methods that can help an organization make these determinations in a far superior process than the outmoded ordinal measures that have previously dominated the field.

## Conclusion

In short, cybersecurity needs to be understood and treated as a core business issue, much like legal and finance. No organization would make a significant business decision without consulting business and finance. In the 21st century very few business decisions ought to be made without considering their cybersecurity aspects.

There are many additional steps an organization needs to take to comprehensively address cyber risk which will be described in succeeding chapters.

Taking the right steps entails reconsidering corporate structure (as discussed in Chapter 3) and using modern cyber risk assessment tools that go beyond the traditional frameworks and checklists (as discussed in Chapter 4), as well as engaging personnel from across the enterprise in addressing a series of specific cyber issues (as discussed in Chapter 6).

To continue learning about the concepts in this chapter the following sources are recommended:

1 D W Hubbard and R Seiersen (2016) *How to Measure Anything in Cybersecurity Risk* Wiley, Hoboken, New Jersey

2 A Bonime-Blanc (2020) *Gloom to Boom: How Leaders Transform Risk into Resilience and Value,* Routledge, Abingdon, Oxfordshire

3 L Clinton and D Perera (2016) *The Cybersecurity Social Contract*, Internet Security Alliance

4 R A Clarke and R K. Knake (2019) *The Fifth Domain*, Penguin Press, New York

5 M Rosenquist (2015) *Navigating the Digital Age,* Caxton Business and Legal, Chicago

## Endnotes

1 Troels Oerting Presentation. G-20 Digital Security Working Group. February 4, 2020. Riyadh, Saudi Arabia

2 Troels Oerting Presentation. G-20 Digital Security Working Group. February 4, 2020. Riyadh, Saudi Arabia

3   National Association of Corporate Directors and Internet Security Alliance. NACD Director's Handbook on Cyber-Risk Oversight 2020, February 25, 2020. www.nacdonline.org/insights/publications.cfm?ItemNumber=67298 (archived at https://perma.cc/W4K9-SANF) [Copyright for this publication is joinly owned between the NACD and the ISA. Permission to republish has kindly been granted by the NACD.]

4   Ernst & Young. EY Global Information Security Survey 2020, 2020. assets.ey.com/content/dam/ey-sites/ey-com/en_gl/topics/advisory/ey-global-information-security-survey-2020-single-pages.pdf (archived at https://perma.cc/DD7Z-G3KJ)

5   Ernst & Young. EY Global Information Security Survey 2020, 2020. assets.ey.com/content/dam/ey-sites/ey-com/en_gl/topics/advisory/ey-global-information-security-survey-2020-single-pages.pdf (archived at https://perma.cc/E7ZZ-HYAV)

6   ESI ThoughtLab. Driving Cybersecurity Performance: Improving Results Through Evidence-based Analysis, June 17, 2020. econsultsolutions.com/wp-content/uploads/2020/06/FINAL_ESITL-Driving-Cybersecurity-Performance_ebook_2020.pdf (archived at https://perma.cc/MQ4M-L8R6)

7   M Hathaway. Patching Our Digital Future Is Unsustainable and Dangerous [blog] Center for International Governance Innovation, n.d. www.cigionline.org/articles/patching-our-digital-future-unsustainable-and-dangerous (archived at https://perma.cc/MD9Z-BJ8K)

8   National Association of Corporate Directors and Internet Security Alliance. NACD Director's Handbook on Cyber-Risk Oversight 2020, February 25, 2020. www.nacdonline.org/insights/publications.cfm?ItemNumber=67298 (archived at https://perma.cc/BS6T-7YZU)

9   J Choi, J Kaplan, C Krishnamurthy, and H Lung. Hit or Myth? Understanding the True Costs and Impact of Cybersecurity Programs [blog] McKinsey, July 27, 2017. www.mckinsey.com/business-functions/mckinsey-digital/our-insights/hit-or-myth-understanding-the-true-costs-and-impact-of-cybersecurity-programs# (archived at https://perma.cc/ZQR5-M6PM)

10  National Association of Corporate Directors. 2019-2020 NACD Public Company Governance Survey, December 11, 2019. www.nacdonline.org/insights/publications.cfm?ItemNumber=66566 (archived at https://perma.cc/G5DY-PQRV)

11  National Association of Corporate Directors, Internet Security Alliance. Cyber-Risk Oversight 2020: Key Principles and Practical Guidance for Corporate Boards, February 2020

12  C Schreiber. Cybersecurity Challenges for Latin America [blog] International Security Studies Group at the University of Granada, September 10, 2018. www.seguridadinternacional.es/?q=es/content/cybersecurity-challenges-latin-america (archived at https://perma.cc/9F2P-K78M)

**13**  CISOMAG. Artificial Intelligence as a Security Solution and Weaponization by Hackers, CISOMAG, December 9, 2019. cisomag.eccouncil.org/hackers-using-ai/ (archived at https://perma.cc/TK4R-JHYD)

**14**  B Cheatham, K Javanmardian, and H Samandari. Confronting the Risks of Artificial Intelligence [blog] McKinsey, April 26, 2019. www.mckinsey.com/business-functions/mckinsey-analytics/our-insights/confronting-the-risks-of-artificial-intelligence (archived at https://perma.cc/SQ3M-Y48G)

**15**  W Dixon and J Farshchi. AI is the Latest Weapon Cybercriminals are Exploiting. World Economic Forum, September 25, 2019. www.weforum.org/agenda/2019/09/4-ways-ai-is-changing-cybersecurity-both-in-attack-and-defense/ (archived at https://perma.cc/JCF9-S7ST)

**16**  B Cheatham, K Javanmardian, and H Samandari. Confronting the Risks of Artificial Intelligence [blog] McKinsey, April 26 2019. www.mckinsey.com/business-functions/mckinsey-analytics/our-insights/confronting-the-risks-of-artificial-intelligence (archived at https://perma.cc/NZ26-8VFY)

**17**  Ernst & Young. EY Global Information Security Survey 2020, 2020. assets.ey.com/content/dam/ey-sites/ey-com/en_gl/topics/advisory/ey-global-information-security-survey-2020-single-pages.pdf (archived at https://perma.cc/57CC-KUYN)

**18**  R A Clarke and R K Knake (2019) *The Fifth Domain,* Penguin Press, New York

**19**  J Boehm, N Curcio, P Merrath, L Shenton, and T Stähle. The Risk-based Approach to Cybersecurity [blog] McKinsey, October 8, 2019. www.mckinsey.com/business-functions/risk/our-insights/the-risk-based-approach-to-cybersecurity (archived at https://perma.cc/S5YD-5Y8C)

**20**  S Ramachandran, N Yousif, W Bohmayr, M Coden, D Frankle, and O Klier. A Smarter Way to Quantify Cybersecurity Risk [blog] Boston Consulting Group, August 9, 2019. www.bcg.com/capabilities/digital-technology-data/smarter-way-to-quantify-cybersecurity-risk (archived at https://perma.cc/S2VC-EPAJ)

**21**  N Davis and A Pipikaite. What the COVID-19 Pandemic Teaches Us About Cybersecurity – and How to Prepare for the Inevitable Global Cyberattack [blog] World Economic Forum, June 1, 2020. www.weforum.org/agenda/2020/06/covid-19-pandemic-teaches-us-about-cybersecurity-cyberattack-cyber-pandemic-risk-virus/ (archived at https://perma.cc/Q8AK-TMPV)

**22**  K Parker, J M Horowitz, and R Minkin. How the Coronavirus Outbreak Has – and Hasn't – Changed the Way Americans Work [blog] Pew Research Center, December 9, 2020, www.pewsocialtrends.org/2020/12/09/how-the-coronavirus-outbreak-has-and-hasnt-changed-the-way-americans-work/ (archived at https://perma.cc/GR2T-U83S)

23  PwC. Digital Trust Insights Pulse Survey, June 2021. www.pwc.com/us/en/
    services/consulting/cybersecurity-privacy-forensics/library/pwc-covid-19-ciso-
    pulse-survey.html (archived at https://perma.cc/57E9-AC7Y)

24  ESI ThoughtLab. Driving Cybersecurity Performance: Improving Results
    Through Evidence-based Analysis, June 17, 2020. econsultsolutions.com/
    wp-content/uploads/2020/06/FINAL_ESITL-Driving-Cybersecurity-
    Performance_ebook_2020.pdf (archived at https://perma.cc/52X7-CPSS)

25  M Sentonas. Global Survey: The Cybersecurity Reality of the COVID-19
    Remote Workforce [blog] CrowdStrike, May 11, 2020. www.crowdstrike.com/
    blog/global-survey-the-cybersecurity-reality-of-the-covid-19-remote-
    workforce/ (archived at https://perma.cc/6SRE-U24P)

26  M Miller. FBI Sees Spike in Cyber Crime Reports During Coronavirus
    Pandemic, The Hill, April 16, 2020, thehill.com/policy/cybersecurity/493198-
    fbi-sees-spike-in-cyber-crime-reports-during-coronavirus-pandemic (archived
    at https://perma.cc/F8PG-P9ZF)

27  PwC. Digital Trust Insights Pulse Survey, June 2021. www.pwc.com/us/en/
    services/consulting/cybersecurity-privacy-forensics/library/pwc-covid-19-ciso-
    pulse-survey.html (archived at https://perma.cc/3K6K-R5Q6)

28  Troels Oerting Presentation. G-20 Digital Security Working Group. February 4,
    2020. Riyadh, Saudi Arabia

29  S Morgan. Cybercrime To Cost the World $10.5 Trillion Annually By 2025,
    Cybercrime Magazine, November 13, 2020, cybersecurityventures.com/
    cybercrime-damages-6-trillion-by-2021/ (archived at https://perma.cc/W6KM-
    ZPNK) [accessed February 1, 2021].

30  www.imf.org/en/Publications/SPROLLs/world-economic-outlook-
    databases#sort=%40imfdate%20descending (archived at https://perma.cc/
    NQZ3-RYD3)

31  E Collins. Yes, 17 Intelligence Agencies Really Did Say Russia Was Behind
    Hacking, USA Today, October 21, 2016, www.usatoday.com/story/news/
    politics/onpolitics/2016/10/21/17-intelligence-agencies-russia-behind-
    hacking/92514592/ (archived at https://perma.cc/HSU8-FSKS)

32  J Fruhlinger. The OPM Hack Explained: Bad Security Practices Meet China's
    Captain America [blog] CSO Online, February 12, 2020. www.csoonline.com/
    article/3318238/the-opm-hack-explained-bad-security-practices-meet-chinas-
    captain-america.html (archived at https://perma.cc/E6TT-NB2A)

33  B Kderner. Inside The Cyberattack That Shocked the US Government, Wired,
    October 23, 2016, www.wired.com/2016/10/inside-cyberattack-shocked-us-
    government/ (archived at https://perma.cc/LUM9-KN4Y)

34  G Lubold and D Volz. U.S. Says Chinese, Iranian Hackers Seek to Steal
    Coronavirus Research, The Wall Street Journal, May 14, 2020, www.wsj.com/
    articles/chinese-iranian-hacking-may-be-hampering-search-for-coronavirus-
    vaccine-officials-say-11589362205 (archived at https://perma.cc/6AXY-K6Z3)

**35**    CrowdStrike. 2020 Global Threat Report, 2020. www.crowdstrike.com/
resources/reports/2020-crowdstrike-global-threat-report/ (archived at
https://perma.cc/J6XE-UPVF)

**36**    Josephine Wolff. The SolarWinds Hack Is Unlike Anything We Have Ever Seen
Before, Slate Group, December 18, 2020, slate.com/technology/2020/12/
solarwinds-hack-malware-active-breach.html (archived at https://perma.cc/
LVS2-RQR6)

**37**    Michael Daniel, Cybersecurity Coordinator, Obama Administration, comment
during meeting with Internet Security Alliance Board of Directors, October 29,
2013

**38**    Adam Janofsky. Companies Struggle to Stay on Top of Security Patches. The
Wall Street Journal, May 29, 2018, www.wsj.com/articles/companies-struggle-
to-stay-on-top-of-security-patches-1527645840 (archived at https://perma.cc/
RL4Z-LSWA)

**39**    RiskIQ. Analysis of an Attack Surface. RiskIQ, February 8, 2019. www.wsta.
org/wp-content/uploads/2020/07/Analysis-of-an-Attack-Surface-RiskIQ-
Research.pdf (archived at https://perma.cc/VDB9-HVM6)

**40**    Protiviti. How Long Does It Take to Implement a Patch? Protiviti, 2017.
www.protiviti.com/US-en/insights/bpro97# (archived at https://perma.
cc/25LT-9V6W)

**41**    C P Chalico. Six Things to Consider when Evaluating Cyber and Privacy Risk
[blog] Ernst & Young, January 8, 2021. www.ey.com/en_ca/private/six-things-
to-consider-when-evaluating-cyber-and-privacy-risk (archived at https://perma.
cc/EG5E-TKFC)

**42**    Microsoft. Ghost in the Shell: Investigating Web Shell Attacks [blog]
Microsoft. February 4, 2020. www.microsoft.com/security/blog/2020/02/04/
ghost-in-the-shell-investigating-web-shell-attacks/ (archived at https://perma.
cc/V7FM-MALD)

**43**    PurpleSec LLC. Ransomware Statistics, Data, & Trends, 2020. purplesec.us/
resources/cyber-security-statistics/ransomware/ (archived at https://perma.cc/
KJD8-6ETG)

**44**    Mission Critical Magazine. The Dark Web: DDoS Attacks Sell for As Low
As $10 Per Hour, Mission Critical Magazine, August 26, 2020, www.mission
criticalmagazine.com/articles/93185-the-dark-web-ddos-attacks-sell-for-as-
low-as-10-per-hour (archived at https://perma.cc/L3MV-ZZBY)

**45**    M Hathaway. Patching Our Digital Future Is Unsustainable and Dangerous
[blog] Center for International Governance Innovation, n.d. www.cigionline.
org/articles/patching-our-digital-future-unsustainable-and-dangerous (archived
at https://perma.cc/E52A-XKU2)

**46**    L McCamy. 7 Things You Can Hire a Hacker to do and How Much it will
(Generally) Cost [blog] Business Insider, November 27, 2018. www.businessin
sider.com/things-hire-hacker-to-do-how-much-it-costs-2018-11 (archived at
https://perma.cc/K9TE-AMA9)

**47**   Digital Shadows. The Ecosystem Of Phishing: From Minnows To Marlins [blog] Digital Shadows, February 20, 2020. www.digitalshadows.com/blog-and-research/the-ecosystem-of-phishing/ (archived at https://perma.cc/WH68-6KQQ)

**48**   Mission Critical Magazine. The Dark Web: DDoS Attacks Sell for As Low As $10 Per Hour, Mission Critical Magazine, August 26, 2020, www.missioncriticalmagazine.com/articles/93185-the-dark-web-ddos-attacks-sell-for-as-low-as-10-per-hour (archived at https://perma.cc/Q8N2-24LX)

**49**   Geoff White. The Lazarus heist: How North Korea almost puled off a billion-dollar hack, BBC, 21 June 2021, www.bbc.co.uk/news/stories-57520169 (archived at https://perma.cc/RP6A-UG29)

**50**   R Anderson and T Moore. The Economics of Information Security, *Science,* 2006, 314 (5799), www.researchgate.net/publication/216757755_The_Economics_of_Information_Security/link/549b102f0cf2d6581ab2e132/download (archived at https://perma.cc/J5V4-WLJD)

**51**   S L Cain. What Happens If Your Bank Account Is Hacked? [blog] Consumerism Commentary, July 15, 2020. www.consumerismcommentary.com/what-happens-if-your-bank-account-is-hacked/ (archived at https://perma.cc/7BR3-Z8Z5)

**52**   R Anderson and T Moore. The Economics of Information Security, 2006, Science 314 (5799), www.researchgate.net/publication/216757755_The_Economics_of_Information_Security/link/549b102f0cf2d6581ab2e132/download (archived at https://perma.cc/4XHV-XVNA)

**53**   M Hathaway. Patching Our Digital Future Is Unsustainable and Dangerous [blog] Center for International Governance Innovation, n.d. www.cigionline.org/articles/patching-our-digital-future-unsustainable-and-dangerous (archived at https://perma.cc/2Q5M-V8WA)

**54**   Booz Allen. 2021 Cyber Threat Trends Outlook, February 5, 2021. http://web.archive.org/web/20210205122428/boozallen.com/content/dam/boozallen_site/ccg/pdf/publications/cyber-threat-trends-outlook-2021.pdf (archived at https://perma.cc/VP52-LC89)

**55**   Security Buzz. Only 1% Of Cybercrimes Prosecuted [blog] Security Buzz, May 29, 2019. www.informationsecuritybuzz.com/expert-comments/only-1-of-cybercrimes-prosecuted/ (archived at https://perma.cc/KNL9-RZDG)

**56**   McAfee. Economic Impact of Cybercrime—No Slowing Down, February 2018. www.mcafee.com/enterprise/en-us/assets/reports/restricted/rp-economic-impact-cybercrime.pdf (archived at https://perma.cc/2XVY-CHJB)

**57**   CrowdStrike. 2020 Global Threat Report, 2020. www.crowdstrike.com/resources/reports/2020-crowdstrike-global-threat-report/ (archived at https://perma.cc/2LJJ-A3KH)

**58**   ESI ThoughtLab. Driving Cybersecurity Performance: Improving Results
Through Evidence-based Analysis, June 17, 2020. econsultsolutions.com/
wp-content/uploads/2020/06/FINAL_ESITL-Driving-Cybersecurity-
Performance_ebook_2020.pdf (archived at https://perma.cc/CUG8-TX2K)

**59**   National Counterintelligence and Security Center. National
Counterintelligence Strategy of the United States of America 2020-2022,
February 10, 2020. www.dni.gov/files/NCSC/documents/features/20200205-
National_CI_Strategy_2020_2022.pdf (archived at https://perma.cc/
5EUR-4X7E)

**60**   McAfee. Economic Impact of Cybercrime—No Slowing Down, February
2018. www.mcafee.com/enterprise/en-us/assets/reports/restricted/rp-economic-
impact-cybercrime.pdf (archived at https://perma.cc/N269-XEZL)

**61**   D Maclean. The NIST Risk Management Framework: Problems and
Recommendations, Cyber Security: A Peer-Reviewed Journal, 2017, 1 (3),
icitech.org/wp-content/uploads/2019/04/The-NIST-Risk-Management-
Framework_Problems-and-Recommendations.pdf (archived at https://perma.
cc/SKU7-FFHX)

**62**   D Hubbard and R Seiersen (2016) *How to Measure Anything in Cybersecurity
Risk,* John Wiley & Sons Inc., Hoboken, New Jersey

**63**   Office of the Secretary of Defense. Annual Report to Congress: Military and
Security Developments Involving the People's Republic of China 2015, April 7,
2015. dod.defense.gov/Portals/1/Documents/pubs/2015_China_Military_
Power_Report.pdf (archived at https://perma.cc/3NT7-2KZW)

**64**   J Rohrlich. The US Military Spent $33 Million on Tech Known to be
Vulnerable to Chinese Cyberespionage [blog] Quartz, July 31, 2019. qz.
com/1679475/dod-spent-30m-on-china-hackable-tech-from-lenovo-gopro-
others/ (archived at https://perma.cc/DES6-H59B)

**65**   National Institute of Standards and Technology. Integrating Cybersecurity and
Enterprise Risk Management (ERM), July 9, 2020. nvlpubs.nist.gov/nistpubs/
ir/2020/NIST.IR.8286-draft2.pdf (archived at https://perma.cc/92RR-URMM)

**66**   PwC. Digital Trust Insights Pulse Survey, June 2021. www.pwc.com/us/en/
services/consulting/cybersecurity-privacy-forensics/library/pwc-covid-19-ciso-
pulse-survey.html (archived at https://perma.cc/EF8K-PCNP)

**67**   ESI ThoughtLab. Driving Cybersecurity Performance: Improving Results
Through Evidence-based Analysis, June 17, 2020. econsultsolutions.com/
wp-content/uploads/2020/06/FINAL_ESITL-Driving-Cybersecurity-
Performance_ebook_2020.pdf (archived at https://perma.cc/N76L-SFFB)

# 02

# Effective Cybersecurity Principles for Boards of Directors

BY LARRY CLINTON, PRESIDENT AND CEO, INTERNET SECURITY ALLIANCE, AND BEN PEIFER, ISA RESEARCH ASSOCIATE

## Five Key Ideas to Take Away from This Chapter

1 It is the board of directors' responsibility to collaborate with the executive team to create a culture of security and effective oversight of executive's cyber risk management.

2 Cybersecurity is not an IT-centric appendage issue, but rather needs to be woven into the full breadth of business decisions on an enterprise-wide basis.

3 There are a core set of board-level cyber risk principles that constitute a de-facto international standard of appropriate cyber risk oversight.

4 Boards should expect that the executive team will provide both technological and organizational structures that will implement the core principles the board has set.

5 Boards should expect management to be able to assess cyber risk in empirical and economic terms consistent with the business plan.

## Introduction

The central thesis of this volume is that cybersecurity is an enterprise-wide risk management issue. It is the board of directors that defines what the enterprise is.

While most readers of this volume may never serve on a corporate board, or even attend a board meeting, it is important to understand the board's role in the cybersecurity ecosystem. The board is not in charge of cyber risk management. Management is in charge of cyber risk management. The board is in charge of cyber risk oversight, which means they set the expectations for management.

## What Role Does the Board Play in Cybersecurity?

This does not mean that the board does not have a role in addressing cyber risk. It has a critical role. It is the board's role to provide the vision of the enterprise, to set the tone for the organization's culture, to work with management to define the enterprise's risk-appetite, and to oversee management in assuring that they are fulfilling their cyber risk management responsibilities. As we will detail later, boards have certain cybersecurity responsibilities they must execute within the context of board itself. However, to have a fully functioning enterprise-wide cyber risk program the board and management need to be communicating and cooperating with each other in order to understand their roles and responsibilities—to both the enterprise and to each other—and assure that they are fulfilled effectively.

## The Evolution in Corporate Board Thinking on Cybersecurity

Almost since the dawn of the digital era, cyber practitioners and policymakers have called for greater involvement from corporate boards in addressing cyber threats. What that plea generally translated to was practitioners wanting to teach board members about IT, hoping that if they fully understood the technology they would better appreciate and focus on the cyber threat.

> The Year 2000 Problem (also referred to as the millennium bug or Y2K bug) refers to problems related to the formatting and storage of calendar data for dates beginning in the year 2000. Problems were anticipated and arose because many programs represented four-digit years with only the final two digits—making the year 2000 indistinguishable from 1900. The assumption of a twentieth-century date in such programs could cause various errors, such as

the incorrect display of dates or the inaccurate ordering of automated dated records or real-time events. Very few computer failures were reported when the clocks rolled over into 2000.

What emerged from consultants and IT professionals in these early days were a series of tutorials on information technology ostensibly written for board members, but largely disembodied from the goals and interests of the supposed target audience. Not surprisingly, these attempts were largely unsuccessful. Board members initially had difficulty appreciating cyber threats as more than a marginal cost of doing business, akin to pilfering or the technical "Y2K" disruptions at the turn of the century.[1]

Over time, however, leading directors and the organizations representing them increasingly realized the extent of the cyber threat and appreciated the link between the economic imperatives of digital transformation and the downside risks of such business development represented by the lack of cybersecurity.

In 2013 the National Association of Corporate Directors (NACD), together with AIG, formed a partnership with the Internet Security Alliance (ISA) and launched a project to clarify the messaging about the cyber threat. A major theme was to cast cybersecurity from a director's perspective, as opposed to a strictly IT-practitioner perspective. The vision was to create a program wherein cybersecurity would flow from the top down starting with the board, as opposed to the previous paradigm wherein cyber security was expected to bubble up from the IT departments.

This new approach sought to embed cybersecurity issues in the business context that boards could more readily appreciate. Instead of insisting that directors learn the language of IT, a new approach was initiated that would instead attempt to cast cybersecurity in the language of business which the boards and business managers were more comfortable with.

So instead of explaining ISO standards, NIST frameworks and vulnerability growth, the new approach focused on business issues directors care about, such as innovation, growth, profitability, and PE ratios. Instead of describing where the vulnerabilities in the new software were, boards were challenged to ask—what cybersecurity issues are raised when launching a new product? What potential cybersecurity issues occur when conducting a merger or acquisition? The new approach raised cyber from primarily an IT issue and conceptualized it for the boards as a business issue.

## Developing and Validating Board-Level Principles of Cybersecurity

The core product of the new approach was the creation in 2014 of the NACD-ISA Cyber Risk Handbook. The Cyber Risk Handbook quickly became the most popular publication the NACD has produced. It has been updated and expanded twice with new editions in 2014 and 2020. In addition, the NACD model has now been adapted and embraced by similar organizations including the Organization of American States, European Conference of Director Associations, the Japanese Federation of Business, The Cyber Security Council of Germany, and the Association of India Communications and Multimedia and Infrastructure. It is now available on four continents in five different languages.

Governments have also embraced the new model. The adapted Cyber Risk Handbooks were the first private sector publications to be endorsed by the US Department of Homeland Security and the US Department of Justice. The handbooks have also been adapted and endorsed by the German Federal Office of Information Security (BSI) as well as the Organization of American States (OAS). Perhaps most importantly, and uniquely, the handbooks have been independently assessed and found to generate actual pro-security outcomes. In their Global Information Security Survey, PWC reported that:

> Guidelines from the National Association of Corporate Directors advise that Boards should view cyber risks from an enterprise-wide standpoint and understand the potential legal impacts. They should discuss cybersecurity risks and preparedness with management and consider cyber threats in the context of the organization's overall tolerance for risk.[2]

> Boards appear to be listening to this guidance. This year we saw a double-digit uptick in board participation in most aspects of information security. Deepening board involvement has improved cybersecurity practices in numerous ways. As more Boards participate in cybersecurity budget discussions, we saw a 24% boost in security spending.[3]

> Notable outcomes cited by survey respondents include identification of key risks, fostering an organizational culture of security and better alignment of cybersecurity with overall risk management and business goals. Perhaps more than anything, board participation opened the lines of communication between the cybersecurity function and top executives and directors.[4]

The positive impact of these programs has also been attested to by board members themselves. On December 14th, 2020, the NACD published its latest survey of corporate directors and found that 33% of directors agreed with the statement that "my board's oversight of cybersecurity has improved over the last 3 years". Only 8% of respondents disagreed with that statement.[5]

There is also ongoing work to make this process more sophisticated and elevate cyber risk management at the board-level and integrate empirical metrics similar to how boards traditionally calculate other risks. In late 2020, the World Economic Forum joined the ISA and the NACD in a collaboration to more rigorously define methodologies that would enable the more precise measurement of how the use of consensus principles for corporate boards to generate positive security outcomes. In Chapter 4 we will discuss some of the techniques that are being developed to make cyber risk assessments more tailored to business needs in an empirical and economic context.

## INTEGRATING CYBER INTO THE ENVIRONMENTAL SOCIAL AND GOVERNANCE (ESG) FRAMEWORK
*By Andrea Bonime-Blanc, JD/PhD*

Since 2018, Larry Fink, Chairman and Founder of Blackrock, the largest asset manager in the world, has issued his annual letter to CEOs underscoring the importance of businesses focusing on purpose, stakeholders and ESG (environmental, social and governance) as part of business strategy. In late 2019, the Business Roundtable, a powerful group of around 200 CEOs from the largest US corporations, joined the ESG wave by issuing their Purpose Statement, stating that companies needed to go beyond shareholder primacy and also consider the interests and expectations of other key stakeholders like employees, customers and suppliers.[6]

The ESG lens now widely championed by the investment community has become not a wave but a tsunami in the past couple of years, accelerated and amplified even more by the COVID-19 pandemic which exposed a number of deep seated environmental, social, health, diversity, equality, and governance problems worldwide. The pandemic also revealed vast cyber-vulnerabilities in many businesses and industries (as well as governments) as the still-unraveling SolarWinds case discovered in late 2020 has dramatically underscored.

What this all means is that the management and board of any business must ensure that there is an effective and tailored enterprise risk management

(ERM) system that takes into account all major ESG and technology risks (or what I call ESGT in my book, *Gloom to Boom*), that are relevant to their business operations, products, services, strategy, and stakeholder expectations.[7]

Given the intense, groundbreaking and constantly changing nature of technology and digital transformation including an array of issues, risks and opportunities in cyber-space, company boards and management have an obligation to incorporate ESGT considerations into both ERM and strategy. In other words, management and boards need to undertake a holistic ESGT (ESG plus technology) approach to risk management, risk governance and business strategy development and oversight.

A business that does not consciously and purposefully incorporate cyber risk management and oversight in an interdisciplinary manner is not only creating grave potential cost and risk to the business, they are also missing out on ESGT and cyber opportunity for resilience, value protection and value creation.

For example, a pharmaceutical company that is developing a pandemic-related vaccine or other treatment has super valuable intellectual property that becomes a juicy target for cyber-criminals or even nation-states. The imperative for such a company to have an evolved ERM system that includes a sophisticated, interdisciplinary team of risk and security professionals—including risk, audit, legal, financial and yes, IT experts—understanding their full array of ESGT risks is enormous. Only through such a coordinated ESGT ERM approach to cybersecurity, risk management and governance can a business develop the proper defenses in terms of policy, practices and culture, as well as the selection of the right IT infrastructure tools.

## Process for Developing the International Principles for Boards and Cybersecurity

The process used to develop these handbooks was grounded in research primarily generated through focus groups. The groups were populated with cybersecurity experts generated though the partner organizations. Prior to the outreach process, ISA, working in partnership with the NACD, researched the existing literature on cybersecurity and boards of directors. Based on this literature and input from the ISA board and NACD membership and staff, an initial draft handbook was developed. This draft, based on the literature review, was deemed useful to help structure and focus the discussions with other participants in the process.

Following the development of the initial literature-based draft, 10 in-person workshops were conducted covering four continents—North America, South America, Europe and Asia. These were then supplemented by 15 international webinars. Sessions generally included 10–15 participants, although in some cases as many as 40 individuals would participate in a session. In each region a draft handbook was created by ISA and its regional partner based on the input, comments, and suggestions from the sessions. The adapted drafts based on the sessions were then circulated to all participants in the region's sessions. Participants were encouraged to make in-line written comments/suggestions to whatever degree they felt appropriate. ISA stressed in all sessions that the intent was to allow the participants to "make the handbook yours—for you and your colleagues' use". Session participants were also encouraged to circulate the drafts to interested colleagues who may want to participate in the process. ISA was tasked with taking the final written comments and integrating them into the text. The regional partner was given final editorial sign off to assure that the final handbook represented the needs and views of their region's participants.

Over 600 cyber experts from indigenous business, government, and academic entities participated in developing the handbooks either by participation in the workshops, webinars, or by providing written comments to the drafts that were generated by the sessions.

Special attention was given to assure that individuals who sit on corporate boards were recruited for these groupings (as boards are the target audience), but all workshops and webinars as well as written reviews were also available to management, government and academic personal. The Internet Security Alliance Board of Directors—which consists of 25 cybersecurity experts representing virtually all critical industry sectors served as the technical authority and "red-team" for the handbooks. The result of this process is the closest thing currently available to a de-facto standard of board of directors' theory and practice for cybersecurity internationally.

## Five Consensus Principles for Effective Cybersecurity at the Board Level

In February 2021 the World Economic Forum issued the following declaration:

> The first step in resolving the board's role in overseeing cyber risk is to establish the principles to guide directors' behaviors and choices. When leading businesses

adopt common principles into practices, the practices can, in turn, become widely accepted standards that the business community comes to expect. That ripple effect can be transformative.[8]

All the handbooks referenced previously in this chapter are organized through a series of core principles followed by a set of "tool-kits" designed to walk through various specific cyber security issues, such as managing insider threats, supply chains, developing metrics or developing relationships among the board, management and the cybersecurity team. The following chapters in this book are largely matched up with the principles and tool kits in the director's handbooks. As directors increasingly adopt and use these handbooks the expectations for managers will presumably follow this model, and the current volume is intended as a management guide to meeting the director's expectations.

One of the most impressive findings of this process was that the participants from all areas involved in the programs came to broad, nearly unanimous agreement on five key principles as to what should guide board process for cybersecurity. Although, there were slight modifications in some of the terminology used in the various handbooks, five consensus core principles are the foundation of all the handbooks. There was, however, some substantial divergence on the various tool kits included in the international editions largely based on the cultural differences of the various regions. The consensus core principles and can be summarized as:

**Principle One:** Cybersecurity is not an "IT" issue. It's an enterprise-wide risk management issue.

**Principle Two:** Directors should understand the unique legal implications of cyber risks as they relate to their company's specific circumstances.

**Principle Three:** Boards should have adequate access to cybersecurity expertise, and discussions about cyber risk management should be given regular and adequate time.

**Principle Four:** Directors should set the expectation that management will establish an enterprise-wide cyber risk management framework with adequate staffing and budget.

**Principle Five:** Board-management discussions about cyber risk should include identification and quantification of financial exposure to cyber risks and which risks to accept, mitigate, or transfer—such as through insurance—as well as specific plans associated with each approach.

It is noteworthy that all five of these principles were supported by all the organizations collaborating on developing these handbooks, despite a number of distinctions in the structures and composition of the boards in various regions.

For example, in the US, there is a fairly consistent structure of one independent board with oversight responsibility over management—and implicitly labor. In parts of Europe (particularly in Germany), there is a dual-board structure with both a supervisory board and a labor board. Some German companies are mandated to have boards while others use a voluntary board. As a result, Principle One in the German edition advises to assess if they have a primarily supervisory function or a more direct management function. Japan, similarly, has a structure in which many boards are more heavily weighted in terms of management than the US independent oversight model. In contrast, in Latin America there is very often a substantial family constitution to the boards, which may dramatically affect both culture and oversight. Notwithstanding the variations in cultural board structures, the dominant role of a board of directors—even if heavily influenced by management—is vision, oversight, and strategy.

## Outlining the Board Cybersecurity Principles

### Principle One

Directors need to understand and approach cybersecurity as a strategic enterprise risk, not just an IT risk.

Principle one is arguably the most comprehensive and foundational of all the principles, as it describes how cybersecurity ought to be understood in the full organizational context irrespective of the variations of board structure.

One of the main roles of a board is to establish the vision for the organization. How the organization thinks about its mission, its goals and its responsibilities needs to emanate from the top down. In a 2019 survey, CEOs of the largest 200 global companies rated "national and corporate cybersecurity" as the number one threat to business growth and the international economy in the next 5 to 10 years.[9]

This principle (from which this volume takes its title) underlines the need to treat the security of an organization's cyber systems as a strategic risk instead of simply as a segmented operational issue. The former antiquated thinking based on an industrial age model and reinforced by industrial age structures (which will be dealt with in greater detail in Chapter 3) has proven to be an inadequate model for generating the sorts of defenses organizations need to properly address modern attacks.

In the context of the digital age, thinking of cybersecurity as essentially an IT issue, is both mistaken and dangerous.[10] This broad misunderstanding of cybersecurity is one of the main reasons that, despite rhetoric about the seriousness of the threat for over a decade, we are not only not resolving the problem, but we are also arguably losing ground at a massive rate. "We are defending inherently vulnerable systems that are getting technically weaker all the time. We are almost always playing catch up, as the attackers have first mover advantage and, there is virtually no law enforcement."[11]

Cybersecurity obviously has a technical component, but it is not exclusively a technical issue and the board needs to understand this and convey that understanding down through the enterprise to establish the appropriate culture of security as well as a clear cyber risk appetite. The World Economic Foundation's research on cybersecurity concluded that "strong and effective cybersecurity adds value to the business. Controlling cyber risk means coordinating and collaborating with business units throughout the enterprise including the CEO and the board. Ensuring the entire enterprise, not just the IT department is addressing cyber risk furthers the organization's culture of cybersecurity".[12]

In Chapter 3 we will discuss the structures that can facilitate this enterprise-wide model. Creating a culture of security will be addressed in multiple chapters, but in particular Chapter 12.

## Principle Two

Directors should understand the legal implications of cyber risks as they relate to their company's specific circumstances.

The legal and regulatory landscape with respect to cybersecurity, including public disclosure, privacy and data protection, information-sharing, and infrastructure protection requirements is complex and constantly evolving. Boards should stay informed about the current compliance and liability issues faced by their organizations—and, potentially, by board members on an individual or collective basis. The 2020 NACD survey of US board members found that only 14.8% of current directors feel that their board is "deeply informed about the legal, disclosure and liability of cyber risks".

Cyber requirements at the US state level vary widely, and each industry faces increasing requirements from US federal regulators. Outside of the US, jurisdictions are increasingly adopting their own cyber regulations, such as the European Union's Network and Information Security Directive, and data security and breach requirements such as the General Data Protection Regulation. Some of these requirements now include governance structures, rapid notification of incidents, oversight of third-party vendors, and (in California) statutory damages through class-action for many notable data breaches.

Boards should understand whether management has an effective compliance program to meet changing requirements, reporting responsibilities, and related obligations. While some of these regulations are highlighted in successive chapters and throughout the Director's Handbooks, they are examples and far from all-inclusive. Chapter 7 in this volume provides a detailed description of how the legal and general counsel's office can assist in cyber risk management.[13]

High-profile attacks may spawn lawsuits, including (for public companies) shareholder derivative suits accusing the organization of mismanagement, waste of corporate assets, and abuse of control. Plaintiffs may also allege that the organization's board of directors neglected its fiduciary duty by failing to take sufficient steps to confirm the adequacy of the company's protections against data breaches and their consequences. Exposures can vary considerably depending on the organization's reliance on technology and data, as well as their sector, and operating locations.

The US business judgment rule may protect directors, so long as the board takes reasonable oversight in advance of and investigation steps following a cybersecurity incident. Other considerations include maintaining records of boardroom discussions about cybersecurity and cyber risks; staying informed about industry-, region-, or sector-specific requirements that apply to the organization; and determining what to disclose in the wake of a cyberattack. It is also advisable for directors to participate with management in one or more cyber breach simulations (or table-top exercises) to better understand their roles and the company's response process in the case of a serious incident as we will discuss in Chapter 10.

## Principle Three

Boards should have adequate access to cybersecurity expertise, and discussions about cyber risk management should be given regular and adequate time on board meeting agendas.

Only 45% of directors believe their board's "understanding of cyber risk is strong enough to provide effective oversight".[14] A study from EY reported that less than half of organizations believed their board and executive management have a sufficient understanding of cybersecurity to fully evaluate preventative measures and cyber risks.[15] When asked to assess the quality of information provided by the board to senior management, information about cybersecurity was rated lowest, with nearly a quarter of public-company directors reporting that they were dissatisfied or very dissatisfied with the quality of information provided by management about cybersecurity. Less than 15% said they were very satisfied with the quality of the information they received.[16]

Even in organizations that have implemented good board education programs on cybersecurity, leading directors recognize that this education needs to be regularly refreshed. A recent NACD survey found that a majority of boards see cybersecurity as "an area where board knowledge can grow quickly stale. Since threats are nearly limitless and constantly mutate, directors must assume their current understanding of cyber risks has an expiration date".[17]

As the cyber threat has grown, the responsibility (and expectations) of board members also has also grown. Directors need to do more than simply understand that threats exist and receive reports from management. They need to employ the same principles of inquiry and constructive challenge that are standard features of board-management discussions about strategy and company performance. As a director at an NACD forum observed: "cyber literacy can be considered similar to financial literacy. Not everyone on the board is an auditor, but everyone should be able to read a financial statement and understand the financial language of business".[18]

Leading boards now understand that cybersecurity is not simply a separate discussion item to be addressed for a few minutes at the end of a board meeting. Rather, cybersecurity is an essential element of many board-level business decisions and needs to be integrated into discussions about issues like mergers, acquisitions, new product development, strategic partnerships, and the like at an early stage. As a result, boards need to be accessing information not simply from IT and technical operations, but from a wide range of sources including human resources, finance, public relations, legal/compliance. Several models for soliciting a wide range of perspectives and inputs are discussed in Chapter 3.

*Principle Four*

Directors should set the expectation that management will establish an enterprise-wide cyber risk management framework with adequate staffing and budget.

Principles Four and Five of the *Cyber Risk Handbook* differ in some respects from the first three principles in that the first three principles focused specifically on what the board should be doing itself, whereas Principles Four and Five focus more on what the board should be expecting from management.

In order for boards to engage in effective oversight, it is important to fully understand the responsibilities that management has in addressing the organization's cybersecurity. Thus, the ultimate success or failure of employing this risk oversight framework may lie in its execution.

However, the existing reporting structures and decision-making processes at many companies are legacies of a siloed operating model, where each department and business unit make decisions and manage risks relatively independently and without fully taking into account the digital interdependency that is a fact of modern business.

Directors should seek assurances that management is taking an appropriate enterprise-wide approach to cybersecurity. Specifically, boards should assess whether management has established both an enterprise-wide technical framework as well as a management framework that will facilitate effective governance of cyber risk. An integrated risk model should consider cyber risk not as unique or separate from other business risks, but rather as part of a comprehensive risk-management plan. Having an integrated approach to risk allows businesses to more effectively address cybersecurity risk across the entire enterprise.

> Given the unique circumstances of each corporation and its board of directors, there is no single implementation model. Each board must determine its own appropriate execution methodology.[19]

The organizational structural issues and options available to enterprises are discussed in greater detail in Chapter 3.

*Principle Five*

Board-management discussions about cyber risk should include identification and quantification of financial exposure to cyber risks and which risks to accept, mitigate or transfer, such as through insurance, as well as specific plans associated with each approach.

Managing financial exposure to cyber risk is a critical component of board risk oversight. Managing cyber risk—as with all risks in general—is a continuum, not an end state. Beyond existing security initiatives and compliance discussions, understanding cyber risk in economic terms is increasingly important as related to enterprise cyber risk oversight.

Boards need to understand how management has determined the effectiveness of the firm's controls and processes in reducing the exposure to cyber risk to an acceptable level. This level of quantification of effective cyber risk management allows the company to make better risk-informed decisions about its strategy and, in turn, its resource-allocation choices.

There is a growing consensus among existing scholarship that the board needs time on its agenda to understand and oversee risks associated with the protection of confidential information and intellectual property. In addition, by allocating board time to these issues, the board elevates the importance of IT issues and cybersecurity within the management team and the company. Quite simply, attention by the board underscores that IT and cybersecurity concerns are a priority. Care should be taken to ensure that adequate time is reserved by the board.[20]

Increasingly, business leaders and regulators are looking at quantitative means for expressing information risk.[21] It is important to note that the US Securities and Exchange Commission's updated 2018 cybersecurity guidance has incorporated quantitative cyber risk reporting requirements, and as such, publicly traded companies need to form an understanding of their quantitative financial exposure to cyber risk. Moreover, credit rating agencies are beginning to incorporate a financial quantitative measurement related to cyber risk exposure, signaling that cyber risk will necessarily become a core component to overall corporate financial management. Leveraging these mathematical and scientific methods for improved analyses can allow for more effective decision making compared to qualitative types of risk scoring and heat map risk reporting.[22]

Traditional risk assessment approaches have had difficulty fulfilling these requirements. Historically, cyber risk assessments tended to follow long check lists of highly technical information or control requirements; often 500 or more that treat cyber risks as a generic item rather than tailoring spending to the specific risk posture of the organization. The 2021 PWC Global Digital Trust Insights found that "more than half (55%) of businesses and technology experts surveyed lack confidence that cyber spending is aligned to the most significant risks".[23]

These methods have historically not been qualitative assessments and have not assessed cyber risk through economic terms.[24] However, quantitative economic assessments of cyber risk have matured to the point where cyber risks can now be quantitatively assessed. Accordingly, just as other disciplines financially model major risks—such as market, credit, insurance, and strategic risks—cyber risks can now be modeled quantitatively to improve risk-management performance.

Several methods have emerged in recent years for expressing cyber risks in economic terms in place of subjective ordinal scales. These more contemporary methodologies, such as X-Analytics, Factor Analysis of Information Risk, and various cyber-Value at Risk (VaR) models tend to view cyber risk not as categories (e.g., supply chains or insiders) but as quantities of potential financial loss. Chapter 4 will discuss these methods in more detail.

By calculating the degree of their financial exposure to cyber risk, organizations can better determine where to place and prioritize their cybersecurity investments to address the greatest, most impactful risks. This provides management with an empirical basis for determining which risks make sense to accept, avoid, mitigate or transfer, and provides the board with a clear basis for conducting their responsibility of cyber risk oversight.

## Conclusion

Cybersecurity is now a serious, enterprise-level risk and strategy challenge. Boards need to continuously assess their effectiveness to address cybersecurity, both in terms of their own fiduciary responsibility as well as their oversight of management's activities. While the approaches taken by individual boards will vary, the principles in the ISA-NACD *Cyber Risk Handbook*, and the several versions adapted for various countries and regions now available around the globe, have been shown to offer a helpful blueprint and timely guidance.

Ultimately, the board's role is to bring its judgment to bear and provide effective guidance to management, in order to ensure the cybersecurity program is appropriately designed and sufficiently resilient given their company's strategic imperatives and the realities of the business ecosystem in which it operates.

To continue learning about the concepts in this chapter the following sources are recommended:

1  Internet Security Alliance and Organization of American States (2019) *The Cyber Risk Handbook for Latin American Boards of Directors in Spanish, Portuguese and English*, ISA. isalliance.org/isa-publications/international-cyber-risk-management-handbooks/

2  Internet Security Alliance and European Confederation of Corporate Boards (2020) *Cyber Risk Handbook for European Boards,* ISA. isalliance.org/isa-publications/international-cyber-risk-management-handbooks/

3  D W Hubbard and R Seiersen (2016) *How to Measure Anything in Cybersecurity Risk* Wiley, Hoboken, New Jersey

4  E Ernst & Young. EY CEO Imperative Study 2019, September 2019

5  J Jones. Understanding Cyber Risk Quantification: A Buyer's Guide, 2019. https://cdn2.hubspot.net/hubfs/1616664/CRQ%20Buyers%20Guide%20by%20Jack%20Jones.pdf

## Endnotes

1  L Clinton. International Principles for Boards of Directors and Cyber Security, *Cyber Security: A Peer-Reviewed Journal,* 2020, 4 (3) July 21, 2020. www.isalliance.org/wp-content/uploads/2021/04/CSJ_4_3_CSJ0005_Clinton.pdf (archived at https://perma.cc/5W2K-JK3D) [The copyright for this article is originally held by Henry Steward Publications, and is republished here with their kind permission.]

2  PwC. Turnaround and Transformation in Cybersecurity: Key findings from The Global State of Information Security Survey 2016, *2015.* www.pwc.com/sg/en/publications/assets/pwc-global-state-of-information-security-survey-2016.pdf (archived at https://perma.cc/7KEF-BV8K)

3  Ibid.

4  Ibid.

5  National Association of Corporate Directors. 2019-2020 NACD Public Company Governance Survey, December 11, 2019. www.nacdonline.org/insights/publications.cfm?ItemNumber=66566 (archived at https://perma.cc/U9L6-C5WJ)

**6**  Business Roundtable. Business Roundtable Redefines the Purpose of a Corporation to Promote 'an Economy That Serves All Americans': Updated atatement moves away from shareholder primacy, includes commitment to all stakeholders. [blog] Business Roundtable, August 19, 2019. www.businessroundtable.org/business-roundtable-redefines-the-purpose-of-a-corporation-to-promote-an-economy-that-serves-all-americans (archived at https://perma.cc/3254-RJX9)

**7**  Bonime-Blanc, A (2020) *Gloom to Boom: How leaders transform risk into resilience and value.* Routledge, Abingdon, Oxon

**8**  F Van der Oord, L Clinton, J Nocera, D Dobrygowski. 6 Principles to Unite Business for Cyber-resilience [blog] World Economic Forum, January 25, 2021. www.weforum.org/agenda/2021/01/cyber-security-governance-principles (archived at https://perma.cc/EKL4-G938)

**9**  National Association of Corporate Directors and Internet Security Alliance. NACD Director's Handbook on Cyber-Risk Oversight 2020, February 25, 2020. www.nacdonline.org/insights/publications.cfm?ItemNumber=67298 (archived at https://perma.cc/SB9A-467M)

**10**  Ernst & Young. How Boards Are Governing Disruptive Technology, 2019. assets.ey.com/content/dam/ey-sites/ey-com/en_us/topics/cbm/ey-how-boards-are-governing-disruptive-technology.pdf (archived at https://perma.cc/CX3A-VA3F)

**11**  L Clinton, et al. (2020) *Incentivizing Cybersecurity: Creating a Sustainable Public-Private Partnership,* Georgetown University, Washington D.C.

**12**  F Van der Oord, L Clinton, J Nocera, D Dobrygowski. 6 Principles to Unite Business for Cyber-resilience [blog] World Economic Forum, January 25, 2021. www.weforum.org/agenda/2021/01/cyber-security-governance-principles (archived at https://perma.cc/TE9W-P2DL)

**13**  National Association of Corporate Directors. 2019-2020 NACD Public Company Governance Survey, December 11, 2019. www.nacdonline.org/insights/publications.cfm?ItemNumber=66566 (archived at https://perma.cc/T9MH-PFM9)

**14**  Ernst & Young. EY CEO Imperative Study 2019, 2019

**15**  Ibid.

**16**  Source: NACD, 2019-2020 NACD Public Company Governance Survey (Arlington, VA: NACD, 2019)

**17**  National Association of Corporate Boards. 2018–2019 NACD Public Company Governance Survey, 2018. www.nacdonline.org/applications/secure/?FileID=295385. (archived at https://perma.cc/C9SH-PMEU)

**18**  National Association of Corporate Boards. Cybersecurity: Boardroom Implications, January 29, 2014. www.nacdonline.org/insights/publications.cfm?ItemNumber=8486 (archived at https://perma.cc/GEY4-JU6W)

**19**  J E Caldwell. A Framework for Board Oversight of Enterprise Risk, 2012. hoacorp.ca/wp-content/uploads/2017/03/CPA-A-Framework-for-Board-Oversight-of-Enterprise-Risk-July-2015.pdf (archived at https://perma.cc/3XG3-Y6FR)

**20**  H J Gregory. Board Oversight of Cybersecurity Risks, March 24, 2014. www.sidley.com/-/media/files/newsinsights/publications/2014/03/board-oversight-of-cybersecurity-risks/files/view-article/fileattachment/board-oversight-of-cybersecurity-risks--march-2014.pdf?la=en (archived at https://perma.cc/5MLR-LC4G)

**21**  D Hubbard and R Seiersen (2016) *How to Measure Anything in Cybersecurity Risk,* John Wiley & Sons Inc., Hoboken, New Jersey

**22**  Ibid.

**23**  PwC. Global Digital Trust Insight Survey 2021, October 2020. www.pwc.com/us/en/services/consulting/cybersecurity/library/assets/pwc-2021-global-digital-trust-insights.pdf (archived at https://perma.cc/RJ7C-T383)

**24**  J Jones. Understanding Cyber Risk Quantification: A Buyer's Guide, 2019. cdn2.hubspot.net/hubfs/1616664/CRQ%20Buyers%20Guide%20by%20Jack%20Jones.pdf (archived at https://perma.cc/9LCV-HMVH)

# 03

# Structuring for the Digital Age

BY LARRY CLINTON, PRESIDENT AND CEO, INTERNET SECURITY ALLIANCE, AND BEN PEIFER, ISA RESEARCH ASSOCIATE

## Five Key Ideas to Take Away from This Chapter

1  Traditional corporate structures for cybersecurity are inadequate to address modern cyber risk.

2  Research demonstrates that the management of the cybersecurity function will be more effective if it is integrated and encourages communication and flexibility on the issue throughout the enterprise.

3  Management of cyber risk is not solely the responsibility of the IT department within an organization, it should be managed across the enterprise.

4  Organizations need to find the right structure to address their cyber risks based on their size, priorities, and industry. There is no one-size-fits-all structure for the digital age.

5  Non-IT executives will play an important role in leading cybersecurity teams in new structures.

## Introduction

In Chapter 1 we described how the cyber threat is evolving both in terms of the sophistication of the attack methods and our understanding of the problem as more than a simple technological and operational issue. In Chapter 2 we discussed how boards of directors are adapting to the growing cyber threat by developing a set of useful principles to guide them in fulfilling their oversight responsibilities and define their role working with management. We will now turn to the similar evolution in corporate structure regarding addressing cyber threats.

## The Move Away from Digital Silos

As digital transformation continues to accelerate and cyber attackers continue to innovate, organizations need to consider adapting their structures to better address the new enterprise landscape. In the past few years, technology has become more integral to business strategy. Management has taken on the role of deploying, managing, and protecting new technology capabilities across the organization. Technology now integrates modern organizations, whether workers are across the hall or halfway around the world. But the existing reporting structures and decision-making processes at many companies are legacies of a siloed operating model, where each department and business unit make decisions and manages risks relatively independently, and without fully taking into account the digital interdependency that is a fact of modern business.

While the default practice in many organizations is to have cybersecurity siloed into a separate category apart from consideration of an entity's most valuable assets, leading organizations are moving toward a more integrated

FIGURE 3.1 The governance, risk and reputation triangle as applied to cyber risk.

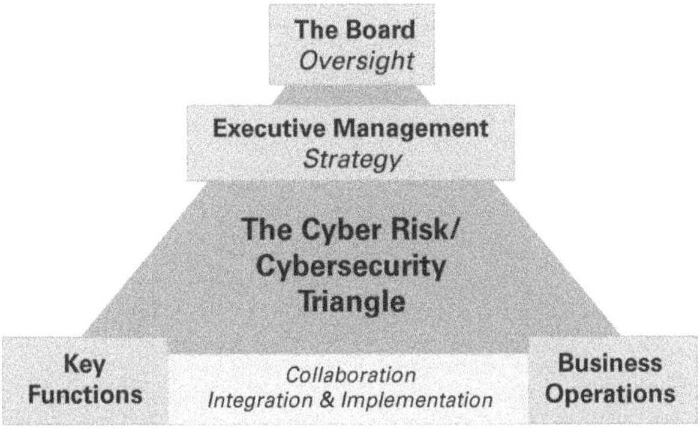


SOURCE © Andrea Bonime-Blanc & GEC Risk Advisory. All Rights Reserved. 2021. Reproduced with permission.

team approach.[1] A recent Conference Board study on Emerging Risk Practices in Cyber recommended a pyramid structure integrating the board with management and operations (see Figure 3.1) noting that:

> Good governance entails an effective triangular relationship between the board, the top leadership (CEO and C-suite), and top management within the organization all working in synchrony on strategy and risk.[2]

An integrated risk model should consider cyber risk not as unique or separate from other business risks, but rather as part of a comprehensive risk-management plan. Having an integrated approach to risk allows businesses to more effectively address cybersecurity risk across the entire enterprise.

## Establishing a Management Framework for Cybersecurity

Consistent with the principle outlined in Chapter 1—that cybersecurity is broader than simply an IT issue—is the realization that cyber risk management should not be thought of as the responsibility of just the IT experts. Even with good technical controls, personnel need to be trained in the proper use of digital assets, hence a secure culture (a construct that will be more fully developed in later chapters), is a critical aspect of cybersecurity. Obviously, compliance and legal issues are critical elements of the overall cyber strategy. With the need for increased and better calibrated cybersecurity budgets, finance is a critical function, as is R and D and marketing. Cyber events can also raise concern regarding reputational risk, making it important for the public relations and communications departments to contribute to cyber risk management. Cybersecurity needs to be managed across the enterprise, and many different parts of the organization need to take responsibility for specific activities and be held accountable for their contribution to an effective enterprise-wide program.

## We are not Integrated Yet

Although some progress is being made, too often cybersecurity is still an afterthought in many organizations, and this works to further undermine security. According to PWC's study of cyber resilience, only 25% of cybersecurity organizations have reframed their team's mission to align with their company's strategic goals—although that may be changing. That same study reported that in the wake of the COVID-19 pandemic, 96% of cyber leaders were considering changing their strategy.[3]

Notwithstanding the attitudes of cyber security practitioners, the corporate structures they operate within have not changed substantially with digital transformation.

> The evolution from introverted technologist to outgoing business partner has yet to take place at many organizations meaning that many cybersecurity teams are working *for the business* rather than *in the business*. The result is that instead of security by design whereby cybersecurity is a central consideration right from the start of each new project, the function finds itself constantly retrofitting protection which will often lead to imperfect and costly security solutions or impractical workarounds. Only by embedding themselves within the organization will they be able to integrate the security agenda into digital transformation programs from the beginning and anticipate the full range of bad actors that might target the business.[4]

The details embedded in the EY study documenting the generally low degree of cybersecurity integration into digital transformation are fairly stark. Despite the fact that one would assume cybersecurity experts would be valuable assets in considering new projects as part of digital transformation, only 41% of organizations involve cybersecurity staff in the early stages of new digital projects. While there is growing concern about the exposure that connected devices might bring, just 4% of Internet of Things-related initiatives drive new spending in cybersecurity. Only 7% of organizations describe cybersecurity as enabling innovation, and only 4% of total cyber-spending is driven toward new business enablement. Meanwhile, 29% of cyber spending is driven by regulatory compliance needs and the vast majority (62%) is risk reduction.[5]

In Chapter 1 we documented the substantial degree of alienation among the cybersecurity function and neighboring divisions, including marketing, finance and even HR. But in truth, even to a slightly lesser extent, the degree of separation between cyber functions and most of the organization is typically distant. Of the nine different divisions EY studied, only the IT function generally rated their relationship with the cybersecurity function as one of high trust and collaboration. None of the other nine departments studied reached a similar degree of collaboration. These numbers caused EY to conclude that: "the cybersecurity team at many organizations currently has little or no relationship with other key functions—especially those involved in innovation, product development and customer-facing activities".[6]

## Siloed Cybersecurity Systems are Counterproductive

While remnants of the traditional siloed status for information security program remain, there is a growing body of evidence that a more collaborative structure is more effective from both a security and a productivity perspective. An independent study conducted by ESI ThoughtLab found that the traditional, narrow thinking about cybersecurity undermined the impact of cyber investments. This study found that "cybersecurity is most effective when it is part of the corporate strategy and treated as a critical business function and not just a function of IT or risk".[7] This finding confirms the research that shows that if the cybersecurity function is more deeply involved in the business environment, both the security function and the likelihood of success in new digital projects is enhanced.

> Companies building a business case for investing in cybersecurity should consider the upside of these investments. In addition to trust and transformation benefits, these include growing shareholder value, enabling innovation, building market share and driving revenue growth. Cybersecurity leaders show the way teaming up with heads of internal business units to facilitate their growth strategies and operational plans.[8]

Those results largely match the results from a similar EY study:

> Cybersecurity cannot fulfill its potential to add value if it is kept at arm's length from the rest of the organization. Organizations that really push for the proactive involvement of security are going to see very significant business benefits in both the near term and the long term.[9]

## How Centralized Ought the Cybersecurity Function be?

Having an enterprise-wide approach means that all the players need to be pulling in the same direction to manage cybersecurity—as opposed to different systems in different parts of the enterprise developing their own strategy. The larger the enterprise the more difficult it is to consistently apply security controls, such as patching, configuration control, policy oversight, or network monitoring. Attackers are adept at finding the last 5% of assets in the company that a control missed. The implication of this is that a company's best chance of success is to centralize as much as possible. This has organizational, financial, and operational implications. Organizationally, if you have security run by each line of business or geographic region with a loose federation, your chances of having each business run equally well are slim. From a financial perspective, a centrally run security function will be less expensive—duplication will be reduced, and you will have more leverage over vendors. Operationally, monitoring from a single location means all potential incidents can be prioritized and acted upon.[10]

However, as digital transformation increases many organizations are considering innovating their structures to keep pace. The ESI survey, which also rated organizations on their cybersecurity effectiveness, found that "as firms transform…cybersecurity leaders are transitioning to hybrid forms of centralization or even decentralization. But these shifts while often necessary because of the size or the underlying organization of the firm can be challenging to orchestrate while maintaining control".[11]

Still, as digital transformation becomes more common the imperative for centralization seems to abate "as firms digitally transform their business divisions often assume responsibility for digital operations. In response, cybersecurity functions are moving away from rigid centralization to central teams sharing budget and staff with other departments".[12]

## Who does the Cyber Leader Report to?

With evolving structures come additional questions as to who the cyber leader reports to, and what implications come with that. Traditionally, the cybersecurity function operated under the IT umbrella and/or under direction of the Chief Information officer (CIO). However, over time it became increasing apparent that, although both the CIO and CISO dealt with technical issues, they often had divergent goals. CIOs typically were charged and compensated for implementing technological innovation to drive revenue growth. As discussed in Chapter 1, many of these technologies and business practices—while great for revenue growth—were problematic from a security perspective, typically the province of the Chief Information Security Officer—the CISO.

Over time this has led to a gradual move away from the CISO reporting to the CIO. The Conference Board 2018 study highlighted the need for senior executive involvement in cyber risk management:

> The CEO and the C-suite must take charge of cyber risk strategy and
> management depending on the cyber risk readiness required at a given company.
> More or less direct CEO involvement on a regular and periodic basis is highly

recommended. The more readiness is needed, the more actual attention, leadership, and support will be needed from the very top of the executive food chain. This may also entail having someone within the executive team or even C-suite who has deep expertise on cyber matters or who has visibility into, and can discuss in informed detail, the cyber risk profile of the company.[13]

Of course, when high-profile breaches hit, boards tend to look to the CEO and senior management to step up and take responsibility, but even setting aside the prospect of a major breach, senior management needs to communicate effectively with the cybersecurity function because it is likely only the senior management team that knows the specific risk/reward balance for this particular enterprise.[14]

One prominent CEO, Larry Jones of Colefire, writing in a compendium of expert analysis on digital transformation, *Navigating the Digital Age*, explained the prioritization and efficiency benefits of involving the senior management team in cyber security issues.

> When cybersecurity programs are managed only at the technical level the focus of the program is at risk of being misdirected…Only senior executives and business unit managers understand the relative importance of specific operations or data…As a senior executive one of the things you should be asking is if your most important systems and your most important data are properly deployed and protected within your system architecture. However, the IT team will never know the *how* to answer that question if senior management does not specifically provide guidance on the relative importance of business functions and their associated systems.[15]

The extent of this evolution was documented in the 2020 ESI survey, which reported:

> Most executives in charge of cybersecurity now report to the CEO, while only about 2 out of 10 report to the CIO. For over three quarters of organizations rated as leaders in cybersecurity, cybersecurity reports into the top management—either the CEO, COO, CFO or the board.[16]

Deloitte's 2019 survey on the future of cybersecurity reported "great success" with organizations who embed cybersecurity specialists within the business units:

> Cyber professionals embedded in the business are an effective approach to manage cyber risk across the enterprise and foster greater collaboration and innovation. In the financial services industry, many banks have business security

officers embedded in the business units... This model becomes a catalyst for better efficiency and risk management.[17]

## Who is on the Cybersecurity Team?

As organizations have increasingly realized that cybersecurity is more than just an IT function, organizational models have been developed that broaden the number of and types of expertise that ought to be involved in managing the cyber security function. One of the earliest, and simplest, models was offered over a decade ago by the American National Standards Institute (ANSI) and the ISA in their joint 2008 publication, *The Financial Management of Cyber Risk: 50 Questions Every CFO Should Ask*. This basic model stresses not only that multiple stakeholders ought to be involved, but also advocates for an identified leader—not from IT—who has cross-organizational authority. It also advocates for a separate cybersecurity budget as opposed to the traditional model of folding cybersecurity into the IT budget. The ISA-ANSI framework outlines the following seven steps:

1 Establish ownership of cyber risk on a cross-departmental basis. A senior manager with cross-departmental authority, such as the chief financial officer, chief risk officer, or chief operating officer (not the chief information officer), should lead the team.

2 Appoint a cross-organization cyber risk management team. All substantial stakeholder departments must be represented, including business unit leaders, legal, internal audit and compliance, finance, human resources, IT (including information security), and risk management.

3 The cyber risk team needs to perform a forward-looking, enterprise-wide risk assessment, using a systematic framework that accounts for the complexity of cyber risk—including, but not limited to, regulatory compliance.

4 Be aware that cybersecurity regulation differs significantly across jurisdictions (among US states, between the United States and other countries, and from industry to industry). As noted in Principle 2, management should dedicate resources to tracking the standards and requirements that apply to the organization, especially as some countries aggressively expand the scope of government involvement into the cybersecurity arena.

5  Take a collaborative approach to developing reports to the board. Executives should be expected to track and report metrics that quantify the business impact of cyber threats and associated risk-management efforts. Evaluation of cyber risk management effectiveness and the company's cyber resiliency should be conducted as part of quarterly internal audits and other performance reviews.

6  Develop and adopt an organization-wide cyber risk management plan and internal communications strategy across all departments and business units. While cybersecurity obviously has a substantial IT component, all stakeholders need to be involved in developing the corporate plan and should feel "bought in" to it. Testing of the plan should be done on a routine basis.

7  Develop and adopt a comprehensive cyber risk budget with sufficient resources to meet the organization's needs and risk appetite. Resource decisions should take into account the severe shortage of experienced cybersecurity talent and identify what needs can be met in-house versus what can or should be outsourced to third parties. Because cybersecurity is more than IT security, the budget for cybersecurity should not be exclusively tied to one department: examples include allocations in areas such as employee training, tracking legal regulations, public relations, product development, and vendor management.[18]

A second conceptual model has emerged over the past few years, originating in the financial services sector but increasingly being adopted by leading organizations in various sectors. This Three Lines of Defense[19] model stresses multiple independent operations within the organization having varied and increasing roles in assessing and checking cyber risk management.

---

The Three Lines of Defense Model was initially created by the Institute of Internal Auditors in 2013 and updated to the Three Lines Model by the IIA in 2020. The term defense was dropped by the IIA in their 2020 update to acknowledge the need in risk management to both seize opportunities and to enact effective defenses. The current model identifies six key principles for itself that were not included in the previous Three Lines of Defense model.

1  Having the right structures and processes to ensure that cyber risk is appropriately managed through governance.

2  Ensuring that responsibility for cybersecurity is appropriately delegated by the governing body and that management has the tools it needs.

3  Management's role is within both the first and second line, and they may be "blended or separated". Second line roles can be assigned to specialists; for cybersecurity this could be a penetration tester challenging the first line.

4  Internal audits "provide assurance and advice on the adequacy and effectiveness of governance and risk management".

5  The internal audit's independence is "critical to its objectivity, authority, and credibility".

6  There must be collaboration among all roles to ensure success.

## Line One

Management owns the risk designs, implements operations, and maintains a constant dialogue while receiving direction from the governing body and its members—such as the CISO. Each business line defines the cyber risk they face and weaves cyber risk and self-assessment into risk, fraud, crisis management, and resiliency processes. Business lines need to actively monitor existing and future exposures and vulnerability threats and assess what impact cyber risk has on new tech deployment, client relationships and business strategies, and maintain appropriate structures and process for risk control.

## Line Two

Defines policy statements and defines the risk management framework. It provides a credible challenge to Line One and is responsible for evaluating risk exposure so that the board can determine risk appetite. Line Two should be established as a separate independent function under management with communication with both internal audit and the governing body. Line Two manages enterprise cyber risk appetite and the risk-management framework within overall enterprise risk. Line Two challenges Line One, determines how to appropriately measure cyber risk, and integrates results into a risk-tolerance statement for the company. Line Two, under management, must communicate and interact with Line Three—internal audit—while maintaining its independence in order to prevent duplication and close any potential gaps in the organization's cybersecurity defense.

The focus of the Line One and Line Two needs to be on effectively managing risk, not on regulatory compliance, although compliance can be integrated into these lines.

### Line Three

Line Three is internal audit. It is responsible for independent evaluation of the Line One and Line Two. It defines roles for each level of defense. Line 3 provides an independent, objective assessment of company processes and controls across Lines One and Two with a focus on operational effectiveness and efficiency. Traditionally, internal audit has focused its testing work on technical IT controls but will need to expand its scope to assess whether cybersecurity is effectively managed as an enterprise risk. Internal audit performs process and control assessments, validates technology infrastructure, reviews controls to mitigate third-party risks, conducts independent penetration testing, and stays abreast of new threats. There is a greater focus on the governing bodies communication with both management and the internal audit in the updated model and less focus on the role of senior management. The internal audit and its importance to cybersecurity will be discussed in greater detail in Chapter 7.

The three-tier model is obviously far more sophisticated than the ANSI/ISA model, but they are alike in attempting to find a structure to bring more voices to the table in assessing an organization's cyber risk and identifying appropriate mitigation methods. It is noteworthy that both approaches bring non-IT executives into leadership roles in guiding cybersecurity policy and practice. This reflects a growing—although not yet dominant—trend toward expanding the team involved in cyber risk in recognition of the varying types of risk the organization may need to address from various types of cyberattacks.

> A diverse leadership team is incredibly helpful at not just responding to the technical problems but also ensuring other areas such as public image, legal ramifications and revenue impact are taken into consideration.[20]

## Finding the Right Structure for the Cybersecurity Team

The Conference Board's study on Emerging Practices in Risk Governance concluded that "one of the important lessons we have learned from (our study) is that there is a strong trend toward cross-disciplinary or cross-functional collaboration".[21] Certainly, getting multiple perspectives on cyber risk is important, but figuring out how to integrate mission owners, IT providers, security personnel and disparate organizational departments is a challenging issue.

Mission owners focus on results, providers focus on efficiencies and the latest technologies, while security personnel aim to keep out—or respond effectively to—entities who seek to attack the system even if that means undermining the mission or the end users. In addition, there is never enough time or money to do it all.[22] Meanwhile, another byproduct of digital transformation is that enterprises may now require specialized expertise for certain projects. A manufacturing business may need help from experts in an industrial systems while IoT professionals may be required to deploy new hardware in a secure fashion, or red-teams may be required to test network strength. Even if consultative expertise can be brought in from the outside, where they sit, who they report to, and where the budget comes from becomes more complicated than in the former centralized models.[23]

There is almost certainly not one, right universal structure. Given the diversity in overall organizational structures, business models, and regulatory requirements, each entity needs to adapt its structure to fit its unique needs.

As innovation in this space proceeds some traditional models can be adapted to address some of these concerns while new models are also being suggested and tested in the field. Some of these are summarized in the following sections.

## Adapting Enterprise Architecture

Enterprise Architecture (EA) offers a comprehensive view of an organization, its mission and strategic vision, as well as the business processes, data and technology that support it. Although EAs have historically been developed to manage the complexities of systems and interconnections, some have argued it can also be used to address security controls at the system process and enterprise levels.[24]

In this model, EA inventories asset and capture relationships and dependencies providing managers with a clean line of sight from the organization's mission and goals through the supporting IT and services. This also facilitates management's ability to assess the impact of proposed change.

EA can be adapted from its historical goal to an organization's cybersecurity needs by providing a common framework. By focusing on mission first, cybersecurity can be driven from the tip of the organization down through it, as opposed to the traditional approach of having security drift bottom-up from the IT department.

> When employed within an effective governance structure, EA can facilitate effective support and resourcing thus bringing the full weight of organizational leadership and resources to bear on the security function.[25]

## Collaborative Models Initiated in the Financial Services Industry

A different—and not necessarily incompatible—approach is being field tested in the financial services sector. McKinsey has reported on financial institutions trying to respond to the massive increases in vulnerabilities associated with digitalization and expanded interconnection by developing a series of alternate organizational models. Adapting these models' institutions can increase collaboration and effectiveness of fighting not only traditional cybercrime but other financial crimes such as fraud as money laundering, all of which have previously been addressed primarily by separate elements in the organization. However, banks are now finding that meaningful distinctions between cyber-attacks, fraud and money laundering are largely disappearing:

> Institutions are finding that their existing approaches to fighting such crimes cannot handle the many threats they are experiencing. For this reason, leaders are transforming their operating models to obtain a holistic view of the evolving landscape of financial crime. This view becomes the starting point of efficient and effective management of risk... In taking a more holistic view of the underlying processes banks can streamline business and technology architecture to support a better customer experience improved risk decision making and greater cost efficiencies.[26]

McKinsey has identified three different variations on the more collaborative model that organizations can adapt based on their size, degree of digital renovation and expansion of their international partnerships and operations.

The first model essentially represents the status quo wherein independent roles and responsibilities are maintained typically in smaller separate units.

This model has the benefit of familiarity both to the institution's staff and applicable regulators. However, it tends to lack transparency across the organization and thus gaps can emerge in overall responsiveness, therefore it fails to achieve possible economies of scope and scale.

A more holistic approach is defined as the partially integrated model for cybersecurity and fraud which is increasingly being grafted into the Three Lines of Defense approach covered previously. In this structure units maintain their independence but develop a consistent framework following mutually accepted rules and procedures. This model creates a consistent architecture for risk identification and assessment which lowers the likelihood that gaps in coverage will occur. However, since the existing structures remain intact, even if cooperating more closely, there is still little transparency since separate reporting is maintained, and benefits of economies of scope and scale remain. Also, with smaller operational units such a partially integrated model may be less attractive to prospective top talent.

The final, unified model is a fully integrated approach bringing together all aspects of financial crime under a single framework with common assets and systems to manage risk across the enterprise. This model creates a single view of the customer and shares analytics. Through convergence and enterprise-wide transparency on threats there is better insight into the most important risks. The model also captures benefits of scope and scale across key roles and therefore enhances the ability to attract and retain top talent. According to McKinsey:

> The integration of fraud and cybersecurity operations is an imperative step now since the crimes themselves are already deeply interrelated. The enhanced data and analytics capabilities that integrating enables are now tools of representation detection and mitigation of threats. Most forward-looking institutions are working toward such integration creating in stages a more unified model across domains based on common processes and analytics.[27]

## Conclusion

As digital transformation becomes a business necessity cyber risks are mounting. Boards at leading organizations are responding by increasingly integrating cybersecurity as a strategic element in their business plans. A natural outcome of this broader understanding of cyber risk has been an evolution in corporate structure sometimes generated by governmental regulatory oversights and sometimes by innovative business thinking. While the specific structures continue to evolve in ways unique to individual enterprise business plans there are some themes that seem to be common. These themes include a flatter, less siloed approach engaging a multi-stakeholder grouping into the discussions on cyber risk, elevating the reporting structure for these responsible for managing cyber risk. Initial research suggests that such structures can both enhance the cyber risk management function and improve business efficiency.

To continue learning about the concepts in this chapter the following sources are recommended:

1  C Troncoso, et al. (2019) *The Cyber Security Body of Knowledge,* The National Cyber Security Centre. www.cybok.org/media/downloads/cybok_version_1.0.pdf

2  G Nott. Organisational Structures for Digital Transformation: 4 Archetypes Emerge [blog] CIO, September 6, 2017. www.cio.com/article/3515498/organisational-structures-for-digital-transformation-4-archetypes-emerge.html

3  A Singh, P Klarner, and T Hess. How do Chief Digital Officers Pursue Digital Transformation Activities? The Role of Organization Design Parameters, *Long Range Planning*, 2020, 53 (3), www.sciencedirect.com/science/article/pii/S0024630116302606.

4  Maarten Wensveen. How Organizational Structure Contributes to Digital Transformation. Forbes Magazine, September 1, 2019. www.forbes.com/sites/forbestechcouncil/2019/09/19/how-organizational-structure-contributes-to-digital-transformation/?sh=3de70a33091f.

5  M Aiello and S Thompson. Upending Tradition: Modeling Tomorrow's Cybersecurity Organization, September 18, 2019. www.heidrick.com/Knowledge-Center/Publication/Upending_tradition_Modeling_tomorrows_cybersecurity_organization

## Endnotes

1  R Anderson et al. (2015) *Navigating the Digital Age the Definitive Cybersecurity Guide for Directors and Officers*, Caxton Business and Legal Inc., Chicago. www.securityroundtable.org/wp-content/uploads/2015/09/Cybersecurity-9780996498203-no_marks.pdf (archived at https://perma.cc/6TSR-BZAX)

2   A Bonime-Blanc. Emerging Practices in Cyber Risk Governance, 2015. pages. conference-board.org/cybersecuritykbi-lp-so.html (archived at https://perma.cc/NU2Q-2SKE)

3   PwC. Global Digital Trust Insight Survey 2021, October 2020. www.pwc.com/us/en/services/consulting/cybersecurity/library/assets/pwc-2021-global-digital-trust-insights.pdf (archived at https://perma.cc/QR5N-UZ9H)

4   Ernst & Young. EY Global Information Security Survey 2020, 2020. assets.ey.com/content/dam/ey-sites/ey-com/en_gl/topics/advisory/ey-global-information-security-survey-2020-single-pages.pdf (archived at https://perma.cc/9UW7-AZQ8)

5   Ibid.

6   Ibid.

7   ESI ThoughtLab. Driving Cybersecurity Performance: Improving Results Through Evidence-based Analysis, June 17, 2020. econsultsolutions.com/wp-content/uploads/2020/06/FINAL_ESITL-Driving-Cybersecurity-Performance_ebook_2020.pdf (archived at https://perma.cc/JDP7-RR75)

8   Ibid.

9   Ernst & Young. EY Global Information Security Survey 2020, 2020. assets.ey.com/content/dam/ey-sites/ey-com/en_gl/topics/advisory/ey-global-information-security-survey-2020-single-pages.pdf (archived at https://perma.cc/97Z4-WVE8)

10   National Association of Corporate Directors and Internet Security Alliance. NACD Director's Handbook on Cyber-Risk Oversight 2020, February 25, 2020. www.nacdonline.org/insights/publications.cfm?ItemNumber=67298 (archived at https://perma.cc/35DW-HJRL)

11   ESI ThoughtLab. Driving Cybersecurity Performance: Improving Results Through Evidence-based Analysis, June 17, 2020. econsultsolutions.com/wp-content/uploads/2020/06/FINAL_ESITL-Driving-Cybersecurity-Performance_ebook_2020.pdf (archived at https://perma.cc/JDP7-RR75)

12   Ibid.

13   A Bonime-Blanc. Emerging Practices in Cyber Risk Governance, 2015. pages. conference-board.org/cybersecuritykbi-lp-so.html (archived at https://perma.cc/GK58-CSWX)

14   R Anderson et al. (2015) *Navigating the Digital Age the Definitive Cybersecurity Guide for Directors and Officers*, Caxton Business and Legal Inc., Chicago. www.securityroundtable.org/wp-content/uploads/2015/09/Cybersecurity-9780996498203-no_marks.pdf (archived at https://perma.cc/DJ34-E3UU)

15   Ibid.

16   ESI ThoughtLab. Driving Cybersecurity Performance: Improving Results Through Evidence-based Analysis, June 17, 2020. econsultsolutions.com/wp-content/uploads/2020/06/FINAL_ESITL-Driving-Cybersecurity-Performance_ebook_2020.pdf (archived at https://perma.cc/JDP7-RR75)

**17**  Deloitte. The Future of Cyber Survey 2019, 2019. www2.deloitte.com/za/en/
pages/risk/articles/2019-future-of-cyber-survey.html# (archived at https://
perma.cc/5VAG-F74E)

**18**  Internet Security Alliance and American National Standards Institute. The
Financial Management of Cyber Risk: An Implementation Framework for
CFOs, 2010. www.isalliance.org/publications/1B.%20The%20Financial%20
Management%20of%20Cyber%20Risk%20-%20An%20Implementation%20
Framework%20for%20CFOs%20-%20ISA-ANSI%202010.pdf (archived at
https://perma.cc/TE6M-6BNP)

**19**  The Institute of Internal Auditors. The IIA's Three Lines Model: An update of
the Three Lines of Defense, July 2020. na.theiia.org/about-ia/PublicDocuments/
Three-Lines-Model-Updated.pdf (archived at https://perma.cc/M56X-Q9MS)

**20**  R Anderson et al. (2015) *Navigating the Digital Age the Definitive
Cybersecurity Guide for Directors and Officers*, Caxton Business and Legal
Inc., Chicago. www.securityroundtable.org/wp-content/uploads/2015/09/
Cybersecurity-9780996498203-no_marks.pdf (archived at https://perma.cc/
2LRS-D5BY)

**21**  A Bonime-Blanc. Emerging Practices in Cyber Risk Governance, 2015.
pages.conference-board.org/cybersecuritykbi-lp-so.html (archived at https://
perma.cc/GR3P-VKMR)

**22**  Didier M Perdu, Rick Lipsey, and Roxanne Everetts. Improving Your
Cybersecurity Posture with Enterprise Architecture, United States
Cybersecurity Magazine, February 19, 2018. www.uscybersecurity.net/csmag/
improving-your-cybersecurity-posture-with-enterprise-architecture/ (archived
at https://perma.cc/WQ6C-3Q6Y)

**23**  Paul DeCoster. The Changing Structure of Cybersecurity Teams, Infosecurity
Magazine, April 22, 2019. www.infosecurity-magazine.com/opinions/
structure-cybersecurity-teams-1-1/ (archived at https://perma.cc/L2MY-PN8J)

**24**  Didier M Perdu, Rick Lipsey, and Roxanne Everetts. Improving Your
Cybersecurity Posture with Enterprise Architecture, United States
Cybersecurity Magazine, February 19, 2018. www.uscybersecurity.net/csmag/
improving-your-cybersecurity-posture-with-enterprise-architecture/ (archived
at https://perma.cc/X98J-R7LL)

**25**  Ibid.

**26**  S Hasham, S Joshi, D Mikkelsen. Cybersecurity in a Digital Era: Financial
crime and fraud in the age of cybersecurity, 2020. www.mckinsey.com/
business-functions/risk/our-insights/cybersecurity-in-a-digital-era (archived at
https://perma.cc/M8UV-5K37)

**27**  S Hasham, S Joshi, D Mikkelsen. Cybersecurity in a Digital Era: Financial
crime and fraud in the age of cybersecurity, 2020. www.mckinsey.com/
business-functions/risk/our-insights/cybersecurity-in-a-digital-era (archived at
https://perma.cc/M8UV-5K37)

# 04

# A Modern Approach to Assessing Cyber Risk

BY JOHN FRAZZINI, PRESIDENT AND CEO, X-ANALYTICS, BOB VESCIO,
CHIEF ANALYTICS OFFICER, X-ANALYTICS, AND CARTER ZHENG,
ISA RESEARCH ASSOCIATE

## Five Key Ideas to Take Away from This Chapter

1 There are flaws with the traditional qualitative cyber risk assessment methods and a modern approach is needed.

2 Cyber risk must be defined in relation to enterprise-wide risk management.

3 Modern cyber risk assessment plays an important role in translating cybersecurity metrics into financial details.

4 Modern cyber risk assessment provides a means for cyber risk evaluation and forecasting financial exposure due to cyber risk.

5 Modern cyber risk assessment provides a set of prioritized remediation and transfer guidance and aligning cyber risk with enterprise-wide risk management reporting.

## Introduction

As a result of digital transformations, engaging in e-commerce activities, and/or other digital customer interactions, all businesses have some level of cyber risk. Similarly, as an organization becomes increasingly digital, its cyber risk also grows. In recent years, this growing cyber risk has been leveraged by a range of attackers resulting in significant, tangible financial losses—some ranging into the billions of dollars. Terms like ransomware, data breach, and malware are becoming commonplace in both the technical circles and boardrooms alike. As such, discussing and assessing cyber risk is now critical to ultimately managing cyber risk for an organization.

Traditional approaches to assessing and understanding cyber risk have proven insufficient, leaving organizations unprepared for their cyber exposure. Part of the reason these traditional methods have proven inadequate is that they have been qualitative in nature. However, innovations in cyber risk methodology have now generated quantitative assessments, which have matured to the point where cyber risk can be effectively assessed precisely and in business terms.

Addressing the deficiencies in traditional methods of cyber risk assessment, these new approaches link deployed technical cybersecurity controls together with the cyber threat and business exposure context that could lead to financial damage.

Today, many Fortune 1000 businesses use key risk indicators (KRIs). KRIs identify risks that could materially threaten a business. In essence, future performance hinges on these risks.

Business leaders have to decide which risks to remediate. This decision generally comes down to risk tolerance and budget. Since the budget is finite, business leaders need a way to compare all risks. This comparison provides a means to prioritize the most critical risks. The key risk register (KRR) is an enterprise-wide, top-level report that organizes the cluster of all KRIs into one view for comparison purposes.

The expression of cyber risk must be in financial terms. This common expression makes it easier for business leaders to contemplate and manage all risks and provides a way to reduce cyber risk that is consistent with the organization's risk tolerance.

## What is Cyber Risk?

A fundamental question in developing a useful cyber risk assessment is to clearly define what we mean when we use the term cyber risk.

Cyber risk is the potential exposure to loss or harm stemming from an organization's information technology, operational technology, or other computer-based technology. The potential exposure ties directly to the probability and severity of incident, while loss and harm are associated with financial damage that stems from theft or loss of property, regulatory fines, customer churn, human casualty, and many other elements.

A good deal of literature has been written discussing various categories of cyber risks. This literature will often classify "insiders" or technology such as "the cloud" as cyber risks. While these are all critical elements of business operation—which we will cover in successive chapters —these are just categories within which cyber risk can reside.

Cyber risk is not a category, it is a quantity indicating how much harm comes from a cyber exposure understood in the context of the enterprise mission. Cyber risk is not usefully expressed as a color (like red or green), a letter grade (like A- or B+), a credit looking score (like 750), or any other arbitrary value that does indicate actual loss from exposure. Cyber risk is most usefully represented in financial terms within the context of the business.

Cyber risk needs to be understood as part of the larger ecosystem or in context with all other risk in the organization. By representing cyber risk in financial terms, an organization has a way to compare and contrast with all other risk in the ecosystem and organization at large. Executive and corporate directors will not understand vague or confusing values. They expect to understand cyber risk in a way that drives informed risk management decisions that improve the health of the organization, improve shareholder value, and articulate necessary due diligence and due care. As an example, if a board member asks a senior manager, "what is our cyber risk in relation to a merger, launching a new strategic partnership, or deploying a new technology?", then they want to understand if such a decision will compromise revenue, increase expenses, or cause any other harm to the organization that cannot be withstood. Each organization needs to define their risk tolerance. The risk tolerance defines the delineation between the amount of risk that the organization cannot withstand and the amount of risk the organization can easily withstand.  If cyber risk is above this defined tolerance, then the executive and corporate directors may decide to remediate, transfer, or avoid that risk.

Cyber risk, in the business context, is most usefully understood not as a category but as a quantity.

When a board member asks a senior manager what the cyber risk is in a business context, what they generally mean is how much value (usually financial) might we lose from a cyber incident and how likely are we to face that sort of incident?

When that calculation is made, it can then be compared to the degree of risk tolerance—often called the risk appetite—the organization has, and it can make intelligent judgments as to how to deal with this degree of risk.

In other words, cyber risk is a business quantity that represents the potential of financial loss, disruption, or damage to the reputation of an organization as a result of its use of its information technology.

## Comparing Traditional Cyber Risk Methods

Traditional cyber risk assessments are flawed because the results don't easily connect with enterprise-wide risks. On the other hand, a modern assessment must solve this problem. As we laid out in Chapter 2, traditional risk assessments have struggled with fulfilling the task of helping business leaders and board members understand the quantitative financial exposure to cyber risk. Traditional cyber risk methods seldom express cybersecurity in financial detail from vulnerability assessments to compliance checklists.

As discussed in Chapter 1, the pass-fail traditional check-the-box model fails to address cybersecurity as a continuum. Meeting the minimum requirements does not protect entities from evolving cyber threats. In fact, many high-profile cyber breaches in the last decade were of companies passing security checklists and meeting compliance requirements. Though compliance may be required by regional or industry regulations, compliance does not always address relevant risk to the organization; therefore, compliance should be viewed by business leaders as a component of their overall business strategy and not as a risk reducing strategy.

Traditionally, various subjective terms are used to portray cyber risk using qualitative scales such as high, medium, and low (or some variation therein), or pseudo-quantitative scales such as multiplying a maturity score with a severity score and calling it "risk".

While qualitative or subjective approaches may be sufficient for audit or compliance objectives, the significant number and magnitude of cyber related losses over recent years suggest a more robust approach to measuring and communicating cyber risk is needed to inform business leaders of *current* and *actual* cyber risk, better inform the business and financial impacts of various cyber events, and provide the business rationale for future cyber-related decisions.

The compliance method and those outlined through the rest of this chapter fail to identify the factors impacting the business. Hence, they fail to connect with the ways business leaders make decisions that align with the goals of their businesses and properly inform overall risk management strategy.

In this chapter, there will be a direct comparison between traditional methods and a modern method. To set the stage, please see Table 4.1 as a side-by-side comparison.

Further explanation and detail will be provided throughout this chapter.

TABLE 4.1  Side by side comparison of traditional methods to a modern approach

| Traditional Method | Issue with Traditional Method | Modern Approach | Improved Decision Management |
|---|---|---|---|
| Security Rating Solution | Security ratings are arbitrary values that lack business context. | Uses the exposure profile to create a business context. | Business leaders have a way to define strategic initiatives based on factors impacting their businesses. |
| Vulnerability Assessments | Technical metrics don't link to financial loss categories. | Translates traditional technical metrics to financial details. | By linking to financial details, business leaders can focus where it matters most. |
| Event Monitoring Platforms | In isolation, monitoring platforms can mislead remediation efforts and waste money. | Combines multiple sources of metrics and ties to financial details. | By combining multiple metrics and linking to financial details, business leaders better align resources. |
| Compliance Checklists | Compliance checklists don't link to probability and loss values. | Combines exposure profile, compliance checklist, and empirical data to forecast financial loss due to cyber. | Business leaders can use the loss forecast to set risk tolerance, trend progress, and understand the benefits of countermeasures. |
| Cyber Maturity Assessments | Tend to assume that all controls and businesses are the same and can mislead remediation efforts. | Uses a set of what-if simulations to establish a prioritized remediation plan. | Business leaders can use the prioritized remediation plans to strategically avoid or minimize financial damage from cyber risk. |
| Cyber Risk Heatmaps | Arbitrary scales don't align well with other risk reported in financial terms. | Displays cyber risk in financial terms, which makes it easy to combine into enterprise-wide reporting. | Business leaders have the ability to compare cyber risk with all other business risks. |

*NOTE  The above table is purely a summary and does not constitute the plethora of traditional cyber risk assessments.

## A Better Approach

Businesses can manage cyber risk. It just requires the adoption of a modern approach that includes:

- a means to identify and quantify cyber risk in financial terms;

- a set of options to accept, remediate, and transfer cyber risk; and
- an ability to combine with all other business risks.

As such, business leaders need to consider cyber risk in a particular way. They need to understand how cyber risk affects revenue and margin. If the consequences are too great, then the business leaders will seek remediation and transfer options.

Risk management is a continuum and changes over time, both externally and internally, which is why a modern approach to assessing cyber risk needs to include a method that is standard and repeatable.

Business leaders are not pursuing perfect cybersecurity. In fact, they understand that perfect cybersecurity is unrealistic. Instead, they are pursuing treatment of cyber risk that fits within their context of risk tolerance.

This raises an important question when viewing cyber risk from a business perspective: "How much cyber risk can a business tolerate?". The answer can vary widely from business to business but is fundamental in aligning cyber risk to business objectives.

The answer to this question comes down to understanding:

- how much damage the business can sustain due to one or more cyber incidents;
- if the business leaders stomach large swings in the value of the business due to one more cyber incidents; and
- if the business is operating on a time horizon that dictates the willingness to accept and recover from cyber-related financial loss.

## The Modern Risk Assessment

Business leaders do not rely on intuition and arbitrary values to manage cyber risk. Instead, business leaders can adopt a modern approach to assessing cyber risk. A modern approach to assessing cyber risk will:

- simplify the contemplation of cyber risk;
- translate traditional cybersecurity metrics into financial details;
- provide a means for a standard and repeatable cyber risk evaluation;
- forecast financial exposure due to cyber risk;
- provide a set of prioritized remediation and transfer guidance;
- align cyber risk with enterprise-wide risk management reporting.

A basic model for accessing cyber risk will:[2]

- find the best available data to assess possible attack scenarios;
- focus on which scenarios are probable and cause enough loss to matter;
- calculate best, worst, and most likely cases;
- determine to what degree loss is acceptable (risk appetite);
- determine what investment is needed to mitigate loss to an acceptable level;
- use advanced modeling (e.g., Monte Carlo simulations).

## Simplify the Contemplation of Cyber Risk

Business leaders need a simple and elegant way to understand cyber risk. They need a solution that produces results in a business context. A modern risk assessment encompasses an understanding of the factors impacting the business. More specifically, it incorporates the exposure profile.

The exposure profile sets the stage for what matters. It indicates if the business should be more concerned about business interruption versus data breach.

**Exposure Profile:** The exposure profile is an understanding of which assets, suppliers, and conditions expose a business. It requires that a business knows its:

- annual revenue;
- operating hours;
- operating regions;
- list of suppliers;
- data record types (such as personally identifiable information);
- data record volumes;
- value of intellectual property and trade secrets;
- other conditions that expose the business.

In addition, the exposure profile establishes the volume or range of each factor impacting the business. For business interruption, it may contemplate financial damages from 30 minutes of interruption to 30 days of interruption. But for a data breach, it may contemplate financial damages from 500 records to 500 million records. The volume or range is critical in understanding the full range of possible financial damage.

Like with all other business risks, cyber risk needs to be associated with loss types or loss categories.

**Loss Categories:** The loss categories are a summarization of the cyber incidents that lead to financial loss. Most financial loss can be categorized:

- **Data breach** is any malicious or error-based cyber incident that exposes confidential employee or customer records to an untrusted environment. Volumes can range from 500 records to 5 billion records.

- **Business interruption** is any malicious or error-based cyber incident that makes a computer or computer-based system unavailable. Volumes can range from 30 minutes of inactivity to 3 months of inactivity.

- **Misappropriation** is any malicious cyber incident that leads to the intentional, illegal use of the property, ideas, or funds of another organization for one's own use or other unauthorized purpose. Volumes can range from insignificant value (such as commonly known intellectual property) to extreme value (such as intellectual property that is transforming an entire market). Volumes can also be represented as an estimated value in relation to annual revenue.

- **Ransomware** is a malicious cyber incident that holds an organization's data or systems hostage with an aim to collect a ransom before freeing what was held hostage. The volume can range from 30 minutes of hostage duration to 3 months of hostage duration.

- **Cyber-physical** is any malicious or error-based cyber incident that causes physical property damage or physical harm to an individual. The volume can range from limited damage (such as inexpensive property) to catastrophic damage (such as loss of life).

Beyond understanding the factors impacting their business, business leaders need a way to make decisions that align with the goals of their businesses. As an example, business leaders may decide to:

- accept all business interruption damage that are less than eight hours in duration; and

- seek cyber insurance to partially cover business interruption damages from incidents that are longer than eight hours in duration.

The exposure profile should not remain static. As the business changes, the exposure profile also changes. The following circumstances should necessitate an update of the exposure profile:

- acquisitions;
- divestments;

- revenue growth;
- customer growth;
- regional expansion;
- addition of suppliers;
- invention of intellectual property;
- many other business profile changes.

With the ability to contemplate cyber risk in a business context, business leaders have a way to define strategic initiatives.

## Translate Traditional Cybersecurity Metrics into Financial Details

Business leaders are not cybersecurity experts, and most do not understand cybersecurity jargon. Business leaders need a method that produces results in a language they understand. A modern risk assessment translates traditional cybersecurity metrics into financial details.

Technical metrics are important. They provide an understanding of threat, vulnerability, and control implementation. They can inform tactical plans and show proof of improvement. However, it is unclear how they tie directly to the financial health of the business.

**Technical Metrics:** Technical metrics are most commonly used by Chief Information Security Officers (CISO) and Information Security Officers (CIO) to better understand IT infrastructure. Most technical metrics are a product of technical solutions or tools. Some of those tools and solutions include

- vulnerability scanning tools;
- compliance management tools;
- security event monitoring platforms;
- incident management platforms.

A modern risk assessment will combine the business's exposure profile, the business's technical metrics, and empirical data. The exposure profile defines the context of the business, the technical metrics define current cybersecurity practices, and the empirical data defines known financial damages and incident probability. The combination of all three variables produces results in financial terms that are specific to the business.

Empirical data is the backbone of a modern risk assessment. It is the variable that ensures integrity and sets financial definition.

**Empirical Data:** Empirical data is the collection of information via observation or experimentation. As related to cyber, this is mainly a collection of incident patterns that inform incident probability and ranges of financial damage. A deeper observation into the data will also indicate there are patterns within patterns. These deeper patterns, when combined with a business's exposure profile, provide amazing insight.

A financial quantification model is a necessary component in a modern risk assessment. This model is the means of combining the business's exposure profile, the business's technical metrics, and empirical data in order to derive financial results. X-Analytics, Value at Risk (VaR), and Applied Cyber Economics for Cyber Risk are three examples of financial quantification models for cyber risk.

A modern risk assessment will calculate the best-case to worst-case for all possible cyber incidents. As an example, a modern risk assessment calculating the range of financial damage for a one million-record data breach might consider the following impact values:

- low impact = $1.10 million;
- median impact = $18.25 million;
- high impact = $41.63 million;
- worst-case impact = $130.93 million.

Additionally, a modern risk assessment will calculate the estimated financial loss per year.

For each financial value, business leaders can decide how they treat cyber risk:

- **Insignificant:** in this case they may decide to just absorb the risk.
- **Moderate:** in this case they may decide to remediate where it is cost effective.
- **High:** in this case they may decide to remediate where it is cost effective and transfer the rest to a cyber insurance policy.

When cyber risk is expressed financially, business leaders have the power to focus risk remediation activities on assets where it actually matters. This also means they can choose to limit focus where it does not matter.

## WHEN COMPARED TO TRADITIONAL CYBER RISK METHODS...

Traditional cyber risk methods seldom express cybersecurity in financial detail. From vulnerability assessments to compliance checklist, these methods fail to translate the cybersecurity metrics into financial details. Hence, they fail to properly inform overall risk management strategy.

As an example, a Tenable vulnerability assessment may indicate that there are 500 high-severity vulnerabilities (or technical weaknesses) out of 1,000 devices scanned. To put it another way, one out of every two devices has a technical weakness that could be exploited by a cyber-attack. It would be easy for a business leader to find this value concerning. But what does it really mean? Does it mean that the organization is going to experience a 1 million-record data breach? Without tying it back to the exposure profile and loss categories, business leaders cannot make informed risk management decisions.

## Provide a Means for a Standard and Repeatable Cyber Risk Evaluation

Business leaders generally review financial metrics every 90 days (or quarterly). Business leaders use this cadence to understand financial shifts in the business and to modify strategy.

Just like there are standard accounting practices, there should be standard cyber risk practices that produce repeatable assessments. Business leaders need to understand how financial exposure due to cyber risk is trending from quarter to quarter.

A modern risk assessment needs to be based on a standard set of practices. These practices should dictate the following characteristics:

- structure;
- data collection;
- modeling;
- integrity;
- reporting.

The structure should be based on the fact that all cyber losses are the intersection of a threat and an asset. The structure provides a consistent framework to connect technical metrics with empirical data. As an example, a human that losses a laptop could result in a data breach:

- asset = laptop;
- threat = human error;
- loss category = data breach.

The data collection process is a consistent practice of collecting information related to the exposure profile, the technical metrics, and the calibration of backend variables using empirical data. This practice should be documented for posterity, and the execution of this practice should be governed by key stakeholders, such as:

- The corporate directors and senior management govern the entire practice by way of established policies and procedures.
- Business line managers, CISOs, and CROs govern the data collection practice by implementing adequate controls (as related to established policies and procedures) for collecting information related to the exposure profile and technical metrics.
- Model experts (in-house or external parties) govern the data collection practice by implementing adequate controls (as related to established policies and procedures) for collecting and updating backend variables and by periodically validating that the model is working as intended.
- Internal audit governs the data collection process by ensuring all components are in compliance with established policies and procedures.

The model is the algorithm that quantifies the exposure profile, technical metrics, and empirical data into financial results. Any changes to the model should be reviewed carefully since consistent reporting is dependent on the model remaining consistent.

Business leaders need to know they can trust the results they are receiving. Business leaders expect evaluation integrity. Integrity guarantees that:

- the exact same inputs will result in the exact same outputs; and
- any changes to the method or model are noted and reported.

The report is the way to communicate the results. Business leaders expect to see results reported in an easy-to-understand and consistent format. In some cases, the business leaders may provide report recommendations to help align cyber risk with other business risks.

Business leaders can use the standard and repeatable cyber risk evaluation to:

- guide strategic and tactical plans;
- trend cyber risk results; and
- determine if the business is operating within its risk tolerance.

---

**WHEN COMPARED TO TRADITIONAL CYBER RISK METHODS...**

Traditional cyber risk methods are actually designed for recurrence. From event monitoring platforms to compliance checklists, these methods to provide consistent structure, data collection, modeling, and reporting. However, they fail to quantify financial results.

As an example, a Splunk's Enterprise Risk Management platform could indicate 500 web application attack events. The 500 means that the organizations web applications were hit with 500 cyber-attacks. But what specifically does that mean? Is this value high or low? How does it relate to a data breach or business interruption? Without this context, business leaders cannot guide strategic or tactical plan or determine if their business is operating within its risk tolerance.

---

## Forecast Financial Exposure due to Cyber Risk

As a risk management concept, business leaders depend on the forecasting of financial risk to:

- set strategy;
- allocate capital and operational expenses; and
- to identify procedures to avoid or minimize the forecasted financial risk.

As related to cyber risk, business leaders need a way to forecast cyber-related damages. A 12-month forecast is generally sufficient for cyber risk.

In order to forecast cyber risk, a modern risk assessment will quantify expected loss.

**Expected Loss:** Expected loss is the sum of values of all possible losses, each multiplied by the probability of that loss occurring.

- Each loss table should include a range that is defined from the exposure profile.

- Each position in the loss table should have a probability value that is quantified from empirical data and the model.

- Each position in the loss table should have a loss value that is quantified from empirical data, the exposure profile, and the model.

- For each position in the loss table, the loss value should be multiplied by the probability value.

- The sum of all loss values multiplied by probability values becomes the expected loss value.

Expected loss should be quantified for each loss category. The sum of expected loss for each loss category becomes the total expected loss as shown in the following example:

- data breach expected loss = $2.6 million;

- business interruption expected loss = $35.6 million;

- misappropriation expected loss = $16.8 million;

- ransomware expected loss = $21.2 million;

- total expected loss = $77.19 million.

As part of a modern risk assessment, expected loss value can be used to:

- trend financial exposure amongst recurring evaluations;

- determine the benefit of future cyber risk countermeasure.

Business leaders can use the expected loss values to determine if financial exposure due to cyber risk is something that can easily be absorbed or if it needs to be remediated.

Additionally, business leaders can use expected loss trending to determine if their business is working toward its risk appetite or if strategy needs to be adjusted.

---

### WHEN COMPARED TO TRADITIONAL CYBER RISK METHODS…

Traditional cyber risk methods seldom forecast cyber risk. From qualitative assessments to compliance checklist, these methods fail to forecast financial loss due to cyber. Hence, they fail to inform risk acceptance and remediation.

As an example, a compliance checklist may indicate that an organization has a compliance score of 50%. The 50% means that only one out of every two controls is implemented. But what does it really mean? Does it indicate that the business will experience significant loss over the next 12 months? Without tying it to probability and loss, business leaders cannot determine if cyber risk can easily be absorbed or if it needs to be remediated.

## Provide a Set of Prioritized Remediation and Transfer Guidance

After the forecasting and evaluation of financial risk, business leaders need a set of procedures to avoid or minimize the impact of that risk. As related to cyber risk, business leaders need a set of prioritized remediation and transfer guidance.

**Remediation guidance** provides a way to reduce the probability of cyber loss. Examples of remediation guidance are better hardware inventory, software inventory, or vulnerability management. The guidance can be specific to threat patterns or asset groups.

A modern risk assessment should be able to quantify remediation and transfer guidance.

Prioritized remediation guidance should be based on running a set of what-if simulations. The what-if simulations provide a means to compare a current risk profile with a future (or what-if) risk profile. There are basically two approaches to take for remediation-based what-if scenarios.

**Cyber control what-ifs:** Cyber controls are countermeasures that businesses can implement to reduce cyber risk. NIST Cyber Security Framework (NIST CSF), Payment Card Industry Data Security Standard (PCI DSS), and Center for Internet Security Critical Security Controls (CIS CSC) are examples of control frameworks. The following steps are an example of a cyber control what-ifs in action:

1 Define current expected loss (current expected loss = $10 million).
2 Define current control implementation (current implementation = 50%).
3 Set a what-if control implementation (what-if implementation = 80%).
4 Run the what-if simulation (assumes a new risk profile where the control is 80% implemented).
5 Document the what-if expected loss (what-if expected loss = $8 million).
6 Calculate the delta between current and what-if expected loss values ($10 million - $8 million = $2 million).
7 Document that delta as the benefit (what-if benefit = $2 million).
8 Repeat steps 1 through 7 for each control.
9 Rank the what-if benefits to create the prioritized remediation plan.

**Cyber project what-ifs:** Cyber projects are initiatives directly tied to technology implementation, corporate policy, or strategy. Just like controls, they are countermeasures that businesses can use to reduce cyber risk. However, they come with nuance and may partially align with one or more cyber control. Implementing Splunk Enterprise Security or focusing on integrated risk management (which is a NIST CSF concept) are two examples of cyber projects. The steps for the cyber project what-ifs are the same as the cyber control what-ifs with one exception. Each step that indicates control should be swapped with the project.

Prioritized transfer guidance should be based on reviewing the impact and probability tables for each cyber loss category. The loss tables serve as means to determine where risk transfer makes sense and the limit to seek within the transfer mechanism. Risk transfer comes with caveats.

**Where to transfer risks?** Part of this decision is not entirely up to the business. Cyber insurance carriers and third-party vendors will have a significant say in this decision. Insurance carriers are only willing to insure risks below a certain probability. Third-party vendors are only willing to take on limited liability. However, businesses can determine to only transfer losses that matter to them. As an example, a business may decide to transfer losses between a 4.0% probability and a 0.1% probability.

**How much to transfer?** Again, part of this decision is not entirely up to the business. Insurance carriers are only willing to cover certain losses. Third-party vendors are only willing to pay back so much in credits or guarantees. However, businesses can select the transfer mechanism and the limit they are willing to buy. As an example, a business may decide to purchase business interruption coverage with a limit that covers up to a 30-day interruption incident.

Outside of remediation and transfer guidance, there are a few more ways to avoid or minimize impact from cyber risk:

- Custom what-if scenarios could be used to determine which technologies to avoid.
- Custom what-if scenarios could be used to determine divestments.
- Cyber evaluations could be used to determine which acquisitions or mergers to avoid.

Business leaders can use a set of prioritized remediation and transfer guidance to avoid or minimize the impact of cyber risk.

WHEN COMPARED TO TRADITIONAL CYBER RISK METHODS...

Traditional cyber risk methods attempt to determine a vague relationship between exposure and control implementation.  Exposure is usually expressed as arbitrary and non-financial values. The guidance generally assumes that all controls are equal or that all businesses are the same. Arbitrary rankings or control gaps are used as a means to define prioritization. From consulting-led assessments to compliance checklist, these methods fail to provide prioritized remediation and transfer guidance in financial detail. Hence, they fail to inform the use of finite budgets and limited business resources.

As an example, a maturity-based cyber risk assessment could indicate that the business is a two on a five-point scale. The two means that the business has intermediate cyber hygiene. The consulting firm wants to help the business achieve a three (or good cyber hygiene). So, the consulting firm provides a list of all controls that are less than three as the prioritized remediation plan. But does this guidance actually matter? Do all the controls reduce financial exposure in the same way? Without this context, business leaders cannot focus on controls or projects that offer the most risk reducing benefit.

## Align Cyber Risk with Enterprise-Wide Risk Management Reporting

Business leaders use key risk indicators (KRIs) to identify risks that could materially threaten their business. Most KRIs are specified in financial detail.

If cyber risk is considered a material risk, then it must be reported as a KRI. Since a modern risk assessment produces results in financial detail, business leaders can easily report cyber risk as a KRI.

The following values are an example of cyber risk amongst other risks:

- economic downturn forecast = $105 million;
- cyber risk forecast = $77 million;
- regulatory forecast = $22 million;
- customer churn = $15 million.

With the example above, business leaders could easily determine that economic downturn and cyber risk are the most concerning.

# Conclusion

At an enterprise-wide level, business leaders have to decide which risks to remediate. This decision generally comes down to risk tolerance and budget. Since budget is finite, business leaders need a way to compare all risks. This comparison provides a means to prioritize the most critical risks. The key risk register (KRR) is an enterprise-wide, top-level report that organizes the cluster of all KRI's into one view for comparison purposes.

---

**WHEN COMPARED TO TRADITIONAL CYBER RISK METHODS…**

Traditional cyber risk methods seldom integrate well with other business risks. From heatmaps to compliance checklists, these methods fail to articulate cyber risk in financial detail. Hence, the results have limited use and cannot easily be incorporated into enterprise-wide reporting.

As an example, a risk heatmap would indicate that a certain risk is red. Red indicates high risk. But what does this actually mean? Does it mean that the forecast of cyber risk is greater than all other business risks? Without this context, business leaders cannot compare cyber risk with all other business risks and set enterprise-wide strategy.

---

To continue learning about the concepts in this chapter the following sources are recommended:

1 S Ramachandran, et al. A Smarter Way to Quantify Cybersecurity Risk [blog] BCG, August 09, 2019. www.bcg.com/capabilities/digital-technology-data/smarter-way-to-quantify-cybersecurity-risk

2 D W Hubbard (2009) *The Failure of Risk Management: Why It's Broken and How to Fix It,* Wiley, Hoboken, New Jersey

3 D W Hubbard and R Seiersen (2016) *How to Measure Anything in Cybersecurity Risk* Wiley, Hoboken, New Jersey

4 J Boehm, et al. The Risk-based Approach to Cybersecurity, October 08, 2019. www.mckinsey.com/business-functions/risk/our-insights/the-risk-based-approach-to-cybersecurityz

5 K Stine, et al. Integrating Cybersecurity and Enterprise Risk Management (ERM), October 2020. nvlpubs.nist.gov/nistpubs/ir/2020/NIST.IR.8286.pdf

# 05

# The Role of HR Functions in Scaling Cybersecurity and Building Trust

BY TIM McKNIGHT, CHIEF SECURITY OFFICER, SAP, NIALL BRENNAN,
CHIEF LIAISON OFFICER, SAP,
AND ELENA KVOCHKO, CHIEF TRUST OFFICER, SAP

## Five Key Ideas to Take Away from This Chapter

1 The cyber threat is a complex issue affecting all enterprises. It needs a cross-functional collaboration between security teams and other key functions, including HR.

2 Comprehensive understanding and visibility into employees' access points lays the foundation for stronger resilience.

3 In the fast-changing work environment HR functions play a crucial role to ensure that employees are educated and are able to comply with complex standards and regulations.

4 HR and CHROs are important partners in leadership decisions, as well as in driving the culture, building and retaining diverse teams, and throughout the employee lifecycle.

5 Ensuring sustainability, continuous testing and improvement of partnerships and processes provides a basis for long-term success.

# Introduction

Employees are the greatest asset of any organization. They can also present a significant vulnerability in the context of cybersecurity. Whether motivated by a nefarious intent or simply lacking sufficient digital hygiene and sophistication to recognize offensive cyber maneuvers, employees—due to their privileged insider access—represent the most effective means by which a malicious actor can compromise an organization's network.

As organizations become increasingly reliant on technical solutions and business processes become completely networked and digitized, their vulnerability surfaces have grown exponentially. The COVID-19 pandemic and the anticipated transition to more distributed work options will increase the number of remote access points into an organization's network. Thus, it will further expand the vulnerability surface and raise the destructive potential of any individual breach. Organizations across all business sectors have recognized this evolution and have, in recent years, begun to incorporate cybersecurity more holistically into operations. A once peripheral concern has now become a core business process and is now recognized as existential. Rapid advancements in technologies—such as artificial intelligence and machine learning—have also greatly improved the quality and capacity of cyber defense.

As a result, malicious actors have shifted their focus to targets with less resilient defenses and more permeable attack surfaces. The human element in any organization—with its privileged network access and variable level of cybersecurity sophistication—often proves to be the "soft" attack surface that malicious actors need to penetrate cyber defenses. Attacks that rely on disgruntled insiders or manipulating human error—such as phishing and business email compromise schemes—now significantly outnumber external viruses, spyware or malware attacks. In addition, a practice known as "shadow IT", in which employees download or use a new information technology system or rely on technology with which they may be more familiar, creates additional exploitable vulnerabilities by which a malicious actor can pierce the organization in an attempted data breach.[1]

Accordingly, the most effective cyber defense strategies are those which address and mitigate the vulnerabilities inherent in technology, business processes and human behavior. As such, organizations with advanced enterprise-wide cybersecurity programs incorporate state-of-the-art digital security tools with effective human resource management techniques to optimize a security-minded culture and mitigate the vulnerabilities created by human errors.[2] In so doing, organizations become more effective at managing vulnerabilities presented by human behavior across the enterprise and throughout the employee lifecycle.

This chapter will explore how—by developing a security-minded culture through all phases of the human capital management cycle—organizations can reduce the vulnerability posed by the human factor. In so doing, leaders will empower their workforce to serve as an effective shield in the early identification and neutralization of digital threats.

## Insider Threat: The Achilles Heel

An insider threat is an organizational threat that originates from an internal entry point. In the typical scenario, a threat actor employs or manipulates individuals with legitimate access credentials or fraudulently obtains valid access credentials to bypass security measures, then gains entry to an organization's facilities or information systems and causes harm to an organization.[3] The damage usually takes the form of fraud, theft of assets, data or intellectual property or sabotage. Insider threats can be difficult to recognize because they do not involve an obvious breach of perimeter security defenses but rather rely on seemingly legitimate access privileges and knowledge pertaining to the location of valuable digital assets. As such, the forensic indicators of compromise are often harder to detect or slower to manifest than in the case of an external breach where there is a clear entry point external to the network. There are three general types of insiders: malicious, negligent and infiltrative.

**Malicious insiders** take advantage of internal access and abuse their authority to cause damage to an organization. Some are disgruntled current or former employees seeking revenge for perceived mistreatment. Others are employees who have been compromised or deliberately deployed by competitors or hostile nation-states to conduct industrial espionage and steal valuable intellectual property or other proprietary information.

**Negligent insiders,** on the other hand, do not act out of malicious intent. But they do put their organizations at risk through unintended errors or poor digital security hygiene. This may occur by simply disregarding digital security policies within an organization to save time or due to ignorance, thus allowing external malicious actors to breach otherwise effective defenses. Weak password policies, unsafe downloads and unprotected email gateways are common causes of negligent insider breaches. Phishing and social engineering are among the other common methods by which external malicious actors compromise negligent insiders. Over 90% of attacks start with a phishing email. Poor stewardship of valuable data by insiders can result in a compromise. As an example, in 2006, a data analyst working at the Department of Veteran Affairs downloaded the personal data of 26.5 million US military veterans—including the information of undercover US agents still in covert positions—to his laptop.[4] One evening his laptop was stolen from his home during a burglary. In another example, in 2019, Facebook lost personal and financial data of tens of thousands of employees when an employee left a corporate laptop in a car and it was stolen.[5]

**Infiltrative insiders** are actually external malicious actors, who fraudulently obtain seemingly valid credentials, pose as a valid credential-holder, and use the fraudulent credentials to cause harm to an organization. The costliest insider threat per-incident is theft of credentials and malicious account takeovers. These incidents have increased significantly in frequency and cost. In fact, the frequency of incidents per company has tripled since 2016 from an average of 1 to 3.2, and the average cost has increased from $493,093 to $871,686 in 2019.[6] On an annual basis, organizations are spending more to deal with insider negligence but the per-incident cost is much lower.

While the intent of malicious and negligent insiders is different, they are both capable of causing incredible damage. Given the existential impact the human factor can present, managing employee behavior is an essential element of any organization's digital security strategy. HR professionals are an important asset as part of the cybersecurity team due to the skills they bring toward reducing the vulnerability of the human factor.

In its standing guidance on countering the insider threat, the US Department of Homeland Security's Cybersecurity and Infrastructure Security Agency (CISA) encourages organizations to incorporate HR professionals as part of multi-disciplinary threat management teams to effectively detect, deter, and mitigate insider threats. Since HR acts as a central repository for personnel information, HR professionals are in the best position to identify patterns, behavior, and trends that will help mitigate potential harm to an organization and its employees. CISA encourages HR departments to actively participate in insider threat mitigation efforts by establishing an evaluation framework that includes threat indicators, data profiles, and behavioral signals.[7] A comprehensive understanding of data flows and visibility into potentially anomalous activities—while respecting privacy and security—will lay the foundation for stronger resilience. Anomalous activities can be an opportunity to investigate the deviation, provide insightful reporting and prevent escalations, while managing the volume of such investigations.

Holistically, knowing the different types of threats and motivations, monitoring critical assets and *crown jewels*, recognizing anomalies and responding appropriately will help scope the protection program. It is not enough to simply deploy the tools and technologies, but an organization must educate its users on how to use these digital tools securely and how to ensure proper configurations with the right permission levels. Auditing, reporting and profiling capabilities will provide leadership and operational teams with the current and historical data to make decisions and adjustments. Many significant cyberattacks in recent years remind us how mismanaged and compromised identities present enormous risk and provide access for attackers to valuable assets and *crown jewels*. Having a robust identity and access management program is a critical element in addressing these risks. An integrated response plan also needs to account for insider risks and threats. While the first step is building out the capabilities, what is potentially even more challenging long term is ensuring sustainability and scalability of these efforts. Routinely testing, adjusting and improving on the processes and technologies will help address and reduce the risk surface.

## Remote Work: The Newest Complication

Since March of 2020, the COVID-19 pandemic has impacted the global economy in ways that Americans have not seen since the Great Depression. The pandemic ushered in the largest alteration in history of how humans "go to work".[8] In the space of a week in mid-March, the US workforce transformed from one in which about "21% of workers at least occasionally used online facilities to work from home to a workforce wherein approximately 80% of the workforce did roughly 100% of their work online at home".[9] This change has vastly altered the configuration of most proprietary digital networks, exponentially increasing the number of remote access points. This shift represents a massive security challenge and significantly expands the perimeter that must be protected. As with any seismic shift in organizational activity, the rapid move to wide-scale remote work has created opportunity for cybercriminals and other malicious digital actors to develop new threat vectors aimed at penetrating the cyber defenses of vulnerable organizations.

Prior to the COVID-19 pandemic, the World Economic Forum estimated the annual cost of global cybercrime to total around $2 trillion per year and estimated it would grow to upwards of $10 trillion in just a few years.[10] While it is difficult to know how these estimates will be impacted by the massive shift to remote work, indications are that it will be significant. A study performed by IBM and Ponemon Institute in 2020 examined the impact of COVID-19 and the massive shift to remote work on digital security. 71% of respondents predicted that remote work would increase the time to identify a data breach while 70% agreed that it would increase the cost.[11] While workers are at home on their computers, the potential for human error increases the likelihood of a breach. The average time to identify and contain a data breach in 2020 was 280 days (about nine months). It is estimated that the average savings from containing a breach in less than 200 days (about 6 and a half months) is $1 million.[12] The study found that the impact of remote work on the average cost of a data breach comes out to an estimated $127,000.

The expanded attack surface that large-scale remote work creates—as well as higher access levels across cloud and personal networks—broadens the threat environment and represents yet another significant risk in the modern digital world. Nonetheless, the flexibility and work-life balance advantages that remote work options offer have been widely embraced. Numerous surveys across multiple industries indicate that remote work has allowed many organizations to maintain similar or, in some cases, improved productivity during the pandemic. While there is not enough data surrounding these findings to be conclusive, it is safe to assume that remote work, in some form, will remain a viable option for the future even after the pandemic is no longer a factor. As a result, organizations must review and supplement their security policies to account for a significant percentage of the workforce to access the network remotely. Once these policies are updated, HR should play the lead role in ensuring that the workforce is properly educated in the proper use of the organization's digital tools. Technical cybersecurity experts can monitor the network for anomalous activity but the best form of protection for any organization is to imbue a security-minded culture in its workforce.

## Developing a Security-Minded Culture

As previously mentioned, attacks that exploit human errors, such as simple phishing emails or business email compromise campaigns, now greatly outnumber viruses, spyware and malware attacks, both in attempts and success rates. In fact, 9 out of 10 cyberattacks begin with phishing emails. Accordingly, a successful cybersecurity program relies upon not only state-of-the-art defensive technology but also a highly skilled and digitally aware workforce. It is essential that this workforce is appropriately trained to recognize threats to the organization, to escalate concerns, and to adhere to assigned security processes and controls.

As such, a special emphasis should be made to recruit, onboard, train and manage personnel with the skills and aptitude to utilize organizational data and information systems securely. HR has a vital role in facilitating this important organizational cultural evolution. While the technical personnel manage the digital equipment and tools, HR has engagement expertise which ensures that all segments of the employee population are properly trained to play their part in organizational cybersecurity and that they execute that responsibility every day. This includes creating an environment where it is not only safe to inquire about cybersecurity policy, but expected. A process and a mechanism to safely report suspected and potential incidents should be established for employees. In addition, a process to identify and reward champions of newly implemented security practices will emphasize their importance to the workforce. HR assists the leadership team members in change management, inspiring current and new leaders, setting up leadership practices and helping managers lead by example. All of these are key to instilling security-minded organizational behavior.

Mature cybersecurity is a multi-dimensional professional discipline where the holistic solution must focus as much on the human element as on machines. Skilled practitioners must manage all the essential variables—people, process, technology—that may open the door to the vulnerabilities, attack surface and defense line of any organization. Security suites and malware protection are an essential part of managing risk; however, technology is not the one-way ticket to deter intruders. To address the human element, HR professionals are increasingly recognized as critical players in building, developing, scaling and maintaining effective cyber defenses.

## Developing Process and Operational Controls

In order to effectively educate and encourage the workforce to adopt a security-minded culture, HR must provide them with clear guidance on how to execute their role as a "human firewall" against cyberattacks. In addition, earning and maintaining the trust of employees and customers by demonstrating an ability to protect their privacy and proprietary information is critical to business success. Information governance, process and operational controls are the key measures used to protect data assets. Thus, HR and technical components of the digital security team must collaborate to develop logical information governance policies and procedures and communicate them to all segments of the employee population.

Placing effective controls on the information an organization has, and the access to that information is the cornerstone of its digital security strategy. That means understanding the different categories of information possessed and the various levels of protection required for each category. Then, it is important to determine who needs access to what information and to place controls over that access ("need to know"). Maintaining access to the data that will need to be accessed in the future is key, as well as knowing when to dispose of the data after that timeline has been realized. Holistic data and process analysis aids in scaling and building cyber defenses. Technologies used to compensate for human errors—such as email gateway security and user behavior analytics—provide an additional layer of defense, enabling access control, security monitoring detection and response. HR must ensure that the human operators at all phases of this complicated web of information management are appropriately trained and facile with the policies, processes and controls relevant to their position.

There has been a substantial increase in insider threat activity in cloud deployments due to poor product configurations that can be prevented. Following product security guidelines supplemented by additional monitoring will go a long way in securing deployment of cloud technologies. Alerting and risk-scoring of anomalous behavior can prevent a threat before it results in a bigger impact for an organization. All the processes and technologies should be integrated with core underlying business processes.

## The Value of HR in Cybersecurity

As was discussed in the previous chapters, the notion of what is involved in enterprise-wide cybersecurity has significantly evolved in recent years. Modern conditions demand that cybersecurity employ a much more diversified skillset. As more functions of the business process become digitized and the threat environment becomes increasingly diversified, boards of directors and business leaders are approaching cybersecurity as a strategic function that must be applied across all other business processes. As illustrated in

Chapter 3, leading organizations are developing new structures to accommodate the reality that cybersecurity has moved from a peripheral concern to a core business function. Cybersecurity has rapidly become everyone's business. As a result, human resources professionals occupy an important position as members of the enterprise-wide cyber risk team by lending expertise on the human element in cybersecurity.

Human resources maintain sensitive personnel and employee data, such as full names, addresses, dates of birth, social security numbers, payroll and financial information, personal and family history. This is the type of data that is constantly targeted by malicious actors because, depending upon its contents, it can be coopted for a myriad of different purposes, ranging from criminal fraud schemes to espionage. Protecting this data was once considered the singular function of the IT team. However, understanding the role human behavior can play in facilitating technical compromise—as illustrated in Chapter 3—cybersecurity is now an enterprise-wide responsibility. As such, HR professionals have a significant role in ensuring that their digital and business processes are structured appropriately to protect this data. Due to the relative value of the data and the ease by which it can be compromised, HR departments must lead the enterprise cybersecurity team in helping to ensure the confidentiality and proper handling of this data in home offices, develop and promote digital and business processes, and encourage employees to be role models in handling information securely.

Just as the threat environment is in a constant state of evolution, integrated security teams must ensure that an organization's security program is constantly evolving. This involves not only anticipating and developing preemptive protocols but also learning from mistakes. Developing processes to analyze and learn from incidents is an excellent tool by which an organization remains agile and constantly improves its security posture. As will be discussed more in Chapter 6, any consequential cybersecurity incident should be followed by an assessment and lessons learned session. This is a great opportunity for the organization to learn from and avoid mistakes in the future.

HR professionals have a unique vantage point in interacting with and observing employee behavior throughout the entire employee lifecycle, from recruitment and hiring, onboarding and training, day-to-day personnel matters, disciplinary issues and off-boarding and separation. As partners of the enterprise-wide security team, human resources professionals need to identify anomalous or troubling behaviors which, if left unchecked, could lead to intentional or unintentional compromising activity on the part of the employee that could be damaging to the enterprise. Examples of such behaviors could be everything from severe financial concerns that could leave an employee open to manipulation by a malicious actor or consistent failure to observe basic cybersecurity protocols which may lead to potential unintentional compromise. The HR team must work closely to identify, report and mitigate potential problems early in an efficient and discrete manner.

HR teams are routinely called upon and asked to join security teams in leadership meetings for questions ranging from employee privacy and access, rolling out and developing trainings, notifications and resolutions, as well as prevention of security and privacy events. From driving security-focused culture in organizations, to global regulatory and internal standards compliance, to helping manage through risk decisions and operational consequences, organizations should be building out stronger partnerships between operational and HR teams. In the times when most employees are working remotely, partnership with HR can help elevate the importance of information security and adhering to security controls and standards and making sure that they are well known to employees.

As Chief Security Officers spearhead security implementation in the organizations, it is important to emphasize the role of Chief HR Officers in providing leadership and ownership for data privacy security, employee access and awareness and operational support for critical security matters. CHRO acts as the steward of information targeted by many attackers. Yet, an IBM study shows that in most organizations the engagement gaps still persist—60% of CHROs do not feel adequately engaged to make cyber risks decisions. Similarly, potentially due to engagement gaps, 61% of CHROs think that cyber security strategy in their surveyed organizations is not well established and are not involved in cross-functional efforts. Moreover, only 57% of CHROs were actually involved in rolling out trainings for employees. Establishing regular routines on a cross-functional basis will allow for security organizations to tap into valuable HR expertise.

## Recruitment, Hiring and Retention

Cybersecurity professionals are currently in high demand. With the global cost of cybercrime estimated to reach over $6 trillion annually by 2021 and the market demand for cybersecurity positions estimated to grow by 145%, there is intense pressure to fill those positions.[13] Nonetheless, there is often a gap between the required skills and those possessed by the average applicant. According to The ISACA State of Cybersecurity 2020, 70% of companies believe fewer than half of cybersecurity applicants are professionally qualified for the positions they seek and 32% believe that it takes six months or more to fill an open cybersecurity position with a qualified candidate. Over 55% of the surveyed professionals say they have unfilled cybersecurity positions on their team and 62% report being understaffed. Given this complicated employment and staffing landscape, HR professionals are uniquely qualified to assist in the effort to identify, recruit and hire new talent. The same skills and processes that HR professionals employ generally to identify and recruit talent are vital in the effort to recruit and hire the right candidates for cybersecurity positions. Just like every other aspect of business, technology has transformed the process of recruitment and hiring in recent years and new tools have been added to the quiver of HR professionals, providing improved access to a larger pool of candidates, more efficient tracking and more detailed vetting.

The National Initiative for Cybersecurity Education (NICE) describes the Workforce Framework for Cybersecurity (NICE Framework), as a fundamental reference for describing and sharing information about cybersecurity work.[14] The benefit of the NICE framework is that not only does it help students to develop relevant cybersecurity skills, but also helps job seekers demonstrate competencies, and employees to accomplish tasks. This framework may serve as a reference for all those involved in the hiring into and applying to companies within cybersecurity.

In a recent study from 2020, one of the issues that companies face when hiring cybersecurity personnel is their relationship with the internal human resources team. 72% of surveyed companies indicated that the HR department does not regularly understand their needs.[15] For that reason, technical, security and HR professionals should partner closely to develop a collaborative recruitment plan. This partnership should be ongoing and highly interactive. Security and IT should convey clearly to HR the various skills, both technical and personal, that are required for the position and should regularly consult with their HR counterparts throughout the search and screening process. Once effective communication and a solid plan are put in place, the HR team can conduct a more focused search to find the right candidates.

A fundamental element of effective recruiting and hiring begins with knowing where to look. HR professionals can assist organizations to recruit and hire candidates with strong cybersecurity skills by focusing their efforts on incubators of the most promising sources of both new and experienced talent. In the search for new talent, many organizations have achieved success by forming innovative development partnerships at colleges and universities with strong programs in the digital sciences. These partnerships can take many forms such as simple recruiting fairs and campaigns or more elaborate arrangements where private organizations provide funding for educational programs and internship opportunities. In well-constructed internship programs, promising students can gain experience working alongside practicing professionals. In these arrangements, both the student and practitioner benefit symbiotically; the practitioner provides the student with experience and the student provides the perspective of current scholarship on various relevant issues and their energetic labor. These programs provide the additional benefit of identifying and evaluating talent in a non-binding manner and beginning the training process prior to formal hire.[16]

HR teams can help keep recruiting managers accountable to interview diverse candidates and build diverse teams, as well as lead new managers through building and retaining their teams. Building out targeted programs to recruit students and young professionals tailored to specific geographies is important in the constant competition for talent.

As an illustrative example, Georgetown University's School of Continuing Studies has now offered a partnership with the information technology and cybersecurity company Telos Corporation for nearly two years. With this partnership, Georgetown students in the Applied Intelligence and Cybersecurity Risk Management graduate programs will benefit from the joint cybersecurity events and training. Not only are they engaging directly with professionals and learning from them, but students are also grappling with current cybersecurity issues and formulating their own solutions. In the end, students not only study the risk management practices this book is attempting to shine light on, but these young professionals gain internships with a leading cybersecurity company responsible for protecting high-profile federal clients.[17]

The most effective HR professionals possess the ability to network well and maintain a good understanding of how organizations across entire industry segments are situated with respect to talent. Given the rapidly evolving nature of the digital economy, the industry's increasing reliance on talent with technical skills, and the difficulty filling those positions, the trend toward increased mobility within the industry is only expected to increase. Keeping track of the top talent across the industry provides a strong competitive advantage to organizations' HR teams as they evolve.

Social media has become an increasingly useful tool in the identification, recruitment and vetting of suitable candidates. According to a CareerBuilder survey, 70% of employers already use social media to screen candidates before hiring.[18] In addition, nearly 45% have found content on a social networking site that caused them to hire the candidate.[19] A digitally nimble HR professional can use social media and other technical and software tools to post positions, identify candidates and track recruitment processes while maintaining regular communication with the operational managers to arrive at more effective hiring decisions.

Just as important as identifying and hiring talented professionals is retaining them. In the ISACA report referenced above, 66% of companies polled lamented the difficulties they have in retaining talented professionals who are either recruited by other companies or leave because of the high stress level that comes with the job, or the lack of development opportunities, financial incentives and management support.[20] HR professionals have experience and can aid in translating functional cybersecurity staffing needs into positions with defined career paths and develop employee services which develop a more positive employee experience. By providing a pathway to career progression and a positive employment experience, organizations can optimize the retention of high-quality talent.

## Training: A Continuing Commitment to Security

HR professionals are vital in ensuring that new employees understand an organization's commitment to cybersecurity. But the training should not stop after onboarding.

Corporate culture change certainly starts with the newest employees. Employee cybersecurity training is becoming an important best practice for organizations, and for good reasons. In fact, more than half of small business owners name employee error as the biggest information security risk to their companies.[21] While percentage estimates vary from year to year, experts agree that most data breaches result from some human error exploited by malicious actors to access encrypted channels and sensitive information. Thus, a cornerstone of any effective cybersecurity strategy must be to reduce that percentage by increasing awareness and "upskilling" its workforce. In so doing, organizations can better combine technical solutions with a human firewall and transform their greatest vulnerability into their best asset.[22]

Of course, transforming culture is easier said than done. It requires a firm and dedicated commitment at all levels of an organization and only occurs effectively over time. One of the fundamental ways of bringing about cultural change within an organization is to focus on the beginning of the employee lifecycle. Moving beyond this point in the employee lifecycle by continuing to train employees consistently is the best way to reaffirm the company's cybersecurity culture and communicate its importance to employees. Forming new culture starts with forming new habits. Research suggests that new habits can form after only 60 days. Therefore, consistent implementation and reward for the right behaviors can go a long way in shifting rooted practices that might no longer service business processes.

The National Association for Corporate Directors regards culture as a corporate asset. In today's world of instant communications, culture can immediately influence business outcomes either positively or negatively.[23] The research shows that 96% of organizations plan employee cybersecurity training within the next year, but only 7% say such training has been extremely successful in building a broad-based cybersecurity culture. This indicates that training programs have effectiveness gaps. However, virtually all companies find business benefits from improved cybersecurity culture.[24] At the same time, most businesses are finding a culture gap between where they are and want to be—only 5% do not have such a gap.

## Off-boarding

As determined earlier on, upon resignation, separation or termination, both the IT and the HR team will play a critical role in offboarding an organization's staff. Ideally there are already policies in place—and if not, they are being formed—yet ultimately, this is the final point of contact between human resources and an employee, giving the company one last opportunity to secure their data. Time and time again, organizations have paid the price for cutting corners. Nearly twenty years ago, an employee who was terminated from Omega Engineering Inc. deleted all of the company's programs, which cost the Bridgeport, N.J., organization $10 million in contracts and sales.[25]

Particularly when an employee's function involves the use of critical data or assets, off-boarding and removal of access should be effected within 24 hours of resignation. This helps address potential risks including data loss, business reputation harm, cost control and ensures compliance with internal and regulatory standards. That would include not only laptops, but also mobile and storage devices, keys, badges, and other access points to organization's data after an employee no longer occupies the role or moves to a different function.

In the 2020 Cost of a Data Breach Report, conducted by IBM Security and the Ponemon Institute, malicious insiders or criminals caused 52% of all breaches. What this means is that not only are malicious attacks the most common, they are also the most expensive. These can be prevented with particular emphasis on always doing the right thing when it comes time to following security practices. Properly transferring technology between the hands of those who the company's technology used to belong to and giving it back to the company is only the first step. Prior to officially off-boarding an employee, there should be initiatives in place which ensure that one no longer has access to files, data, or information that previously required them to do their job. Physical transfers of technology are not the only important aspect of off-boarding. Ensuring that usernames, IDs and passwords will no longer grant someone access is vital.

## Conclusion

Cybersecurity today has left the tech silo and is moving into the business front lines, where HR must play a key role in the people side of implementation. A policy is a guide for individual behaviors, and HR must be an active participant in any policy change. It is important that the top management—or above—demonstrate and regularly communicate the importance of security to all the employees. As indicated in Chapter 4, cyber risk as a whole is a business quantity that represents the potential of financial loss, disruption, or damage to the reputation of an organization as a result of its use of information technology. Each department has a role in mitigating risk to minimize the overall loss of a business quantity. After all, cybersecurity is everyone's business.

The team of authors would like to thank Caitlyn Herrick for her support of this chapter.

To continue learning about the concepts in this chapter the following sources are recommended:

1   G Kurtz, J Scambray, and S McClure (2012). *Hacking Exposed: Network Security Secrets and Solutions,* McGraw-Hill, New York

2   R A Clarke (2012) *Cyber War: The Next Threat to National Security and What to Do About It,* Ecco, New York

**3** K Mitnick and W L Simon (2003) *The Art of Deception: Controlling the Human Element of Security,* Wiley, Indianapolis

**4** B Schneier (2004) *Secrets and Lies: Digital Security in a Networked World.* Wiley, Indianapolis

**5** Marc Goodman (2015) *Future Crimes: Everything Is Connected, Everyone Is Vulnerable and What We Can Do about It,* Doubleday, New York

## Endnotes

**1** J Higgins. Internet Security Alliance Response to DHS CISA on Cross-Sector Priorities and Needs During Coronavirus Pandemic, April 2020. https://insidecybersecurity.com/sites/insidecybersecurity.com/files/documents/2020/apr/cs2020_0145.pdf (archived at https://perma.cc/3MWD-NWLP)

**2** J Abbott. Five Ways HR Can Improve Cyber Security [blog] Personnel Today, July 1, 2019. www.personneltoday.com/hr/hr-role-in-cyber-security/ (archived at https://perma.cc/6LTR-3RGV)

**3** M Rosenthal. Insider Threat Statistics You Should Know: Updated 2021 [blog] Tessian, June 1, 2021. www.tessian.com/blog/insider-threat-statistics/ (archived at https://perma.cc/9959-ASJ2)

**4** Reuters. U.S. Says Personal Data on Millions of Veterans Stolen, The Washington Post, May 22, 2006, www.washingtonpost.com/wp-dyn/content/article/2006/05/22/AR2006052200690.html (archived at https://perma.cc/N4FL-H3PQ)

**5** Abdul Ghani N. A Thief Stole Unencrypted Hard Drives Filled With 29,000 Facebook Employees' Information [blog] Bloomberg, December 13, 2019. www.bloomberg.com/news/articles/2019-12-13/thief-stole-payroll-data-for-thousands-of-facebook-employees (archived at https://perma.cc/4UDY-25BX)

**6** Ponemon Institute. 2020 Cost of Insider Threats Global Report, 2020. cdw-prod.adobecqms.net/content/dam/cdw/on-domain-cdw/brands/proofpoint/ponemon-global-cost-of-insider-threats-2020-report.pdf (archived at https://perma.cc/7MMR-2PCH)

**7** Cybersecurity & Infrastructure Security Agency. Human Resources' Role in Preventing Insider Threats, n.d. https://www.cisa.gov/sites/default/files/publications/HRs%20Role%20in%20Preventing%20Insider%20Threats%20Fact%20Sheet_508.pdf (archived at https://perma.cc/UX7X-WM6D)

**8** L Clinton. The Word of the Day Is Not Virus, It Is Agility [blog] PECB Insights, August 18, 2020. insights.pecb.com/the-word-of-the-day-is-not-virus-it-is-agility/ (archived at https://perma.cc/42J2-4UQX)

**9**  J A Lewis. The Cybersecurity Workforce Gap, January 29, 2019. www.csis.org/analysis/cybersecurity-workforce-gap (archived at https://perma.cc/BQS9-4DD5)

**10**  Steve Morgan. Cybercrime to Cost the World $10.5 Trillion Annually By 2025, Cybercrime Magazine, November 19, 2020. cybersecurityventures.com/cybercrime-damage-costs-10-trillion-by-2025/ (archived at https://perma.cc/LYJ6-XA6R)

**11**  A D Wright. How Proper Offboarding Can Help Prevent Data Breaches [blog] SHRM, August 16, 2019. www.shrm.org/resourcesandtools/hr-topics/technology/pages/how-proper-offboarding-can-help-prevent-data-breaches.aspx (archived at https://perma.cc/RB7A-JMKX)

**12**  D Swinhoe. What Is the Cost of a Data Breach? [blog] CSO, August 13, 2020. www.csoonline.com/article/3434601/what-is-the-cost-of-a-data-breach.html (archived at https://perma.cc/Y8HN-X5SA)

**13**  A Oweda. 5 Reasons to Consider a Career in Cybersecurity [blog] ESET, March 3, 2020. https://www.welivesecurity.com/2020/03/03/5-reasons-consider-career-cybersecurity/ (archived at https://perma.cc/5Z3W-CH2D)

**14**  R Petersen, D Santos, M C Smith, K A Wetzel, and G Witte. Workforce Framework for Cybersecurity (NICE Framework), November 2020. nvlpubs.nist.gov/Nistpubs/SpecialPublications/NIST.SP.800-181r1.Pdf (archived at https://perma.cc/DQE2-6ZME)

**15**  D Brecht. How to Work with HR or Recruiters to Improve Your Cybersecurity Hiring Strategy [blog] Infosec Resources, April 25, 2020. resources.infosecinstitute.com/how-to-work-with-hr-or-recruiters-to-improve-your-cybersecurity-hiring-strategy/ (archived at https://perma.cc/C9A5-4V3L)

**16**  J Haller and S Merrell. Best Practices for National Cyber Security: Public Private Partnership, 2010 (CMU/SEI- 2010-SR-010). Software Engineering Institute, Carnegie Mellon University.

**17**  A Howard. Georgetown University Partners with Cybersecurity Company to Augment Graduate Programs [blog] Telos Corporation, March 12, 2019. www.telos.com/georgetown-university-partners-with-cybersecurity-company-to-augment-graduate-programs/ (archived at https://perma.cc/8N63-89LY)

**18**  L Salm. 70% of Employers are Snooping Candidates' Social Media profiles [blog] CareerBuilder, June 15, 2017. www.careerbuilder.com/advice/social-media-survey-2017 (archived at https://perma.cc/X2W6-XNRE)

**19**  D Brecht. How to Work with HR or Recruiters to Improve Your Cybersecurity Hiring Strategy [blog] Infosec Resources, April 25, 2020. resources.infosecinstitute.com/how-to-work-with-hr-or-recruiters-to-improve-your-cybersecurity-hiring-strategy/ (archived at https://perma.cc/PG6E-M8EV)

**20**  Ibid.

**21** N Feather. New Employees Can Be a Cybersecurity Risk. Here Are 5 Simple
    Practices You Can Teach Them During Onboarding [blog] Inc, November 27,
    2019. www.inc.com/neill-feather/new-employees-can-be-a-cybersecurity-risk-
    here-are-5-simple-practices-you-can-teach-them-during-onboarding.html
    (archived at https://perma.cc/HNG5-NHH8)

**22** J Goodchild. How HR and IT Can Partner to Improve Cybersecurity [blog]
    Dark Reading, November 4, 2019. www.darkreading.com/edge/theedge/
    how-hr-and-it-can-partner-to-improve-cybersecurity/b/d-id/1336256 (archived
    at https://perma.cc/6UGK-U9MN)

**23** F Scholl. How HR Can Become a Cybersecurity Ninja [blog] Human Resource
    Executive, February 21, 2019. hrexecutive.com/how-hr-can-become-a-
    cybersecurity-ninja/ (archived at https://perma.cc/DW9T-SLA3)

**24** F Scholl. How HR Can Become a Cybersecurity Ninja [blog] Human Resource
    Executive, February 21, 2019. hrexecutive.com/how-hr-can-become-a-
    cybersecurity-ninja/ (archived at https://perma.cc/DW9T-SLA3)

**25** David W Chen. Man Charged With Sabotage Of Computers, The New York
    Times, February 18, 1998. www.nytimes.com/1998/02/18/nyregion/man-
    charged-with-sabotage-of-computers.html (archived at https://perma.cc/
    774Q-49L6)

# 06

# Cybersecurity and the Office of the General Counsel

BY JIM HALPERT, PARTNER, GLOBAL DATA PROTECTION,
PRIVACY AND SECURITY PRACTICE, DLA PIPER US, AND CAITLYN HERRICK,
ISA RESEARCH ASSOCIATE

## Five Key Ideas to Take Away from This Chapter

1 The General Counsel and General Counsel's Office can play an important role in addressing organizations' cybersecurity risk, both proactively and reactively. Cyber risk is such a dynamic and complex risk area that a GC should embrace the role and see it as an important contribution to their organization.

2 This role differs from and complements the CISO's role because the GC is consulted on many business decisions that the CISO is often not consulted on, including legal and regulatory compliance, corporate governance, investigations, mergers and acquisitions, contracts with third parties, new product reviews, engaging and terminating employees and contractors.

3 The basic functions that all GC's Offices should own are following and driving compliance with

   a) rapidly changing legal, regulatory and contractual cybersecurity requirements (which often vary by business sector); and

   b) evolving conditions to protect sensitive information under legal privilege or attorney work legal doctrines.

**4** The advanced roles that GC's Offices should play, including

    **a)** playing an active role in their organization's understanding of cyber risks it faces and voicing those risks to senior management;

    **b)** driving incident preparation including, improving incident response plans and helping to run tabletop exercises;

    **c)** co-leading incident responses with the CISO during breaches;

    **d)** leading post-breach assessments; and

    **e)** overseeing proactive cyber risk assessments.

**5** By playing these roles actively, the GC and GC's Office can significantly improve the cyber risk posture of their organizations.

## Introduction

The General Counsel is positioned to play an important role in advancing cybersecurity risk management in organizations. The General Counsel is part of the C-Suite and typically reports directly to the CEO, because their advice is integral to a host of business decisions.[1] The General Counsel is the organization's authority on legal risk and is typically consulted on and involved in a host of important business decisions that bear on cyber risk. These include legal and regulatory compliance, corporate governance, investigations, mergers and acquisitions, contracts with third parties, new product reviews, engaging and terminating employees and contractors, as well as, of course, cyber risk management itself—the focus of this book.

Through these responsibilities, the GC has contact with most key functions across an enterprise. They also present at many important meetings where the CISO is not, and by raising relevant cybersecurity risk considerations can help fulfill the important goal of ensuring that cybersecurity risk is addressed across the organization's functions and businesses.

This chapter provides a roadmap for GCs and their offices to play both proactively and reactively this important role in mitigating cyber risk. It divides the potential GC functions in this regard into basic and more complex types. Ideally, the GC or a lawyer on the GC's team should be an active participant in cyber risk management performing all of these functions.

## Why Cybersecurity Demands a Proactive Approach by the GC

Cybersecurity is typically ranked as one of the greatest risks for most enterprises.[2] As explained in Chapter 2, cybersecurity is not an IT issue, but an enterprise-wide risk management issue that must be addressed across many parts of the enterprise in order to mitigate the risk successfully. The GC is an authoritative voice within the organization on legal risk and is uniquely situated to raise this risk in settings where the CISO is often not present or on which the CISO has less authority.

Currently, the majority of businesses' cybersecurity practices are reactive. For example, a VMWare study indicates that 80% of enterprise IT security investments are reactive and only 20% are preemptive.[3] Successful cybersecurity management requires addressing cyber risks proactively to avoid or mitigate potential incidents, instead of detecting and reacting to them. This involves repeatedly identifying, weighing and devising appropriate risk mitigation strategies for changing cybersecurity threats and business developments.

Although cybersecurity legal compliance is certainly part of the General Counsel's responsibility, the most effective cyber risk management is forward-looking and very different than a check-the-box compliance exercise. Simply following today's legal requirements is not enough. Leadership should steer the organization towards addressing emerging requirements pre-emptively, preparing for upcoming changes in the business, and escalating threats. This proactive risk management approach should be infused throughout the organization because, as explained in Chapter 2, cybersecurity risk management is an enterprise-wide issue. The GC and GC's Office have specific responsibilities described in the basics section below, but beyond that the GC has a unique role to play in driving better cyber risk management across the enterprise, which is the focus of later sections of this chapter.

## Key Responsibilities—The Basics

The General Counsel's principal responsibilities relating to cybersecurity risk management typically includes:

- monitoring and advising on changes in statutory, regulatory and sectoral requirements;
- overseeing management of contract requirements and liabilities imposed by and imposed on the organization;

- overseeing legal privilege and attorney work product protection;
- overseeing breach preparation activities;
- co-leading the incident response with the Chief Information Security Officer (CISO) during breaches; and
- leading post-breach assessments.

## Monitoring and Advising on Changes in Statutory, Regulatory and Sectoral Requirements

As noted above, the mission of the GC's Office includes advising on legal requirements—whether statutory, regulatory or contractual—to which the organization is subject. Statutory and regulatory requirements typically vary based upon the sector the organization operates in, but SEC requirements apply to publicly listed companies, and some requirements apply to specific types of information.

Traditionally, government is seen as adopting a carrot-and-stick relationship with private sector entities. A business is rewarded with tax cuts or subsidies to support compliance, and punished with fines, threats of license revocation, or private lawsuits when it is not in compliance. This relationship is at worst adverse, and at best asymmetrical. However, the ISA's view is that these adverse and/or asymmetrical relationships are detrimental to every party's cybersecurity interests because they create non-cooperative and potentially antagonistic relationships between organizations and their regulators. The real antagonists in the cybersecurity ecosystems are the attackers, and the regulators and private sector should instead collaborate by repeatedly fortifying defenses against rapidly innovating attackers. In other words, the private and public sectors should be working together identifying emerging cyber threats and vulnerabilities and improving risk management, instead of focusing primarily on following or enforcing regulatory requirements that often become outdated. To be sure, civil enforcement can help deter seriously inadequate security measures, but an active public-private partnership is vital to addressing complex cyber threats.

## Regulatory Requirements

In the US, regulatory requirements exist at both the federal and state levels.

## Federal Laws and Regulations

Federal requirements generally focus on specific sectors. Prominent federal regulatory examples include:

**Health Insurance Portability and Accountability Act (HIPAA)** and **Health Information Technology for Economic and Clinical Health Act (HI-TECH)** regulations: These federal regulations generally regulate protected health information processed by health care providers, health plan payers, health-care clearinghouses and their business associates (service providers). The cybersecurity dimensions of these regulations impose quite specific data security obligations for patient health data and require regulated entities to conduct security risk assessments regarding their handling of these data.[4]

**The 1999 Gramm-Leach-Bliley Act:** This federal law, also known as the Financial Modernization Act of 1999, removed many regulations on financial institutions. However, Title V of the law established privacy and security obligations on financial institutions and some related service providers (including accountants). Data security regulations issued under Title V, the Gramm-Leach-Bliley Safeguards Rules, impose process-based data security regulations on entities subject to the rules.[5] Federal functional regulators who oversee the safety and soundness of banking institutions conduct oversight of regulated institutions' cybersecurity programs, and have issued detailed and extensive cybersecurity guidance regulating these institutions and their use of service providers. Financial services entities that are licensed by the NY Department of Financial Services (NYDFS) must also comply with the NYDFS cybersecurity.

**The Federal Information Security Management Act (FISMA):**[6] an amendment to the 2002 Homeland Security Act, requires each federal agency to develop, document, and implement an agency-wide program to "provide information security for the information and systems that support the operations and assets of the agency, including those provided or managed by another agency, contractor, or other sources".[7] A long list of federal agency regulatory requirements apply to government contractors and vary by sector. For example, in early 2020, the Department of Defense issued the Cybersecurity Maturity Model Certification (CMMC),[8] a unified standard for implementing cybersecurity across the defense industrial base (DIB), which includes over 300,000 companies in these supply chains. As Chapter 8 illustrates, ecosystem cybersecurity is only as strong as its weakest links, many of which are smaller subcontractors with fewer cybersecurity resources than the prime contractor.

**The Federal Trade Commission (FTC) Consumer Protection Bureau** uses its enforcement authority under Section 5 of the FTC Act against deceptive and unfair business practices to launch investigations and obtain data security consent decree settlements. These investigations focus on data security of consumer data and usually hinge upon false statements that a business is keeping data secure or significantly inadequate data security practices. The FTC has issued guidance that draws general principles from its specific enforcement actions on security and groups them in categories: security by design, secure authentication, protection of sensitive personal information, network segmentation and monitoring, securing remote access, vendor management, ongoing cyber risk and vulnerability management, and securing physical documents, media and devices.[9] State Attorneys General, who often have similar consumer protection authority under their state consumer protection laws, also bring enforcement actions in similar circumstances and occasionally investigate other areas of particular interest to their offices.

**The Securities & Exchange Commission** has authority to protect investors and retail brokerage accounts, trading platforms and critical market infrastructure. Of broader concern to public companies, the SEC has issued interpretive rules guidance for publicly traded companies to disclose material cyber risks and cyber incidents that the GC's Office may need to address.[10] In addition, the Cybersecurity Unit within the SEC's Enforcement Division focuses on cybersecurity controls at regulated entities, trading on the basis of hacked nonpublic information, and cyber-related manipulations, such as brokerage account takeovers and market manipulations using electronic and social media platforms.[11] What is more, cybersecurity is a priority of the SEC's National Examination Program for market participants.[12]

### State Laws

There are extensive insurance sector cybersecurity regulatory requirements—including in states that have transposed the NAIC Model Insurance Cybersecurity Law, or in New York, the NYDFS cybersecurity regulations—state government contractor security laws, state data breach notice laws for specific types of data, and state data security laws.[13]

**State Insurance Sector Requirements.** Insurers are subject to state, not federal, regulation. This is not to the industry's advantage in cybersecurity, as the sector is subject to varying and unusually stringent requirements in relation to the types of personal data it holds. The principal state cybersecurity requirement is the NAIC Model Cybersecurity Law. It sets out standards and best practices that insurance companies should include in their information security programs, including a comprehensive information security program, information security requirements for third party vendors, an incident response plan and breach notification requirements in the event of a breach.[14] A growing number of states have adopted this law. The NYDFS cybersecurity regulations[15] predate the NAIC model law and contain some additional requirements, as well as a catch-all breach notice requirement to notify the NYDFS if a licensee must notify any other regulator. As noted above, the NYDFS regulations apply to financial services and insurance sector entities that are licensed by the agency.

**State Government Contractor Security Requirements:** There are a number of state laws, such as in Connecticut and New York, that impose particular data security and breach notice requirements on government contractors generally, or for a particular sector (New York's applies to education sector contractors). These are generally less extensive than federal requirements but require individualized review, as they in some cases apply over and above requirements imposed in the government contract.

**State Data Breach Notice Laws:** These widely varying laws in all 50 US States, most US territories, the EU and an increasing number of other countries require organizations that have been breached or should reasonably believe that they have been breached to notify regulators or affected individuals of security breaches of personal information that creates some risk to the affected individuals. Security breach notice laws typically have varying provisions regarding: (1) who must comply with the law (some laws apply to non-profit organizations and governments, others do not), (2) what range of "personal information" triggers the notification requirement, (3) what activity constitutes a breach (e.g. acquisition, access to or unavailability of) the personal data, (4) whether there is a lack of risk of harm exception or other exception (e.g. for encrypted or redacted personal data); (5) whether regulators or individuals must be notified; (6) the time deadline(s) to notify; (7) notice content requirements; and (8) any obligation to provide identity theft prevention assistance to affected individuals.

**State Data Security laws:** Most of these data security laws require businesses that own, license, or maintain personal information about a resident of that state to implement and maintain "reasonable security procedures and practices" appropriate to the nature of the information and to protect the personal information from unauthorized access, destruction, use, modification, or disclosure.[16] The most menacing of these laws is California's because it is enforceable through class action lawsuits for minimum statutory damages of $100 to $750 per violation, which may be interpreted as per individual affected. Civ. Code § 1798.150(a). The law applies to personal information—other than username and password data—that is subject to breach notification requirements in the state. It contains an exception for encrypted and redacted data, and enforceable class action waivers can also serve to defeat class action lawsuits under the law. Other noteworthy state laws include the following:

- Massachusetts' cybersecurity regulations that contain more particular requirements, including a data encryption requirement for "breach notice personal data";[17]
- Nevada's encryption mandate and safe harbor law for breach notice personal data outside the premises of the employer;[18]
- the New York Shield Act;[19] and
- Ohio's safe harbor law for entities that follow a federal data security law or established cybersecurity standard.[20]

## Sectoral Requirements

In addition to general regulations, businesses must comply with requirements applicable to their specific sector. The Department of Homeland security monitors, analyzes, and responds to security incidents that affect critical infrastructure industry sectors. These sectors are areas in which both public and private organizations provide vital assets, services, systems, and networks to the citizens of the United States. A cyberattack to any of these sectors could lead to disastrous effects on the security of the nation, the US economy, or public health and safety of US citizens.

US sectors classified "critical infrastructure" are typically subject to significant additional cybersecurity requirements. Although regulator enforcement authority varies significantly across sectors, contractual and reputational risks are also heightened. The US sectors include: energy services, dams, financial services, nuclear reactor, material and waste, food and agriculture, water and wastewater system, healthcare and public health, emergency services, transportation systems, chemical, communications, information technology, defense industrial base, and critical manufacturing (metals, machinery, automobile and transportation equipment, electrical equipment producers). EU law contains a quite similar list of "essential services" sectors, but adds information technology as a distinct "essential services" sector.

## Contractual Requirements

Over and above requirements imposed on organizations by government statute or regulation, an organization's cybersecurity requirements can be, and often are, bound by contractual requirements through transactions with other parties. Organizations are often subject to more extensive contractual cybersecurity requirements than regulatory ones. As specialization and rationalization of business functions increases, so do outsourcing and teaming arrangements through which organizations share data, depend on IT systems of their partners to deliver key services, and sometimes have their networks interconnect directly with one another. All these arrangements increase cybersecurity risk. Increasingly common ecosystem arrangements in which multiple businesses team together to provide services magnify this risk further—from "third party" to "nth party" risk.

In this increasingly complex environment, organizations need to manage third party or, in the case of ecosystem arrangements, "nth party" risk by imposing contractual requirements that exceed specific regulatory requirements, as regulations are often too specific and outpaced by the dynamic nature of cyber risk.

Contracts are legal documents squarely within the GC's Office's expertise and responsibility. Although procurement functions (on the buy side) and sales or business development functions (on the sell side) drive most contractual arrangements, it is important that the General Counsel's Office manage contractual cybersecurity risk. Unless it does so, the day-to-day imperatives of clinching sales or getting the lowest price on an agreement will often overshadow significant cybersecurity risk. In doing this, the General Counsel's Office should work with the CISO on what requirements make sense to impose or accept in contracts, and also work with outside counsel to develop negotiation playbooks on both the buy and sell sides that both satisfy legal requirements to which the organization is subject and mitigate larger cybersecurity risks identified by the CISO. The General Counsel's Office also needs to work with procurement and sales to ensure that a clear structure is in place to systematize use and application of the playbook, with mandatory escalation to the General Counsel and CISO if an exception is being considered.

There is more work to do regarding the many contracts that the organization has already entered into. This includes:

- Conducting a review and mapping of cybersecurity obligations, including breach notice deadlines, that the organization has committed to.

- A review and mapping of obligations that the organization has entered into with its third parties, as well as any risk designation flagged by vendor management in relation to each such third party. This information is often best presented on a chart with the date the contract is up for renegotiation.

- Targeting in consultation with the CISO over-commitments to third parties, or deficiencies in commitments obtained from third parties that are flagged to be fixed when the contract can be renegotiated.

## Legal Privilege Protection

This is another area where the GC's Office is uniquely positioned to help the organization mitigate risk. Because cybersecurity is such a complex and significant risk, protecting the confidentiality of communications about potential negligence or regulatory violations and about areas in need of improvement is itself an important risk management function. The GC's Office, teamed with outside counsel, is the only part of the enterprise positioned to maximize the chances of privilege applying.

Enforcement authorities and plaintiff's lawyers are particularly interested in obtaining assessments that note cybersecurity failures or serious vulnerabilities from any outside security expert the organization has hired. In the event of a security incident, they also are interested in obtaining any admissions by employees or contractors that security measures or the response were deficient.

Reports or assessments are of particular interest because they provide an outside assessment by someone trusted by the organization of the organization's security posture and summarize conveniently large amounts of technical information that is difficult for lawyers and laypeople to understand. They should be protected by privilege whenever possible, including when auditors ask to view them.

Similarly, analyses by outside counsel of legal theories the organization may raise or may be raised against it can be protected by attorney work product doctrine and also should be rigorously protected, if possible.

These doctrines vary widely by country, and it is important to review carefully requirements in the jurisdictions an organization is exposed to. If your organization has an international footprint, this includes planning where to base investigations of cyber incidents in order to take advantage of privilege protections available in some countries. For example, the US and

UK both protect legal privilege, whereas China does not recognize it. For an overview of privilege rules by country in 49 countries, see DLA Piper's Legal Privilege Global Guide, available at https://www.dlapiperintelligence.com/legalprivilege/.

Legal privilege applies to legal, as opposed to routine business, communications. Those communications must be designed to protect the company against legal risk. In-house counsel can be deemed to be providing business advice and not to provide a sufficient basis for privilege. For this reason, involving outside counsel often helps to strengthen privilege arguments and it is advisable to engage outside counsel in most incidents that create legal risk to an organization.

Attorney work product doctrine, in jurisdictions where available, applies more narrowly to information generated in anticipation of litigation.

Because some recent US court decisions are narrowing the availability of privilege and work product protections in cybersecurity investigations, it is important to seek advice immediately about how to structure internal communications and how to engage all vendors to maximize these protections.

Generally speaking, the General Counsel—and in the UK and often in the US—outside counsel should be included in communications. It is also critical when an incident occurs that vendors be engaged by the General Counsel (not IT or the CISO) and ideally through outside counsel in a new engagement agreement that follows an agreement form that has been upheld by a court as sufficient to support privilege.

Also, in jurisdictions where privilege is available, it is best that all forensic or other reports qualitatively assessing an organization's security posture or recommending changes to it be screened through outside counsel. Outside counsel should display drafts to the organization via online communications software (e.g., WebEx, Zoom or Teams) and work with it on modifications to finalize the report without any copy of drafts being stored on the organization's systems. The reason for this approach is that enforcement authorities and plaintiff's lawyers often seek copies of drafts of reports and scour them for changes made to drafts at the request of the organization or its counsel.

In addition, final reports and legal memoranda by counsel, where possible, should not be shared outside the organization (unless an additional legal privilege, such as a bank examiner legal privilege applies). If disclosure is required, then it is best to prepare a non-privileged factual summary that removes qualitative assessments. Where privilege with regard to engagement of a forensic vendor is at risk or not available, in some cases it may be safest either to not to generate a report at all, or to commission a narrower report on what happened and commission a second, more sensitive report for purposes of supporting outside counsel's advice on protecting the organization against legal risk.

Because they both can be waived, legal privilege and work product protection require establishing and training team members to follow protocols for internal and external communications and for handling forensic reports and written advice from counsel. It is very important that the organization's incident response plan reflects the privilege protocol (see next section). Furthermore, because of the complex conditions for these protections and their importance for risk management, tabletop exercises should include practicing the protocol and adjusting it to ensure that the protocols to protect privilege are workable.

## Advanced Risk Management Functions of the GC

### Role of the General Counsel in Cybersecurity Risk Management

The General Counsel rarely has technical expertise. However, they have unique insight into legal risk and should actively address legal dimensions of cyber risk and risk management in board and management meetings, partnering closely with the CISO and the insurance risk manager. This includes active involvement in the organization's cyber risk management plan; active partnership with the CISO to work toward active management of cyber risk both internally and vis-à-vis third parties; articulating legal cyber risks clearly to help ensure that those risks are mitigated to the extent practicable, including with sufficient cyber insurance; and supporting the mission of the CISO to improve the organization's cyber risk posture. Particular opportunities for the GC to do this arise in corporate governance advice, arranging for and participating in cybersecurity briefings for corporate directors and senior management, insurance reviews, compliance and new product reviews, merger and acquisition due diligence and integration, certain internal investigations, higher risk business partnering negotiations and vendor risk management generally, employee onboarding and termination procedures, and advice on network monitoring, among other situations.

Moreover, the General Counsel should lead engagement with regulators with supervisory authority over the organization (e.g., critical infrastructure regulators). This should include: proactive outreach to regulators with supervisory authority over the organization (e.g. functional regulators or critical infrastructure regulators), responses when a cybersecurity rule is being proposed by the regulator, the response to an examination by a regulator that addresses cybersecurity, and the response to any investigation by a regulator of the organization or of individuals associated with the organization.[21]

## Incident Preparation

The General Counsel's Office should take the lead ensuring that the organization has pre-engaged through outside cybersecurity counsel forensic, ransomware negotiator, PR vendor, and notification vendors under a separate agreement that reflects latest privilege guidance. In the event of an incident, a statement of work can be added to this engagement letter Pre-establishing the engagement letter increases the likelihood of privilege protection applying quickly, while saving valuable time during the tense period following discovery of an incident that may require outside support.

Further, the General Counsel should establish or refine the organization's incident response plan attorney-client privilege and work product protocols, including that the GC's Office with outside counsel help direct the incident response jointly with the CISO. It is very important that the GC participate in tabletop exercises and that the GC's Office helps design tabletop exercises that test and improve the privilege protocol.

## Role of the GC in Incident Response

The GC's Office should co-lead the IR effort with the CISO wherever there is potential legal risk for privilege reasons and to improve the quality of risk assessment and risk management in response to the incident.

Specific tasks that the GC's Office performs, typically in conjunction with outside counsel where they are engaged are as follows:

- Instructing team members that the privilege protocol applies to communications and any reports generated, and that in a transnational investigation the GC's Office and CISO jointly approve the jurisdiction where the investigation should be centered in light of practical and privilege issues.

- Considering whether to engage outside counsel and overseeing activities of outside counsel when engaged.

- In the event of a breach of a third party that holds organization data or supports organization operations, leading negotiations with the third party in conjunction with internal organization relationship manager and managing all communications with the third party.

- In consultation with CISO, considering whether to engage forensic investigation firm to start work immediately.

  o If that forensics firm is not pre-engaged under privilege, the GC's Office should ensure that outside counsel engages it appropriately and as soon as possible.

  o If the forensics firm is already working for the organization in a proactive capacity, it is very important for privilege and work product protection to apply, to ensure that the firm provides an entirely different team, engaged through the GC's Office and outside counsel, using a different source of funds (not a pre-established retainer).[22] In some jurisdictions, additional measures may be required,[23] so it is important to confirm the approach with outside counsel.

- In consultation with the CISO, Communications and HR, considering whether to engage other third-party vendors (e.g., ransomware negotiation consultant, public relations, identity theft remediation) under the privilege protocol.

- Evaluating the terms of cyber insurance and overseeing risk manager or outside counsel discussions with the organization's cyber insurer (if any) to confirm coverage.

- In consultation with IR Team, determining whether/when senior management and the board and/or employees should be notified and participating in any such briefing with the CISO and other firm management.

- In consultation with IR team, determining whether to notify law enforcement and what information to disclose to law enforcement (considering the waiver of legal privilege that applies to information shared). Also, managing participating with corporate security in any organization outreach to law enforcement. This may be performed by outside counsel or the forensic vendor but should be managed by the GC's Office.

- Determining what statutory, regulatory and contractual breach notification requirements are likely triggered and overseeing legal review of obligations.

- In a public company, determining whether to close the securities trading window for insiders who are aware of the incident to avoid insider trading risk and whether to make a disclosure in an SEC 8-K filing.

- Assessing whether the cyber incident likely raises any litigation or other regulatory issues (e.g., current or anticipated litigation, regulatory investigations, settlements with the government or private litigation) and leading the strategy to manage those issues.

- Where other hazards or significant risks to the organization are possible, leading the process that identifies those hazards or risks, their potential consequences and likelihood of occurring,[24] as well as the ultimate assessment of likely harm from the incident.

- Reviewing and signing off on all proposed breach-related communications to employees, clients, affected individuals, investors, the general public, and any other third party.

- In a ransomware incident where payment is being considered, assessing whether and if so, in which countries, sanctions risk is an issue and paying ransom may put the organization at risk.

- Leading notice to, communications with, responses to inquiries from, and any other interactions with, regulators.

## Role of the GC in Post-Breach and Any Other Cybersecurity Risk Assessments

Once the dust from the incident has settled, the General Counsel should oversee a lessons-learned session under privilege.

Cyber incidents are common but provide important lessons. It is important to develop processes to learn from significant incidents. This enables both better prevention of incidents and better handling of other types of incidents that inevitably occur in some form in the future. What is more, courts and regulators are more likely to find negligence or violations of regulatory requirements if an organization repeats mistakes in leading to or aggravating subsequent incidents. For all these reasons, any consequential cybersecurity incident should be followed by an assessment and "lessons-learned" session so that the organization does not make the same mistakes again. These reviews should assess changes that have or that need to be made in the organization's security posture and incident response. They should assess how the organization's incident response plan worked in practice and how to adjust it, if at all, in light of the incident. Finally, working in conjunction with HR, the review should incorporate lessons-learned into cybersecurity trainings and future tabletop exercises.[25]

Because this exercise necessarily notes failures and problems, it is important that it be protected by privilege wherever possible. This means that the GC's Office should convene and co-lead this process, working closely with CISO.

Similarly, other cybersecurity risk or program reviews by third party assessors should be structured to protect them under attorney-client privilege. This requires the General Counsel's Office to engage the third party, often through outside counsel, and to supervise the review or risk assessment while applying the organization's privilege protocol.

## Conclusion

The GC can be an important force in mitigating cyber risk. This chapter provides a roadmap for playing that important role both proactively and reactively, and for doing so in conjunction with the organization's CISO, while helping to build support from the C-Suite and Board of Directors.

## Endnotes

**1** R Walters. A Day in the Life of a General Counsel [blog] Robert Walters, n.d. www.robertwalters.us/blog/a-day-in-the-life-of-a-general-counsel.html (archived at https://perma.cc/2V85-2E2P)

**2** Allianz Global Corporate & Specialty. Allianz Risk Barometer 2020 [blog] Allianz, January 14, 2020. www.agcs.allianz.com/news-and-insights/expert-risk-articles/allianz-risk-barometer-2020-business-risks.html (archived at https://perma.cc/B6LX-25SD)

**3** VMwarebelgium. Three Steps to Restore Confidence in Cybersecurity [blog] VMware July 26, 2019. blogs.vmware.com/emea/be/2019/07/three-steps%E2%80%AF-to-restore-confidence-in-cyber-security/ (archived at https://perma.cc/2FHD-MBCY)

**4** Centers for Disease Control and Prevention. Health Insurance Portability and Accountability Act of 1996 (HIPAA), September 14, 2018. www.cdc.gov/phlp/publications/topic/hipaa.html (archived at https://perma.cc/23DA-FDS3)

5   J De Groot. What Is GLBA Compliance? Understanding the Data Protection
    Requirements of the Gramm-Leach-Bliley Act in 2021 [blog] Digital Guardian,
    July 6 2021. digitalguardian.com/blog/what-glba-compliance-understanding-
    data-protection-requirements-gramm-leach-bliley-act (archived at https://
    perma.cc/DXV9-L5PG)

6   Dark Cubed. Cybersecurity Compliance: A Comprehensive Guide [blog] Dark
    Cubed, n.d. darkcubed.com/compliance (archived at https://perma.cc/A8TB-
    NG7X)

7   Computer Security Resource Center. NIST Risk Management Framework:
    Federal Information Security Modernization Act (FISMA) Background [blog]
    CSRC. csrc.nist.gov/projects/risk-management/detailed-overview (archived at
    https://perma.cc/N7S6-SP54)

8   Federal Register. Defense Federal Acquisition Regulation Supplement,
    September 29, 2020. www.federalregister.gov/documents/2020/09/29/
    2020-21123/defense-federal-acquisition-regulation-supplement-assessing-
    contractor-implementation-of (archived at https://perma.cc/9SAP-EJSA)

9   Federal Trade Commission. Start with Security: A Guide for Business, June
    2015. www.ftc.gov/system/files/documents/plain-language/pdf0205-
    startwithsecurity.pdf (archived at https://perma.cc/X5LM-VPPP)

10  Securities and Exchange Commission. Commission Statement and Guidance
    on Public Company Cybersecurity Disclosures, February 26, 2018. www.sec.
    gov/rules/interp/2018/33-10459.pdf (archived at https://perma.cc/46MP-
    995X)

11  U.S. Securities and Exchange Commission. SEC Announces Enforcement
    Initiatives to Combat Cyber-Based Threats and Protect Retail Investors,
    September 25, 2017. www.sec.gov/news/press-release/2017-176 (archived at
    https://perma.cc/96Q5-ZUVX)

12  U.S. Securities and Exchange Commission. Cybersecurity [blog] SEC, April 24,
    2021. www.sec.gov/spotlight/cybersecurity (archived at https://perma.cc/
    UJ7Q-4VNM)

13  P Greenberg. Security Breach Notification Laws [blog] NCSL, April 15, 2021.
    www.ncsl.org/research/telecommunications-and-information-technology/
    security-breach-notification-laws.aspx (archived at https://perma.cc/8689-
    2S25)

14  TotalHIPAA. A Guide to the NAIC's Insurance Data Security Model Law
    [blog] TotalHIPAA, n.d. www.totalhipaa.com/naic-insurance-model-law/
    (archived at https://perma.cc/R4J5-NMTX)

15  New York State Department of Financial Services. Part 500 Cybersecurity
    Requirements for Financial Services Companies, December 15, 2020. govt.
    westlaw.com/nycrr/Browse/Home/NewYork/NewYorkCodesRulesandRegulati
    ons?guid=I5be30d2007f811e79d43a037eefd0011&originationContext=docu
    menttoc&transitionType=Default&contextData=%28sc.Default%29
    (archived at https://perma.cc/VT67-QB2R)

**16**  P Greenberg. Data Security Laws: Private Sector, May 29, 2019. www.ncsl.org/
research/telecommunications-and-information-technology/data-security-laws.
aspx (archived at https://perma.cc/6PTR-BFXG)

**17**  Office of Consumer Affairs and Business Regulation. 201 CMR 17.00:
Standards for the Protection of Personal Information of MA Residents,
October 19, 2017. www.mass.gov/regulations/201-CMR-1700-standards-for-
the-protection-of-personal-information-of-ma-residents (archived at https://
perma.cc/49UL-ZL83)

**18**  Legislative Counsel Bureau. NRS: Chapter 603A - Security and Privacy of
Personal Information, n.d. www.leg.state.nv.us/nrs/nrs-603a.html#
NRS603ASec215 (archived at https://perma.cc/EBU8-5W36)

**19**  NY Gen. Bus. Law § 899-bb

**20**  Ohio Revised Code. Chapter 1354: Businesses Maintaining Recognized
Cybersecurity Programs, n.d. codes.ohio.gov/ohio-revised-code/chapter-1354
(archived at https://perma.cc/7P2R-NGR7)

**21**  N Champ. Building Effective Relationships with Regulators [blog] Harvard
Law School Forum on Corporate Governance, October 22, 2015. corpgov.law.
harvard.edu/2015/10/22/building-effective-relationships-with-regulators/
(archived at https://perma.cc/YG5S-7T9S)

**22**  *In Re Capital One Consumer Data Security Breach Litigation, 2020 WL
2731238 (E.D. Va. May 26, 2020), aff'd,* 2020 WL 3470261 (E.D. Va.
June 25, 2020)

**23**  *Wengui v. Clark Hill PLC,* Civil Action No. 19-3195 (JEB) (D.D.C. Jan. 12,
2021). casetext.com/case/guo-wengui-v-clark-hill-plc (archived at https://
perma.cc/FF3C-QTN9)

**24**  Ready.gov. Risk Assessment, February 6, 2021. www.ready.gov/risk-assessment
(archived at https://perma.cc/H3GL-42NM)

**25**  G Dhillon. What to Do Before and After a Cybersecurity Breach? n.d. www.
american.edu/kogod/research/cybergov/upload/what-to-do.pdf (archived at
https://perma.cc/CCN4-GEZ2)

# 07

# Cybersecurity Audit and Compliance Considerations

BY ANDREW COTTON, PARTNER, EY, AND KANGKYU LEE,
ISA RESEARCH ASSOCIATE

## Five Key Ideas to Take Away from This Chapter

1 Audit and compliance functions need to continue their evolution from a "check-the-box" approach to cybersecurity and incorporate a strategic, risk-based approach to risk assessment to achieve good cyber governance and effective risk management.

2 While compliance with the various regulatory or contractual regimes are critical, an organization must be mindful that compliance does not equal security.

3 The role of audit is expanding to provide assurance and insight over the controls and activities of critical risk areas and digital transformation efforts.

4 The audit model for cybersecurity has been updated to stress the importance of communication between the "third line" and other lines in the corporate structure to better fit the strategic and operational needs of the organization.

5 The introduction of advanced technologies such as AI and blockchain, while introducing new risks, should eventually serve to enhance audit and compliance activities through effective risk management and increased efficiency.

# Introduction

As cybersecurity truly became an enterprise-wide concern over the past decade, the effective assessment and management of cyber risk has been highlighted as an imperative. The traditional audit processes and compliance requirements did not provide the necessary insight on the maturity of enterprise level cybersecurity. As stressed in a 2019 study by ISACA and Protiviti:

> IT audit cannot let its guard down, and it does not have the luxury of conducting high-level check-the-box audits of areas such as information security, controls, and overall privacy. Security issues are among the greatest concerns for auditors because, if an emergency arises (e.g., data loss, security breach), they can bring most other processes and activities in the organization to a standstill. It's the enduring risk that can strike at any time and requires effective controls to be maintained and updated as needed.[1]

A more comprehensive approach is necessary to properly manage risk and controls for ensuring good governance and provide adequate risk assurance to enterprises. The limitations of the traditional approach are apparent. Many current compliance management solutions appropriately address cybersecurity compliance gaps, but do not incorporate values such as financial risk or prioritized risk mitigation efforts. To address such issues, a more strategic, risk-based approach needs to be employed. This will benefit audit and compliance regimes in providing good cyber governance and more effective risk mitigation for enterprises. By understanding the current landscape and the potential benefits of emerging technologies, corporations can utilize the modern approach to cyber risk, introduced in Chapter 4.

## The Current Landscape of Compliance and Audit Requirements

### Regulatory Imperatives that are Driving Compliance

Data protection within the enterprise and the privacy of customer and employee data is home to a vast landscape of cybersecurity laws, regulations and standards. Unlike the European Union, there is currently no single federal law that regulates information security, cybersecurity, and privacy throughout the United States. Instead, these areas are currently regulated by industry-specific federal laws and state legislation with varying scopes, jurisdiction and penalties for non-compliance (civil or criminal).[2]

As discussed in detail in Chapter 6, within the United States, all 50 states have their own data breach notification laws, and states also have different data privacy and IT security compliance requirements. New York has its own specific cybersecurity regulation for covered financial institutions that is enforced by the Department of Financial Services. Industry standards and regulations include the Health Insurance Portability and Accountability Act (HIPAA) for health and patient data, the Sarbanes-Oxley Act (SOX) for public companies, Graham-Leach-Bliley Act (GLBA) for a broadly defined group of financial institutions, and the Federal Information Management Security Act (FISMA) for federal agencies.

This environment is also one that is changing rapidly. As discussed in Chapter 2, the legal and regulatory landscapes are complex and volatile, hence why Principle Two for board oversight of cybersecurity stresses the importance of evaluating company-specific circumstances. Over the past few years, global regulators have introduced several highly impactful regulations governing data protection including the General Data Protection Regulation (GDPR) for the EU, and the California Consumer Privacy Act (CCPA). Many more regulations are anticipated and exactly how these current and new regulations will be enforced in practice remains an area of significant uncertainty.

As can be easily imagined, organizations that conduct business globally and across all 50 states face a formidable challenge of compliance with this myriad of regulations. Imagine a public healthcare company based in California. At a minimum, that enterprise would be forced to comply with both HIPPA, SOX and CCPA requirements and, if it accepts payments through a point of service (POS) device, then it also needs to meet Payment Card Industry Data Security Standard (PCI DSS) requirements.

For US registrants the U.S Securities and Exchange Commission has shown increased interest and concerns related to cybersecurity. In a January 2020 report, the SEC's Office of Compliance and Inspection (OCIE) noted that:

> The seriousness of the threats and the potential consequences to investors, issuers, and other securities market participants, and the financial markets and economy more generally, are significant and increasing. As markets, market participants, and their vendors have increasingly relied on technology, including digital connections and systems, cybersecurity risk management has become essential.[3]

The report addresses several areas of cybersecurity and its practices where a corporation may seek to enhance cybersecurity preparedness and operation resiliency, encouraging organizations to take action in identifying and assessing cybersecurity risk. The SEC also highlights the need for organizations to disclose cybersecurity risk, material breaches, intellectual property, and more to ensure that organizations are adequately addressing such risks.[4]

Seeking a better understanding of the cybersecurity posture of organizations, some shareholders have advanced proposals seeking increased cybersecurity insights and disclosure. A proposal at Walt Disney Company's 2019 annual shareholder meeting requested the board of directors to publish a report assessing the feasibility of integrating cybersecurity and data privacy metrics into the performance measures of the senior executives. The proposal received close to 27 percent support from shareholders.[5] It is possible that an increased level of interest shown by shareholders may become an additional catalyst for compliance.

The penalties for actual or perceived non-compliance can be severe, both financially and to a company's reputation. A company found to have infringed the requirements of GDPR may be subject to fines of up to €20 million or 4% of the company's global annual turnover—whichever is higher. The NYDFS recently announced their first enforcement action under their cybersecurity regulation. The case is still ongoing, and the results are yet to be determined, but NYDFS is considering penalties for the respondent to be $1,000 per violation, with an additional fine of up to $1,000 for each instance of Nonpublic Information encompassed within the charges.[6]

Many organizations are looking to gain more insight into the unique ways privacy and data protection practices have been affected by the COVID-19 pandemic. While there is no letting up with the compliance work around existing global privacy laws, responding to data subject requests and conducting privacy and security reviews and data protection impact assessments, these new challenges and priorities around teleworking and teleconferencing, processing employee health data, and sharing data with third parties have taken on novel importance.[7]

Although this chapter cannot possibly address the potential nature of penalties by regulator or by jurisdiction, it may be instructive to look at guidance issued by the US Department of Justice Criminal Division (DOJ) regarding how non-compliance cases may be assessed by that organization. Specifically, this guidance states that prosecutors have to assess the compliance program and internal control of the systems of enterprises at the time of offense to determine whether the enterprise has allocated proper investments to manage risk and its remediation efforts. The DOJ states:

> We make a reasonable, individualized determination in each case that considers various factors including, but not limited to, the company's size, industry,

geographic footprint, regulatory landscape, and other factors, both internal and external to the company's operations, that might impact its compliance program.[8]

Common questions that are referenced by the DOJ as being important in the determination of cases that it has prosecuted include:

- Is the corporation's compliance program well designed?
- Is the program being applied earnestly and in good faith? In other words, is the program adequately resourced and empowered to function effectively?
- Does the corporation's compliance program work in practice?

## Other Factors Driving Compliance and its Costs

Regardless of any regulatory requirement, evidence of cybersecurity compliance may also be a necessary pre-requisite of a new or continuing business relationship. With the ubiquity of cloud services and the movement of data beyond corporate perimeters, many organizations are now issuing questionnaires to their third-party vendors seeking a level of comfort regarding the protection of their information assets. Similarly, Request for Proposal (RFP) processes frequently request attestation as to compliance with ISO/IEC 27991, *Statements on Standards for Attestation Engagements* (SSAE) 16 Service Organization Control (SOC) type two reports, and third-party standardized vendor security scorecards.

Organizations are being forced to create a master database of questions and answers to enable accurate and timely responses to these myriad requests. Business opportunities may be lost for those that are unable to demonstrate compliance with the requested levels of security controls. Many small enterprises lack the in-house resources to keep up with their compliance requirements. Large enterprises may have more dedicated resources, but they also will usually have broader geographical footprints, more complex supply chains and data sets to handle and a higher possibility of employee mishandling of data.

A 2020 survey of IT professionals conducted by Vanson Bourne shows that on average, organizations must comply with 13 different IT security or privacy regulations and spend $3.5 million annually on compliance activities.[9] Many organizations are spending a multiple of that amount and are allocating significant resources to simply identify which regulations apply to them and then adjusting to meet the requirements of these multiple and often over-lapping compliance requirements.

FIGURE 7.1  Use of net new funds for cybersecurity

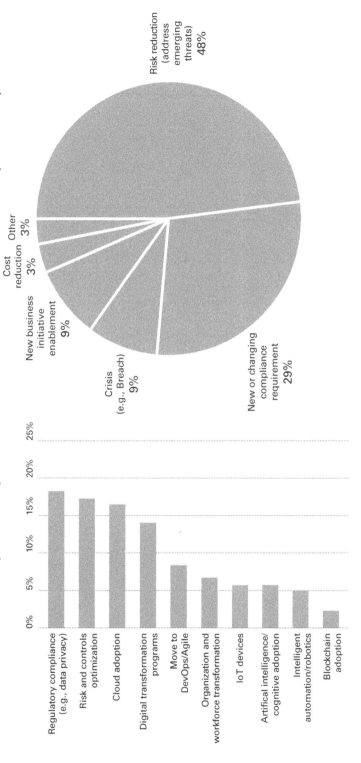

Use of net new funds for cybersecurity

Justification for new or increased cybersecurity funds

Determining the appropriate level of spend on compliance is a very complex task since the penalties are so hard for an enterprise to assess. According to IBM's report, Cost of Data Breach 2020, the average cost of a data breach is approximately $3.9 million and 80% of the data breaches included customer PII (Personally Identifiable Information).[10] A 2017 study by the Ponemon Institute found that the average cost of non-compliance in its population sample was 2.7 times the cost of compliance.[11] However, these are merely two data points and should not be interpreted as being indicative of any enterprise's current exposure.

A closer look at the allocation of funds between competing cybersecurity needs demonstrates the level of significance that enterprises are now placing upon avoiding the pitfalls of non-compliance. A 2020 EY survey found that the demands of regulatory and compliance was the second most common rationale for an increase in budget, trailing only the critical area of risk reduction. It was also noted in the survey that a higher percentage (18%) of any newly added cybersecurity funds were ultimately allocated to regulatory compliance than were allocated to any other area, and that more "new" funds were being spent on compliance than were being allocated to AI, robotics and Blockchain combined.[12]

## Cybersecurity Compliance Within Enterprise Risk Management

With the constantly rising prominence of cybersecurity within the enterprise, the role of compliance and audit needs to be addressed thoroughly.

A well-designed compliance function will address the three key areas, including policy (and its documentation), behavior, and technology. However, as witnessed at the time of the enactment of SOX 404 in 2002 and the 2018 enactment of GDPR, too many businesses rush to channel their limited resources and time into complying with the regulation rather than focusing more comprehensively on building robust controls or security guidelines.

Historically, due to the prescriptive nature of the cybersecurity regulations that it seeks to address, much of the role of compliance has been focused on point-in-time initiatives that may strive to achieve only the bare minimum necessary to meet the rules prescribed by the specific regulator(s). These initiatives will usually be focused on a sub-set of systems or data, rarely encompassing the entire enterprise. Because of this and the fact that it is a point-in-time initiative, this form of assessment can provide no guarantee or level of assurance regarding the untested areas nor that the enterprise's security posture for the areas subject to an assessment will remain compliant immediately following the date of assessment.

As discussed in Chapters 4 and 6, compliance requirements are burdensome and resource intensive, which may hinder enterprise-wide efforts towards building an impactful cybersecurity process. As a result, compliance programs must continue to evolve to improve risk management through effective risk assessment and collaborative efforts between regulators and organizations. With more effective compliance management, cyber resources can be allocated to different areas to pursue innovation and achieve organizational objectives. Ensuring compliance requirements are adequate to avoid the penalties of non-compliance is critical, but it is also important that there is a method to prevent overspending in these areas.

As noted earlier, enterprise cybersecurity is not a matter of pass-fail. An enterprise is not secure or insecure, instead there are gradations of security. Security is a result of the actions taken to protect an enterprise's information. Compliance is the documentation of those actions. While controls may be in place that serve to protect the systems, networks and software, an enterprise cannot prove that the controls are fit for purpose without documentation.

Although the compliance and audit functions within an organization are separate from security/risk management, the closer that these disciplines can all work together, the more value can be provided. Put simply, the security team is responsible for putting in place the systemic controls needed to protect information assets. The compliance team validates that the controls are functioning as planned. Both teams working in alliance will ensure that the security controls are built to scale, and that all the required documentation and reports are accessible for auditing.

## The Role of the Audit Function

The importance of having defined processes, trained and competent cybersecurity resources, and a governance framework to ensure that appropriate actions are taken to address current and emerging threats cannot be overstated. While those being audited may well view it as a business disruption to gather evidence and participate fully in the audit, obtaining the perspective from those that are not responsible for the design and operation of the controls and processes is critical to ensure that the program is meeting the business objectives. The audit process, if performed properly, should build additional accountability and serve to strengthen the control environment.

The role of internal audit in cybersecurity areas of an enterprise has been rapidly evolving, linked to the increased involvement of the board, performing their own oversight over this area. As boards desire more insight on cybersecurity, auditors have to understand and keep up with evolving cybersecurity risks and provide input on the sufficiency of counter measures to better protect enterprises. As stated in an analysis by Focal Point:

> Board members want to gain a comprehensive view of the risks both inside and outside of the organization. As involvement in cyber risks grow and board responsibility to adhere to the FTC's increased standards of care becomes a concern, boards will rely more heavily on Chief Audit Executives (CAEs) and their Internal Audit (IA) team to communicate these risks and effective methods for countering them.[13]

Auditors are well positioned to inform board members on the effectiveness of cybersecurity programs and risk mitigation plans to enhance overall cybersecurity within organizations. Additionally, the company's General Counsel, as illustrated in Chapter 6, will also assist in providing the board with insight and advice regarding changing regulatory requirements.

To achieve the above, the audit's role is expanding to understand the risk from many areas within the organization in order to properly address enterprise-level cybersecurity. These areas include organizational culture, tone and values, transformation adoption and technology implementation, human capital and talent management, third-party risk and supply chain management. As the audit moves out of its traditional functional areas, and works with various counterparties within the business, it can provide more than just an evaluation of compliance and help achieve enhanced cybersecurity.

The global focus on digital transformation of the enterprise opens new areas where an internal audit can operate. Strategic technology projects, including the modernization of legacy infrastructure, operational performance improvement initiatives, and digitization of products and services, are accompanied by the adoption of new software development methodologies—such as DevOps—accelerating the pace of change. Working alongside the development, quality assurance and information security teams throughout all phases of the strategic technology projects, an internal audit team can identify new risks and evaluate the security procedures necessary for the changes in the control environment, particularly those impacting segregation of duties, change management and the related access controls, thereby closing any newly introduced gaps in risk and controls. An internal audit can also review a product team's adoption of DevOps practices and capabilities and assess the quality of training and development. As stated in the ISACA and Protiviti survey:

> By having knowledge of events like new applications coming online, or being pushed out, IT audit can be ready to respond in an agile manner to provide meaningful insights as well as identify and communicate risks of which the IT department should be aware. Most importantly, these actions can happen ahead of time, rather than reactively in response to request or information previously unknown to IT audit.[14]

The survey also shows that there is still room for improvement in order to increase the level of an audit's involvement throughout technology project lifecycles, with approximately a quarter of the surveyed organizations having no audit involvement in the critical planning through implementation phases.[15]

As the role of an audit expands to address cyber risks at the enterprise-level, the criticality of its role as the objective third line of defense will only increase. For example, the past few years have seen a significant acceleration in ransomware cases and in the size of "demands" for the release of data. Many corporations have designed their back up procedures for the threats of earthquakes or other natural disasters and have to update these and build in resilience against this emerging threat. IT audit can play a significant role in determining the sufficiency of processes and controls in such areas as data back-up protocols and recovery time.

## Three Lines of Defense Model

Within the Three Lines model, addressed in Chapter 3, the third line defines the roles and objectives of the internal audit. The primary goal of the third line is to provide an independent, objective assessment of company processes and controls across lines one and two with a focus on operational effectiveness and efficiency. With the new model, the prime objectives of the third line are as follows:

- Maintain primary accountability to the governing body and independence from the responsibilities of management.
- Communicate independent and objective assurance and advice to management and the governing body on the adequacy and effectiveness

of governance and risk management (including internal control) to support the achievement of organizational objectives and to promote and facilitate continuous improvement.

- Report impairments to independence and objectivity to the governing body and implement safeguards as required.

The goal of the new model is to shift away from the traditional, defensive approach on risk to creating and protecting value for the organization. To achieve that, the work of the third line such as audit plans, control testing, and compliance polices must align with the objective of the company to provide good risk assurance. A key and distinctive characteristic of internal audit is its independence from management. This is critical for audit as it eliminates any hinderance and bias in planning and carrying out its goal. However, as the updated model addresses, "Independence does not imply isolation".[16] Communication between the third line and other lines will allow audit to demonstrate that their work is relevant and aligned with the strategic and operational needs of the organization. This is critical in maintaining the independence of internal audit, and when the governing body request assurance on such matters, such activities should be undertaken by a qualified third party.

The audit can take many shapes and have different focuses with respect to cybersecurity governance or technical testing. For programs that are less mature the focus may be on ensuring that the policies, procedures, standards and guidelines are relevant, approved and updated/reviewed in response to business changes. For mature organizations, audit may focus on how current or emerging risk vectors are identified and addressed or on the organization's level of preparedness for material incidents.

## The Role of External Auditors

Current US auditing standards require the external auditor to obtain an understanding of how the company uses information technology and how that technology impacts the financial statements. In the audit, particular attention is usually focused on the IT general controls that are designed to ensure the effective operation of automated controls and the reliability of data and reports produced by the company that are used to generate its external financial statements and disclosures.

The systems and data that are in scope and tested under most external audits will represent only a limited subset of a company's total systems and data. This is because the auditor's focus is risk-based and prioritizes access and changes made to those systems and data that could reasonably impact the financial statements and the effectiveness of the Internal Controls over Financial Reporting (ICFR).[17] Accordingly, those operational systems that do not impact the company's financial reporting are excluded from the audit scope. Additionally, the auditor's focus is upon the controls over the application and database layers of the company's IT environment rather than upon the perimeter (e.g., cloud) and network layers.

With respect to when material cyber incidents are brought to the attention of the external auditor, the auditor's responsibility and level of procedures will vary dramatically, depending upon the nature of the breach and the impacted systems. At a minimum, however, the auditor must determine and conclude upon the impact of the material breach upon financial reporting, including the company's disclosures. This may involve determining the implications to their audit from the applications that were actually accessed but also considering the control implications for any financial statement applications that could have been accessed during the incident. Early notification to, and involvement of, both internal and external audit is key to ensuring that these matters can be addressed in time to allow for timely financial reporting.

As has been made clear from many of the other chapters in this publication, the issues and challenges of cybersecurity are evolving rapidly and both the expectations of shareholders and the requirements of regulators with respect to the extent of an external auditor's responsibility for assessing the design and operating effectiveness of controls over cyber risk will probably both increase.

Although elements of cybersecurity risk management practices may currently be beyond the scope of a typical financial statement audit, CPAs are already in a strong position to play an important role in informing the advancement of these practices and in assisting board members in executing their broader oversight responsibilities related to cybersecurity risks. The CPA profession's commitment to continuous improvement, public service, and investor confidence has recently resulted in a much greater focus on this area by the accounting profession, specifically:

- In 2017 the AICPA developed a cybersecurity risk management reporting framework that assists organizations as they communicate relevant and useful information about the effectiveness of their cybersecurity risk management programs. The framework is a key component of a new

System and Organization Controls (SOC) for Cybersecurity engagement, through which a CPA provides an independent report upon an organizations' enterprise-wide cybersecurity risk management program. This SOC can help senior management, boards of directors, analysts, investors and business partners gain a better understanding of an organizations' efforts.[18]

- To help address the cybersecurity risks from third party vendors, the AICPA released new guidance for reporting on controls related to supply chains, including a new System and Organization Controls (SOC) report specifically for supply chains. Completing this new SOC report can provide assurance to user entities around the security and availability of products and information from suppliers within the supply chain. It offers user entities a window into a supplier's processes and the controls in place to mitigate risks.[19]

## The Role of Technology in the Future State of Compliance and Audit

Advanced technology and data analytics show promise in helping companies address the rising costs and complexity of cybersecurity compliance. A survey of IT professionals conducted in 2020 showed that:

> Nearly all survey respondents (99%) indicated their organization would benefit from automating IT security and/or privacy compliance activities, citing expected benefits such as increased accuracy of evidence (54%), reduced time spent being audited (51%) and the ability to respond to audit evidence requests more quickly (50%).[20]

We have described previously the scale of the undertaking required by an enterprise to simply review the multiple regulatory guidelines necessary to achieve compliance. The introduction of AI and Machine Learning (ML) may serve to reduce the time needed for manual review, decreasing the time taken by risk and compliance management. According to a survey, 42% of surveyed executives view advanced AI as likely to bring more effective risk and compliance management. 75% of the respondents believe that advanced AI has had a moderate or significant positive impact on IT and cybersecurity. In addition, 94% expect positive impacts from AI within two years.[21] Advanced technologies such as AI, ML, and analytics are to be viewed as enablers, as they will enhance the capabilities or the roles of its user. For auditors, advanced technologies could lessen their time spent on information gathering, data retrieval and summation, providing them with more time to be spent on evaluation and analysis of information and data. Areas that have the potential to be improved include, but are not limited to, risk assessment, control testing, and reporting.[22] AI has the capacity and the ability to spot trends and outliers within massive amount of data, which makes it an ideal technology for detecting and protecting against cyber risk.

However, AI is not a panacea. It is still a developing technology that organizations are piloting in limited areas, but there has not yet been widespread usage of AI to assure its sustainability and reliability.

Concerns about the security of AI are still substantial for enterprises. One of the many reasons for such a level of concern is its wide access to data. As mentioned, one of the benefits of AI is its ability to monitor and identify issues from large amount of data sets. Through the process, it will continue to evolve with machine learning algorithms, and for that, it will need greater access to sensitive and personal data. For AI to be effectively implemented, there must be a method to protect such sensitive data as it is processed by the machines.

When dealing with large and complex data sets, AI may employ a neural network; a series of algorithms that endeavor to recognize underlying relationships in a set of data through a process that mimics the way the human brain operates. Organizations need to consider the problem of AI bias before implementing AI systems. AI bias can come from the design of the model itself or from bias data sets that the algorithm uses to train itself.[23] These must be identified and eliminated for AI results to be useful and effective. To address the concerns, it is important that organizations understand how their algorithms work and be able to explain and justify the AI results.

Tying to this issue, regulatory constraints will also be a major issue. Tyrone Canaday, Protiviti's global head of innovation states:

> When you start to look at thing like Deep Learning, where computers are essentially writing their own algorithms, how do you audit that? Can a regulator have confidence even when some people don't understand how AI is coming up with its answers?[24]

Along with AI, blockchain offers great potential in enhancing the efficiency and effectiveness of audits. Blockchain is a peer-to-peer, digital ledger which includes all transaction data since its creation. It offers a decentralized verification through timestamps on transaction data, and alterations of recorded transactions cause mismatch in the public account. It enables direct transactions between two parties without a central processing party as it is a distributed ledger. All active nodes have full copies of the blockchain ledger, eliminating single point of failure and increasing reliability.[25] For audit, it will assist in activities such as reviewing transactions and verifying the existence of digital assets and attesting to consistency between information on a blockchain and in the physical world.[26] Distributed ledger technology may be used to record compliance procedures and tasks undertaken by organizations, providing an opportunity for increased efficiency of compliance activities.[27] Similar to those listed for AI there are, of course, obstacles or concerns over the adoption of blockchain technology. For instance, lack of centralized authority makes it difficult to verify the existence, ownership, and measurement of items recorded on blockchain. Also, the transaction records within a blockchain, although authentic may be unauthorized, fraudulent, or illegal, making such data inappropriate for audit evidence purposes. As with most new technologies, compliance and regulations regarding the technology will need to be addressed at the time of widespread introduction.

## Conclusion

The role of audit and compliance in cybersecurity needs to evolve to effectively address the concerns arising from the evolution of technology and the threats to it. The compliance regime is going through rapid changes with the increasing quantity and complexity of cyber risks. Global emphasis on data and privacy protection requires enterprises to allocate substantial budget toward meeting compliance requirements and keeping an eye on the changed regulations and risks of non-compliance. However, it is crucial that compliance does not become the security standard of organizations.

More extensive effort must be put into addressing security at the enterprise level. Internal and external audit needs to provide insights on risk areas across the enterprise by shifting away from traditional approaches. To do so, the audit needs to engage with other functions in the enterprise to align its activity with the business objectives of the organization and take part in strategic project practice to acquire better understanding of the innovative technologies and methods being introduced to organizations. The audit and compliance organizations may experience substantial change with the introduction of advanced technologies. These are projected to increase efficiency and effectiveness through automation and deep learning processes but will certainly add more risk factors to be considered and managed. At the end, audit and compliance requirements are set to support organizations in achieving business objectives and promote growth while maintaining appropriate compliance. With proper assessment and management more fitted for the evolving market, audit and compliance will play a value-added role in achieving enhanced cybersecurity for organizations.

To continue learning about the concepts in this chapter the following sources are recommended:

1 General Data Protection Regulation (GDPR) Everything You Need to Know about GDPR Compliance [blog] GDPR.eu, April 11, 2019. https://gdpr.eu/compliance/

2 State of California Department of Justice - Office of the Attorney General. California Consumer Privacy Act (CCPA), July 20, 2020. https://oag.ca.gov/privacy/ccpa

3 M G Oxley. H.R.3763 - 107th Congress (2001-2002): Sarbanes-Oxley Act of 2002, July 30, 2002. https://www.congress.gov/bill/107th-congress/house-bill/3763

4 Smartsheet. Maintain, Protect, and Diminish Risk with a Comprehensive IT Compliance Strategy, n.d. www.smartsheet.com/understanding-it-compliance

5 AICPA. System and Organization Controls: SOC Suite of Services, n.d. www.aicpa.org/interestareas/frc/assuranceadvisoryservices/sorhome.html

6 ISACA. "ISACA Expands Cyber Security Resources for Auditors." February 14, 2017. www.isaca.org/why-isaca/about-us/newsroom/press-releases/2017/isaca-expands-cyber-security-resources-for-auditors

## Endnotes

1 ISACA and Protiviti. Today's Toughest Challenges in IT Audit: Tech Partnerships, Talent, Transformation, 2019. www.protiviti.com/US-en/insights/it-audit-benchmarking-survey (archived at https://perma.cc/YY4C-EL7T)

2 N Biradar. Cyberstalking: Breach of Privacy, December 18, 2020. web.archive.org/web/20210218072444/https://ufls.in/cyberstalking-breach-of-privacy/ (archived at https://perma.cc/NP5J-XEEV)

**3**   U.S. Securities and Exchange Commission. OCIE Cybersecurity and Resiliency Observations, January 27, 2020. www.sec.gov/files/OCIE%20 Cybersecurity%20and%20Resiliency%20Observations.pdf (archived at https://perma.cc/35HP-N5KK)

**4**   J Smith and S Klemash. What Companies are Disclosing about Cybersecurity Risk and Oversight, August 7, 2020. www.ey.com/en_us/board-matters/ what-companies-are-disclosing-about-cybersecurity-risk-and-oversight (archived at https://perma.cc/77ZZ-FKY9)

**5**   SquareWell Partners. Clarity on Cybersecurity, December 16, 2019. squarewell-partners.com/wp-content/uploads/2018/07/SquareWell-Cybersecurity-Final-Version.pdf (archived at https://perma.cc/6SRU-WVYY)

**6**   Department of Financial Services. Department of Financial Services Announces Cybersecurity Charges Against a Leading Title Insurance Provider for Exposing Millions of Documents with Consumers' Personal Information. July 22, 2020. www.dfs.ny.gov/reports_and_publications/press_releases/ pr202007221 (archived at https://perma.cc/QK5H-749H)

**7**   M Fazlioglu. Privacy in the Wake of COVID-19: Remote Work, Employee Health Monitoring and Data Sharing, May 2020. iapp.org/media/pdf/ resource_center/iapp_ey_privacy_in_wake_of_covid_19_report.pdf  (archived at https://perma.cc/9UDG-8X2U)

**8**   The United States Department of Justice. Evaluation of Corporate Compliance Programs, June 2020.  www.justice.gov/criminal-fraud/page/file/937501/ download (archived at https://perma.cc/H2VR-6CDV)

**9**   Telos. Survey Finds Compliance Activities and Fines Cost Organizations Nearly $4M per Year [blog] Telos Corporation, October 13, 2020. www.telos. com/survey-finds-compliance-activities-and-fines-cost-organizations-nearly-4m-per-year/ (archived at https://perma.cc/AG87-A7Z6)

**10**   IBM. 2020 Cost of Data Breach Report, 2020. www.ibm.com/security/digital-assets/cost-data-breach-report/#/ (archived at https://perma.cc/W7KX-CUMA)

**11**   Ponemon Institue LLC and Globalscape, The True Cost of Compliance with Data Protection Regulations, December 2017. www.globalscape.com/ resources/whitepapers/data-protection-regulations-study (archived at https:// perma.cc/QJ2S-6NNR)

**12**   EY. EY Global Information Security Survey 2020, February 2020. assets. ey.com/content/dam/ey-sites/ey-com/en_gl/topics/advisory/ey-global-information-security-survey-2020-single-pages.pdf (archived at https://perma. cc/V4LR-P5H4)

**13**   Focal Point. The Future of Internal Audit: 10 Audit Trends to Prepare for in 2020 [blog] Focal Point, January 14, 2020. blog.focal-point.com/the-future-of-internal-audit10-audit-trends-to-prepare-for-in-2020 (archived at https:// perma.cc/33FK-LM25)

**14**   ISACA and Protiviti. Today's Toughest Challenges in IT Audit: Tech Partnerships, Talent, Transformation, 2019. www.protiviti.com/US-en/insights/it-audit-benchmarking-survey (archived at https://perma.cc/YY4C-EL7T)

**15**   Ibid.

**16**   The Institute of Internal Auditors. The IIA's Three Lines Model, July 20, 2020, global.theiia.org/about/about-internal-auditing/Public%20Documents/Three-Lines-Model-Updated.pdf (archived at https://perma.cc/36GH-LMYK)

**17**   CAQ. Cybersecurity and the Auditor's Role, [blog] CAQ. publication.thecaq.org/cybersecurity/the-auditors-role/ (archived at https://perma.cc/8CSB-SKF6)

**18**   AICPA. SOC for Cybersecurity [blog] AICPCA us.aicpa.org/interestareas/frc/assuranceadvisoryservices/aicpacybersecurityinitiative (archived at https://perma.cc/X2HM-P8W4)

**19**   T Bialik. SOC for Supply Chain: Answering the Needs of the Market [blog] LinkedIn, 27 April 2020. www.linkedin.com/pulse/soc-supply-chain-answering-needs-market-todd-bialick/ (archived at https://perma.cc/8UQK-KN9D)

**20**   Telos. Survey Finds Compliance Activities and Fines Cost Organizations Nearly $4M per Year [blog] Telos Corporation, October 13, 2020. www.telos.com/survey-finds-compliance-activities-and-fines-cost-organizations-nearly-4m-per-year/ (archived at https://perma.cc/AG87-A7Z6)

**21**   Protiviti. Competing in the Cognitive Age: How Companies Will Transform Their Businesses and Drive Value Through Advanced AI, February 2019. www.protiviti.com/sites/default/files/united_states/insights/ai-ml-global-study-protiviti.pdf (archived at https://perma.cc/V247-P8P8)

**22**   CPA Canada and AICPA. The Data-Driven Audit: How Automation and AI Are Changing the Audit and the Role of the Auditor, July 20, 2020. www.aicpa.org/content/dam/aicpa/interestareas/frc/assuranceadvisoryservices/downloadabledocuments/the-data-driven-audit.pdf (archived at https://perma.cc/9U7B-7PJR)

**23**   Greg Satell, and Josh Sutton. We Need AI That Is Explainable, Auditable, and Transparent, Harvard Business Review, October 28, 2019, hbr.org/2019/10/we-need-ai-that-is-explainable-auditable-and-transparent (archived at https://perma.cc/97HY-7534)

**24**   Protiviti. Competing in the Cognitive Age: How Companies Will Transform Their Businesses and Drive Value Through Advanced AI, February 2019. www.protiviti.com/sites/default/files/united_states/insights/ai-ml-global-study-protiviti.pdf (archived at https://perma.cc/V247-P8P8)

**25**   CPA Canada and AICPA. "Blockchain Technology and Its Potential Impact on the Audit and Assurance Profession, 2017. www.aicpa.org/interestareas/frc/assuranceadvisoryservices/blockchain-impact-on-auditing.html (archived at https://perma.cc/JHP5-4H6U)

**26**  M Liu, K Wu, and J Jie Xu. How Will Blockchain Technology Impact Auditing and Accounting: Permissionless versus Permissioned Blockchain. *Current Issues in Auditing*, 2019,13 (2), doi.org/10.2308/ciia-52540 (archived at https://perma.cc/Y884-3L53)

**27**  I Camilleri. Blockchain in Compliance [blog] Deloitte Malta, August 17, 2020. www2.deloitte.com/mt/en/pages/risk/articles/mt-blockchain-in-compliance. html (archived at https://perma.cc/ZW5D-RDF2)

# 08

# Cyber Supply Chain and Third-Party Risk Management

BY JEANNIE PUMPHREY, HEAD OF THIRD-PARTY RISK MANAGEMENT
AND CHANGE RISK MANAGEMENT, MUFG UNION BANK, AND LISA HUMBERT,
MANAGING DIRECTOR, OPERATIONAL RISK MANAGEMENT OFFICER,
MUFG UNION BANK

## Five Key Ideas to Take Away from This Chapter

1 Organizations need to strike a balance between the financial opportunities of lower costs and higher efficiencies in cyber risk by creating a flexible supply-chain.

2 Understand the main challenges within supply chain risk mitigation.

3 A step-by-step role for managers and how to reduce their risk with third parties.

4 Acknowledge the reliance on third parties and how to work with them for products and services.

5 Understand that if companies have the right skill set to conduct assessments testing and ongoing monitoring of third-party relationships.

## Introduction

In this chapter we will review the core concepts necessary to achieve effective Cyber Supply Chain Risk Management (C-SCRM) and Third-Party Cyber Risk Management Programs (TPCRM).

Below are the definitions for both Cyber Supply-Chain Risk Management (C-SCRM) and Third-Party Cyber Risk Management (TPCRM), and considerations for both disciplines. In some industries these functions overlap; however, the activities for each are distinctly different.

C-SCRM is the process of identifying, assessing, and mitigating the risks associated with the distributed and interconnected nature of Information and Operational Technology (IT/OT) product and service supply chains. It covers the entire lifecycle of a system (including design, development, distribution, deployment, acquisition, maintenance, and destruction) as supply chain threats and vulnerabilities may intentionally or unintentionally compromise an IT/OT product or service at any stage.[1] As discussed in Chapter 4, one solution to a non-aligned metric reporting mechanism is a state-of-the-art cyber risk management system which consolidates all relevant information in one place. Through this process, key risk indicators present the consistent evaluation across assets to tailor specific risk controls.

Third-Party Risk Management (TPRM) is the standardized process companies use to monitor and manage risk associated with third-parties, subcontractors (also known as fourth, fifth and nth parties[2]) and other service providers to the enterprise throughout the lifecycle of the relationship with the third party.

Third-Party Cyber Risk Management (TPCRM) include those requirements specific to the IT/OT supported products and services that are above and beyond the minimum standards set forth in the enterprise third-party risk management program and are specific to cyber third parties.

C-SCRM is the first line-of-defense for any enterprise engaging a third party to provide products and services, and otherwise support its operations. The value of C-SCRM to the enterprise is dependent upon compliance to the processes and methodologies that are built into its supply chain processes.

The scope and focus of C-SCRM should extend beyond the cyber third party being engaged to provide the actual product and/or services to the enterprise, to also include the subcontractors that have access to the cyber third party's network that, through that access, may have access to the enterprise's network and/or data.

## Approaching Cyber Supply Chain Risk Management

There has been an influx of cybersecurity third parties saturating the market over the last few years, and that population is not shrinking. The former

Chairman of RSA, Art Coviello, agrees, mentioning in the Bank Info Security video interview[3], "when CISOs seek security technology to solve a specific problem, they are faced with 1,500 vendors and the problem is almost insurmountable".[4,5]

The enterprise should be thoughtful and deliberate in the selection of third parties to ensure they are the best solution and fit for the product and/ or service needs of the enterprise. Familiarity and prior working experience with a third party are no substitute for appropriate due diligence; and the application of a sustainable, repeatable cyber supply chain risk management process will support the cyber risk team not only in the initial selection process but also set up a solid basis for the ongoing monitoring throughout the lifecycle of the cyber third party.

Attributes and activities that are driving the need to engage a third party should be identified prior to the start of the cyber supply chain due diligence process. The enterprise needs to identify how the third party will be utilized, access the third party will need, and the required capabilities to support existing—or expanding—operational capabilities where a third party will have access (people, process, facilities, data, technology, etc.).

## Accounting for Cybersecurity Management and IT Governance in the Total Cost of Ownership Calculation

### CASE STUDY: TARGET DATA BREACH

Hackers stole a reported 40 million credit card numbers in one of the biggest data breaches in history.

This breach was a result of stolen credentials from a third-party HVAC vendor. The hackers used the stolen credentials to break through from a "billing, contract submission, and project management" platform.

The following list of settlements were made as a result of the 2013 Target data breach:

- $10 million paid in a class action lawsuit to affected consumers in March 2015;
- $19 million paid to Mastercard in an April 2015 settlement;
- $67 million paid to Visa in August 2015;

- $39.4 million paid to banks and credit unions for losses and costs related to the breach in a December 2015 settlement;

- $18.5 million in a 2017 multi-state settlement. (Target paid a combined $18.5 million dollars to settle investigations led by 47 different state governments. New York Attorney General Eric Schneiderman said it represents the "largest multistate accord ever reached over a data breach".)

These settlements totaled $153.9 million dollars. Target reported that the total cost of the breach was $292 million dollars.

Target had a cyber-insurance policy that helped them cover some of their costs. After the insurance company kicked in, Target's net loss was $202 million. The breach also cost the CEO his job.[6]

The risk-based cost benefit analysis—where the risk and reward are components of the overall total cost of ownership—is a dynamic aspect in the selection of cyber third-parties. The risk-based cost benefit analysis should encompass not only the risk that will be introduced into the enterprise by the third party, but also include the risk the subcontractors will bring into the equation as well as resources required to oversee and manage the third party on a day-to-day basis along with the potential for breach and data loss. The analysis should also identify any cost associated with designing, implementing and maintaining controls necessary to ensure the protection and prevention of data loss and poor performance, alongside the benefit of reward for taking on that risk, including but not limited to faster service delivery; expanded technical capabilities; new and/or changed product and/ or service offerings; and reduced costs. If the upside (benefit) of the equation outweighs the risk (total cost of ownership), then the enterprise has a solid basis for continuing with the due diligence process, and potentially bringing the third party into their cyber ecosystem.

Risk-based cost benefit analysis should not be a one-and-done exercise. As material facts are known, or additional risks are identified, the risk-cost benefit analysis should be updated and reevaluated as appropriate.

An enterprise's cyber governance structure is instrumental for the cyber supply chain to function effectively from a directional guidance perspective. In addition to receiving directional guidance from the cyber governance structure, the cyber supply chain is able to ensure that they are resourcing the necessary staffing against projects that are going to drive both benefits and strategic alignment, as well as avoidance of performing activities that are not within the enterprise's strategic plan.

The enterprise benefits from this type of governance structure by having one overall approval body for all cyber related products and services; it should also be tasked with maintaining the enterprise roadmap and inventory of products and services being leveraged to support the cyber ecosystem and any cyber third parties supporting the cyber ecosystem. Leveraging an enterprise view of cyber products, services and related third-parties also enable the enterprise to understand, track and make informed decisions regarding where they can tolerate, from a risk perspective, having new cyber third-parties supporting additional products and/or services, where there is potential for cyber third-party concentration risk, where the cyber third-parties align in the strategic plan and where there is a potential for a divergence of strategy based on unapproved cyber third parties within the enterprise before the contract execution occurs. This type of governance is instrumental in the support and guidance of a cyber supply chain organization.[7]

## Negotiation Strategies Inclusive of Cybersecurity Insurance Provisions

In Europe, the European Insurance and Occupations Pension Authority, (EIOPA) published a report titled *Cyber Risk for Insurers—Challenges and Opportunities*, in which they assert the need for a cyber resilience framework for European insurers. Most interestingly, the report cites a "well-developed cyber insurance market" as a driver in transforming the digital economy.[8]

The cyber supply chain function should leverage tools in the marketplace as an internal or external control for the cyber third-party risk management program. An example of two valuable tools in the insurance arena are cyber insurance and third-party cyber insurance.

Cyber insurance is insurance that your enterprise can procure to provide financial relief when a data loss occurs to help offset some of the cost. As with all insurance products, the cost is dependent upon a number of factors, including amount of coverage, potential for loss, and credit rating of the enterprise, to name a few.

Third-party cyber insurance provides the clients of the third-party assurance that loss claims can be covered in the event of a loss due to the third party, their processes or subcontractors. The challenge with both insurance products is the identification of the amount of insurance that will be sufficient regarding the potential loss[9] and resulting cost and determining how much insurance is right for your enterprise.

For example, if a third party has ten clients, the amount of insurance coverage obtained in the cyber third-party insurance policy should be at an amount that would cover all ten clients—the same for an internal cyber insurance product. In Figure 8.1, you will notice that 46% of breaches cost considerably more than $50 million.

FIGURE 8.1  Financial exposure to a major third-party incident

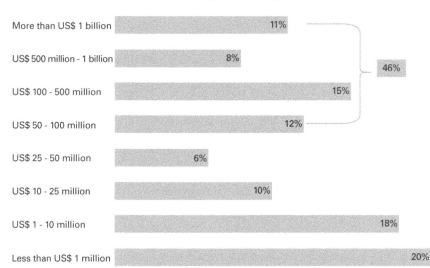

The organization's Chief Financial Officer (CFO) should be engaged to support the determination of the appropriate level of insurance for both internal and external third-party acceptable limits. As shown in the Target Case Study, cyber insurance helped recover $100 million of the cost of losses due to the cyber data breach.

## Implementation of Inclusive Service Level Agreements

Service Level Agreements (SLAs) outline the requirements—in addition to the contract terms and conditions—that the parties in a contract are required to perform. Service level agreements also outline the enterprise's requirements and the cyber landscape that are being supported and/or provided. Service level agreements should reside outside of the contract terms and should be revisited on a regular cadence to ensure that the information is both maintained and that the parties understand and are compliant with the requirements as outlined. At a minimum, service level agreements should outline the following:

- Number of resources, both direct and indirect, that:
  o will be assigned to support the product(s) and/or service(s) being provided by the Third Party; and
  o are assigned to the Enterprise, as well as the lead for each party and their contact information.
- Subcontractors that will have access to support the Third Party, including what access they will have to the data and where they will be located.
- Times and days the product(s) and/or service(s) will be available.
- Location(s) of where the product(s) and/or service(s) will be provided.
- Cyber-related support requirements by both the Third Party and the Enterprise, as well as detailed products and/or services that will be provided and specific requirements for each.
- Performance metrics and scorecard components.
- How the metrics will be measured.
- Resolution for non-performance (penalties and performance bonuses), and escalation paths to senior management for issue remediation.
- Incident management process, including incident response plans and any procedures required to be followed; and notification requirements for data breaches or other cyber incidents.
- Any data and access the Third Party will have; any data of which the Third Party will have ownership or custody; and its location for storage transmission and where—if applicable—the data will be stored.
- Utilization of secondary and masked data where appropriate.
- Access controls that will be utilized, and compensating end user controls for the cyber product(s) and/or service(s).
- Testing schedules, participation in testing and contingency activities.
- Reporting requirements, timing of reports, clarity on who will provide the reports and how the reports will be utilized.

The cyber service level agreements should be detailed, but operational and comprehensible from an independent point-of-view. Avoid jargon and definitions that are not clearly defined either in the contract or the cyber third-party service level agreements themselves. The document will live throughout the life of the contract, and it should be expected that it may pass through several owners during this time.

## Including Cybersecurity in Current Supply Chain Risk Management

As the landscape of cyber third parties continues to grow, and cyber criminals continue to utilize more creative methods to gain access to enterprise data, the cyber supply chain must be hypervigilant with regards to the vulnerabilities that can be exploited to gain entry through multiple, and sometimes the most unforeseen, methods. One of the most relevant examples is the Target data breach case study.

---

### CYBERSECURITY RISK IN THE SUPPLY CHAIN

There are a variety of ways cybersecurity risk emerges in the supply chain. Each new supplier adds security vulnerability, but there are mitigations an organization can take to address these risks. For example:

- understanding which suppliers have data, where it is stored and who has access to it;
- data quality checks and data flow mapping;
- supplier maturity within the FinTech community;
- contract negotiations and terminations;
- employee skill level;
- subcontractors;
- age of contracts;
- internal cybersecurity maturity;
- end-to-end process management and oversight.

---

FIGURE 8.2 Possible supply chain risks

- Exchange rates (volatility)
- Raw material prices
- Energy prices
- Penalties

- Accuracy of billing
- Commercial
- Competition
- Labor costs

- Food safety
- Demand planning
- Quality standards
- Logistics
- Contracts

- Delivery performance and lead times
- Controls
- Security

**Financial**

**Operational**

**Social, ethical & environmental**

**Complex arrangements realize new risks**

**Continuity**

**Strategic**

- Child labor
- Ethical practices
- Health and safety

- Resource consumption
- Waste

- Reputation/brand
- Compliance
- Macro economic
- Geopolitical
- Investment

- Legal/regulatory
- IP/food fraud
- Change programs
- Market changes

- Supplier financial failure
- Food security
- Natural hazards
- Terrorism/food defense

- Poor management
- Key dependencies on personnel/suppliers

Not only was the breach a shock to Target, but to the industry as a whole since the source of the breach was a facility third party—specifically a HVAC company. As HVAC third parties are generally categorized as more of a facilities break/fix and more of an engineering challenge than a cyber-related concern, it was especially surprising that the provision of service to the enterprise would result in such a material breach.

No matter how much an enterprise may probe their own security, a review does not end within a singular business. Even in the first month of 2021, companies were forced to reevaluate their relationships with their third party's security after a hack within SolarWinds' supply chain. Organizations within the public and private sector assessed how they used SolarWinds software after the Austin, Texas-based company disclosed that as many as 18,000 customers downloaded a malicious update.[10] As Chris Inglis—former deputy director of the National Security Agency—put so perfectly, "You can't assume that [supply chains] defend themselves".

## Training Supply Chain Personnel to Recognize Cybersecurity Risk and Enable Mitigation Activities

As discussed in chapter 3, embedding personnel with cyber expertise into functional business units is increasingly becoming an effective method of ensuring both efficiency and security. Locating such expertise in the supply chain function is an excellent example of this sort of modern integration. In some enterprises, it is not feasible to have a supply chain function focused solely on cyber; however, in today's environment not having a cyber Subject Matter Expert (SME) supporting the cyber supply chain exacerbates cyber risk even more than a cyber third party.

Closing this gap can be accomplished through a couple of different methods. One method is training supply chain risk management professionals to recognize when they have a third party that may impact cyber risk, and partner with the CISO enterprise to have a cyber SME assigned to cyber related supply chain events. This ensures that any knowledge gaps are closed throughout the supply chain process. Leveraging the supply chain professional to deploy the supply chain process and having the cyber SME execute the process, in collaboration with the supply chain professional, should ensure that the process remains intact, and that any potential cyber risks are adequately identified and addressed.

Another method that an enterprise may want to leverage is through a consulting or legal firm specializing in cyber-IT/OT products and services to support C-SCRM process.

## Cyber Supply Chain Third-Party Due Diligence

Cyber supply chain third-party due diligence is essential in the proposal, selection and onboarding process of a cyber third party. The cyber supply chain supports the CISO organization by leveraging the cyber supply chain's standard methodology to ensure that a holistic end-to-end process is leveraged with emphasis on the additional activities that are required to ensure that all aspects of the new cyber relationship meet the expectations of the enterprise.

As mentioned in the Approaching Cyber Supply Chain Risk Management section, there are hundreds of cyber third parties providing an unmeasurable number of products and services to the marketplace. An upfront step in the cyber supply chain process is the identification of the activities that will be expected from the cyber third party to support the product and/or services, as outlined by the CISO organization, and input into a proposal document to share with the cyber third parties that have been identified as potentially new cyber third-party relationships. One method of executing this process is through a Request for Proposal (RFP), managed and executed by the C-SCRM Team in partnership with the CISO organization.

The activities listed in the request for RFP should define *what* will be expected to be delivered, and not necessarily *how* the cyber third-party products and/or services will deliver within the enterprise; as that will generally depend heavily on the products and/or services the cyber third party proposes based on the activities defined by the enterprise.

You can think about this process similar in how you would think about starting the building process for a new house; you know you want a house, you know how many square feet you prefer, you know how many bedrooms you want, what type of floors you'd like, what general look and feel you want, but you may not know what type of walls, insulation, roofing materials, foundation, etc. is preferred or cost efficient as you'll likely have those discussions with the architect you select to complete the house design. The exception would be a "stock house" where all the houses are built with the same materials, floorplan etc. and offered as a type of out of the box solution.

It is a similar concept with a cyber third-party request for proposal. You know the activities you want to be performed and can document the details of those in the request for proposal, but the design and delivery can take on many shapes and sizes dependent upon the cyber products and/or services you are seeking, and will be outlined by the cyber third party in response to the request for proposal. The proposal phase will allow the cyber third parties to review your activity and standard requirements (e.g., infrastructure to support IT/OT products and/or services) and submit a proposal—based on the core competencies the cyber third party brings to the table—with pricing associated with design, delivery and support requirements for the proposed cyber products and/or services. The exception, much like a stock house, is an out of the box solution where very few—if any—customizations are available.

The CISO organization can get very specific on the exact requirements they want, the exact cyber product and/or service they are looking for and exactly how they want it delivered. However, in doing so, they risk boxing themselves out of new and potentially innovative solutions that a cyber third party is able to bring to the table or willing to explore via a potential partnership with the enterprise to build.

Identification of potential cyber third parties includes the identification of a supply base capable of providing the defined cyber activities. There are several resources available to support the identification of the supply base and C-SCRM supporting processes to reduce the number of cyber third parties to a manageable number for the proposal. These resources include the following:

- Internal recommendations from the CISO Enterprise;
- Gartner research.

Once you have the potential cyber supply base identified, understanding the potential cyber third party's marketplace strategy, size and capabilities, complexity, financial risk, reputation and current customer base—as outlined in this chapter—will help inform the decision-making process to determine the interim cyber supply base of third parties that will proceed to the proposal phase.

In reviewing the marketplace strategy of the cyber third party, as laid out in their annual report or marketing material, the enterprise should ensure there is alignment with the enterprise's strategy, this will help ensure that the effort put into building a relationship and through the implementation of a solution will not be short-lived if the cyber third party's strategy does not align with the enterprise in the long term.

The size and capabilities of the cyber third party should be assessed to ensure that they can support the products and/or services that are required to executed as defined by the activity in the Request for Proposal (RFP) and the expectations in the Service Level Agreements (SLAs). Cyber third parties that are just opening their doors may offer a more attractive pricing model to alternative, more established cyber third parties, but care must be taken to ensure that the third party has the necessary capabilities and is able to support, and—in conjunction with their marketplace strategy—grow while providing the necessary services.

Alternatively, if the enterprise is seeking a niche or very narrow product or service offering, a larger more established cyber third party may not be willing to provide small scale support to the required for the product and/or service. Moving forward with a larger cyber third party for smaller scale products and/or services, the enterprise runs the risk that they may not have the leverage to get the attention, dedicated staff or required support for the product and/or services that they require.

Complexity can be reviewed through two lenses: legal entity complexity and cyber product and/or service complexity. Legal entity complexity may require a deeper dive into the legal entities to ensure the enterprise has a good understanding of which of the entities they would be considering adding to their supply chain.

Complex products or services will require that the enterprise spend more time analyzing and breaking down the products and services to understand what the product or service will entail; whether the enterprise requires all or part of the product and service; what, if any, additional management may be necessary to participate in the design and implementation of the product and service; and whether the cyber third party can meet the requirements of the offered products and/or services. As noted by PWC in their 2016 *Food Trust Snapshot: Supplier Risk*:

> ...these sourcing and offshoring activities are becoming more extensive and sophisticated in order to capture the next level of service delivery, processing efficiency and cost savings. The extent and complexity of recent sourcing and outsourcing arrangements has increased the likelihood of supplier risks. [11]

Cyber third-party financial risk should be assessed to determine if the cyber third party will pose a greater risk to the enterprise beyond the acceptable level of risk. If a cyber third party has a high financial risk, there is an increased likelihood that the third party could be facing bankruptcy or may have had an internal or external disruption that could signal financial instability. If a cyber third party that has a high financial risk rating makes it to the final stages of the selection process, the enterprise Chief Financial Officer (CFO) should be engaged to conduct a financial review with the cyber third party to assess the level of financial risk to the enterprise.

Assessing a cyber third party's reputation can be the most difficult part of the due diligence assessment in getting to the final selection process. While an enterprise can outsource the cyber products and/or services to a third party, they cannot outsource the risk. If a cyber third party has had reputational damage in the marketplace through faulty or failure of delivery or through a breach incident, there is a chance that the reputational damage can be transferred to the enterprise, through the acquisition or delivery of the products and/or services by its customers and/or shareholders. For example, in the case study of the Target data breach, CNBC published that:

> ...Target's brand plunged by 35 points on BrandIndex's scale, which ranges from a high of 100 to a low of -100. That means that Target's brand score dropped to -9 on December 20, from 26 points the week before the security breach was announced.[12]

In the same article, the loss of brand perception was quantified as, "a billion-dollar blow, given that its brand is valued at $25.5 billion, according to global brand consultancy Interbrand".[13]

Multiple studies and ongoing analysis are conducted regularly on brand impact due to data breaches.

> A Centrify study found that 65% of data breach victims lost trust in an organization as a result of the breach. IDC found that 80% of consumers in developed nations will defect from a business if their information is compromised in a security breach.[14]

The FDIC defines Reputation Risk as:

> ... the risk arising from negative public opinion. Third-party relationships that result in dissatisfied customers, interactions not consistent with institution policies, inappropriate recommendations, security breaches resulting in the disclosure of customer information, and violations of law and regulation are all examples that could harm the reputation and standing of the financial institution in the community it serves. Also, any negative publicity involving the

third party, whether or not the publicity is related to the institution's use of the third party, could result in reputation risk.[15]

The assessment of the cyber third party current and past customer base can support determination of experience applicable to the enterprise industry. In the event that the enterprise is subject to legal or regulatory requirements in the delivery of the products and/or services, prior experience in delivering products and/or fulfilling service requirements for similar customers may be beneficial. In addition, in assessing current customers of the cyber third party the enterprise may find that they are currently supporting a company that has significant reputational risk, that again, could be transferred by association to the enterprise.

## Including Cyber Requirements in the Third-Party Risk Management Program

During the onboarding process of the cyber third party, a detailed control effectiveness assessment should be conducted to ensure that the third party's control environment is effective and acceptable to the enterprise in accordance with internal control objective requirements as identified in the enterprise's policies and standards. While the cyber third party is accountable for their control environment, the enterprise is responsible for the cyber third party's control effectiveness with regards to the products and/or services the third party provides on behalf of the enterprise.

As an example, if the enterprise engaged a cyber third party to host customer statements, one of the requirements the third-party hosting contract should include—among others—is the requirement to be compliant with American's with Disability Act (ADA) 28 CFR Part 35:

> …large print materials; accessible electronic and information technology; or other effective methods of making visually delivered materials available to individuals who are blind or have low vision; (3) Acquisition or modification of equipment or devices; and (4) Other similar services and actions.[16]

While the cyber third party would be accountable to the enterprise for delivery of the services on behalf of the enterprise, the enterprise is accountable for ensuring that their customers have the accommodations necessary to receive the statements and to ensure that the cyber third-party controls are effective and operating as designed. The enterprise maintains the ownership of the risk, requirements to their customers to receive the statements based on their accommodations and that the services are delivered in a safe and sound manner.

In addition to ensuring that regulatory compliance for ADA compliance in the example above, the cyber third party would also be required to have controls in place to secure the data.

The assessment process and cadence, designed to identify and remediate weaknesses and threats, should be performed periodically throughout the lifecycle of the cyber third party on a risk-based cadence. The control effectiveness assessment should have the requirements for both the cyber third party and the enterprise to document the controls that are in place for, at a minimum, the enterprise's information security, architecture, compliance, privacy and business continuity. In addition to these disciplines, additional assessments should be conducted based on applicability of the products and/ or services being provided and any additional control objectives.

Another method of assessing control effectiveness for cyber third parties are on-site assessments at the third party's facilities. Those cyber third parties that are considered critical to the enterprise should receive on-site assessments performed by the enterprise staff that are responsible for assessing the control effectiveness and those that are directly responsible for overseeing the cyber third party's delivery of services on a day-to-day basis.

The purpose of the on-site assessment, much like a remote assessment, is to assess the effectiveness of the control environment to ensure—during the ongoing monitoring of the cyber third-party relationship—the control environment remains intact, is enhanced as necessary and tested on a regular basis, but also to observe the services being performed, that facility controls are being adhered to (e.g., clean desk policies) and to promote relationship building.

## Ensuring Cyber Third-Party Agreements Provide Adequate Controls for Legal Risks and Compliance

Access to confidential or proprietary data, personally identifiable information (PII), sensitive personal information (SPI), or handling of personal health information can, depending in part on the industry sector, expose the

enterprise to higher regulatory risk and require a higher level of due diligence when this data is maintained and/or transmitted by a third party on
behalf of the entity. Failure to adequately secure the data which results in a
data breach is a failure of the enterprise, regardless of the third party's
culpability. Having a contract in place with the third party outlining the
requirements of the cyber third party to safeguard the data may be required
to be in compliance with the legal and regulatory guidance is a necessary
control, For example in the financial services industry the FDIC has stated:

> ...such agreements do not insulate the institution from its ultimate responsibility
> to conduct banking and related activities in a safe and sound manner and in
> compliance with law.[17]

Given guidance from the regulators, and as part of good practices for due
diligence and ongoing monitoring of the cyber third party, control assessments should be conducted on a regular basis to ensure that the controls
in place—both those maintained by the cyber third party and the enterprise—are effective, monitored on a regular basis and any control
deficiencies or gaps identified are communicated immediately and remediated in coordination with agreed upon requirements.

## Conclusion

To continue learning about the concepts in this chapter the following sources
are recommended:

1 NIST. Key Practices in C-SCRM: Computer Security Division, Information
Technology Laboratory. csrc.nist.gov/publications/detail/nistir/8276/final

2 NIST. Interdependency Tool: Computer Security Division, Information
Technology Laboratory. csrc.nist.gov/publications/detail/nistir/8272/
archive/2020-08-25

3 Cybersecurity and Infrastructure Security Agency CISA. Overview of
Cyber Vulnerabilities, n.d. us-cert.cisa.gov/ics/content/overview-cyber-
vulnerabilities

## Endnotes

1    Whitney, Armistead. "Cybersecurity Vendors - How CIOs Are Managing It."
*Apptega,* Apptega Inc, 3 Nov. 2020, www.apptega.com/blog/too-many-
cybersecurity-vendors (archived at https://perma.cc/3B9M-CDKA)

**2**   Information Technology Laboratory. Cybersecurity Supply Chain Risk Management [blog] *CSRC*, 22 June 2020. csrc.nist.gov/projects/cyber-supply-chain-risk-management (archived at https://perma.cc/ATZ5-88Y2)

**3**   RiskRecon. How to Start Thinking About Nth Party Risk - Part 1[blog] RiskRecon, Apr 20, 2020. blog.riskrecon.com/how-to-start-thinking-about-nth-party-risk-part-1 (archived at https://perma.cc/D4WR-3A45)

**4**   T Kitten. Is There Too Much Cybersecurity Technology? Former RSA Chair Coviello Says More Tech Won't Reduce Risk [blog] Bank Info Security, 30 May 2017. www.bankinfosecurity.com/too-many-vendors-hampers-cybersecurity-a-9956 (archived at https://perma.cc/KLW2-7YRK)

**5**   A Whitney. Cybersecurity Vendors - How CIOs Are Managing It [blog] Apptega, Nov 3, 2020. www.apptega.com/blog/too-many-cybersecurity-vendors (archived at https://perma.cc/3B9M-CDKA)

**6**   V Lynch. Cost of 2013 Target Data Breach Nears $300 Million [blog] thesslstore. May 26, 2017. www.thesslstore.com/blog/2013-target-data-breach-settled/#:~:text=With%20Latest%20Settlement%2C%20the%20Cost%20of%20the%202013,being%20compromised.%20The%20timing%20couldn%E2%80%99t%20have%20been%20worse (archived at https://perma.cc/Q5W5-NQDD)

**7**   Coalfire. Third Party Risk Management and the Cloud [blog] Coalfire, March 2020. www.coalfire.com/the-coalfire-blog/march-2020/third-party-risk-management-and-the-cloud (archived at https://perma.cc/3EGN-7LJL)

**8**   Y Golan. 2020 Cyber Insurance Predictions [blog] Attack Solutions, December 20, 2019. attacksolutions.com/2020-cyber-insurance-predictions/ (archived at https://perma.cc/NKN6-MYW7)

**9**   McKinsey & Company. Perspectives on Transforming Cybersecurity: Risk [blog] McKinsey & Company, 2020. www.mckinsey.com/business-functions/risk/our-insights/perspectives-on-transforming-cybersecurity (archived at https://perma.cc/D32M-QVPR)

**10**  David Uberti and Kim S. Nash. SolarWinds Hack Forces Reckoning With Supply-Chain Security, The Wall Street Journal, January 14, 2021, www.wsj.com/articles/solarwinds-hack-forces-reckoning-with-supply-chain-security-11610620200 (archived at https://perma.cc/XN4Z-T36C)

**11**  Pwc. Supply Chain and Risk Management, n.d. www.pwc.com/gx/en/operations-consulting-services/pdf/pwc-supply-chain-and-risk-management.pdf (archived at https://perma.cc/YP4S-LRA5)

**12**  Aimee Picchi. After Security Breach, Target's Brand Takes a Hit, CBS News, 27 Dec. 2013. www.cbsnews.com/news/after-security-breach-targets-brand-takes-a-body-blow/ (archived at https://perma.cc/T7BM-GHYJ)

**13**  Ibid.

**14**   S Hospelhorn. Analyzing Company Reputation After a Data Breach [blog] Varonis Inside Out Security, March 30, 2020. www.varonis.com/blog/company-reputation-after-a-data-breach/ (archived at https://perma.cc/C3UE-VJKA)

**15**   Federal Deposit Insurance Corporation. Guidance For Managing Third-Party Risk Introduction, 2020, www.fdic.gov/news/financial-institution-letters/2008/fil08044a.pdf (archived at https://perma.cc/2QJ2-JZD6)

**16**   Department of Justice. Americans with Disabilities Act Title II Regulations, September 15, 2010. www.ada.gov/regs2010/titleII_2010/titleII_2010_regulations.pdf (archived at https://perma.cc/B9J6-SCD6)

**17**   Federal Deposit Insurance Corporation. Guidance for Managing Third-Party Risk, June 6 2008. www.fdic.gov/news/financial-institution-letters/2008/fil08044a.html (archived at https://perma.cc/HH8F-AZQV)

# 09

# Technical Operations

BY GREG MONTANA, CHIEF RISK OFFICER, FIS, AND KANGKYU LEE,
ISA RESEARCH ASSOCIATE

## Five Key Ideas to Take Away from This Chapter

1  The demands on cybersecurity operations continue to grow as cyber-attacks increase in sophistication and speed.

2  Even firms with the highest budgets and the most sophisticated tools and techniques risk becoming the victims of cyber-attacks due to an inability to consistently execute across constantly changing IT environments, including internal and third-party operations.

3  Defense-in-depth strategy provides multiple controls and techniques to protect data from malicious activities through the combination of prevention, detection, and response operations—as detailed in this chapter.

4  Technical Security Operations, including the Security Operation Center (SOC), is expanding its role at leading firms and can become the independent central program execution hub for a firm's defense-in-depth strategy, thus ensuring the broadest possible coverage and execution of a firm's security strategy.

5  Advanced technologies such as AI and machine learning expand the ability to scale security programs to cover the interaction of cybersecurity and fraud, thus enhancing the effectiveness and efficiency of these efforts.

## Introduction

The demands of managing cybersecurity operations are increasing significantly. Across nearly all industries, the trends of digitization and the importance of data privacy and service availability, coupled with the rising frequency and sophistication of cyber-attacks has made the need to enhance cybersecurity operations more critical than ever.

The 2020 COVID-19 pandemic has accelerated the rate of digitization for many industries and exacerbated security risks with cyber-attacks increasing in both number and sophistication against an increasingly remote-work model for many organizations. According to the UN, for example, phishing is up 600% since the 2020 pandemic started.[1] In one of the most publicized attacks of 2020, the company SolarWinds was used as the springboard for one of the worst-known breaches of US government computer systems in the last five years. In response to this attack, Andy Smith, a leader with cybersecurity firm Centrify, stated:

> The biggest takeaway of this hack is that a layered approach to security is the way to go in the future in light of this hack's sophistication. There's no silver bullet to stop a hack this sophisticated, though. No one strategy or approach could have prevented it.[2]

Smith Adds,

> That initial vulnerability will be there, and you need those layers of security to prevent it, so you need to look at preventive controls, predictive controls and detective controls. All those need to be combined into a single, unified strategy.[3]

## Technical Operations—The Need for Consistent Coordination of Defense-in-Depth

Smith is referring to defense-in-depth. Just like criminals in the physical world look for the easiest way into a building, cybercriminals will exploit the easiest entry point into an organization's system. Having a cybersecurity operations group that inventories all assets, like a retailer inventories its physical stores or a bank, its branches, is required on a real-time basis to provide the foundation for securing those assets, assigning owners and measuring their adherence to the prevention, detection and response programs concurrently managed by the security operations team.

FIGURE 9.1 Defense-in-depth.

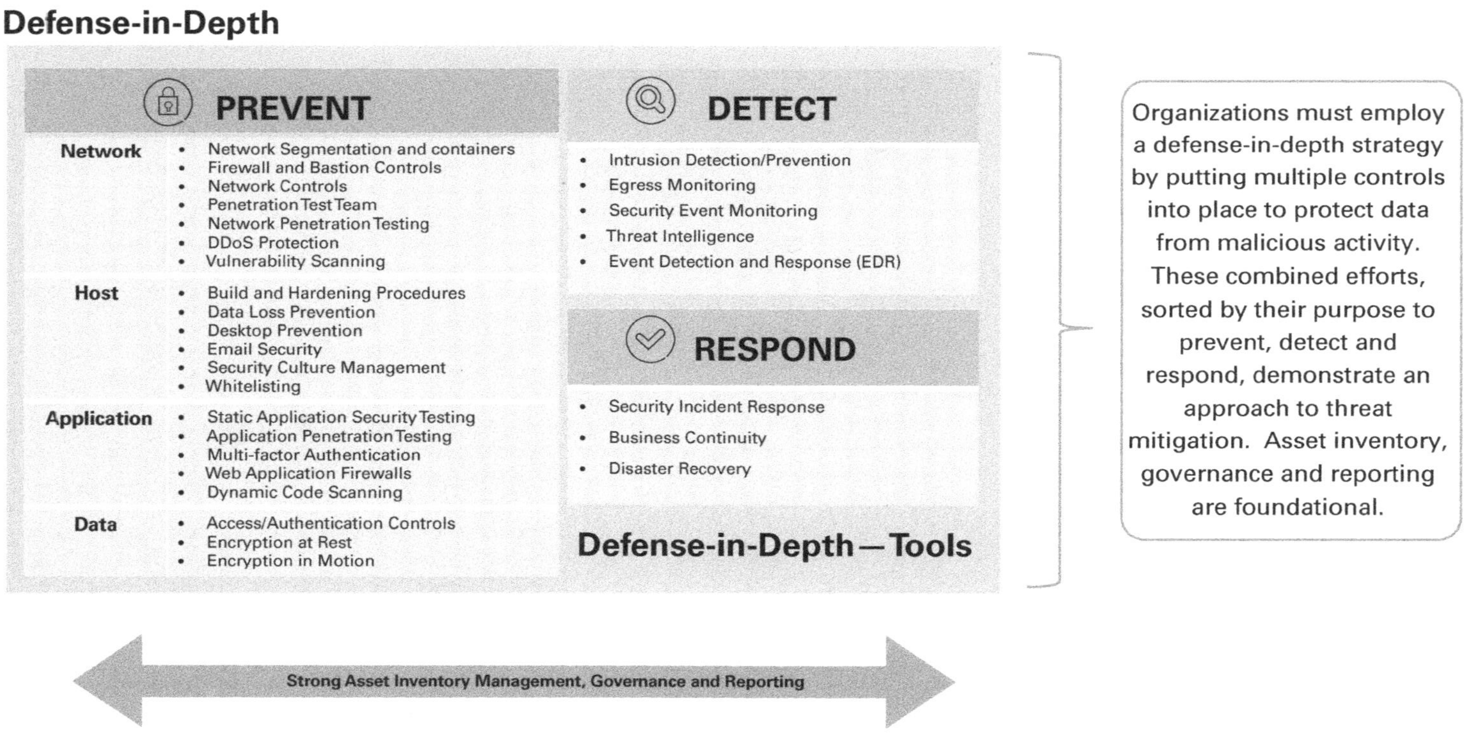

# Defense-in-Depth

Organizations must employ a defense-in-depth strategy by putting multiple controls into place to protect data from malicious activity. These combined efforts, sorted by their purpose to prevent, detect and respond, demonstrate an approach to threat mitigation. Asset inventory, governance and reporting are foundational.

## PREVENT

**Network**
- Network Segmentation and containers
- Firewall and Bastion Controls
- Network Controls
- Penetration Test Team
- Network Penetration Testing
- DDoS Protection
- Vulnerability Scanning

**Host**
- Build and Hardening Procedures
- Data Loss Prevention
- Desktop Prevention
- Email Security
- Security Culture Management
- Whitelisting

**Application**
- Static Application Security Testing
- Application Penetration Testing
- Multi-factor Authentication
- Web Application Firewalls
- Dynamic Code Scanning

**Data**
- Access/Authentication Controls
- Encryption at Rest
- Encryption in Motion

## DETECT

- Intrusion Detection/Prevention
- Egress Monitoring
- Security Event Monitoring
- Threat Intelligence
- Event Detection and Response (EDR)

## RESPOND

- Security Incident Response
- Business Continuity
- Disaster Recovery

## Defense-in-Depth—Tools

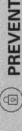

Strong Asset Inventory Management, Governance and Reporting

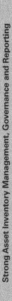

This is why an inventory of authorized and unauthorized devices and software are the first and second of the Center for Internet Security Institute *Top 20 Critical Security Controls*, and are foundational to the NIST (National Institute of Science and Technology) and PCI (Payment Card Industry) cybersecurity guidance.

If a bank's physical security team cannot tell you the number of branches the organization has in their physical network upon request, you would think the group less than competent. The same should be true of the team charged with cybersecurity defense, which should have a process for independently inventorying all information technology assets including servers, desktops, laptops, mobile devices, storage devices, network equipment, Internet Protocol (IP) addresses and URLs including whether each is accessible from the public internet.

The case for empowering a central security operations team with the independent management and oversight of a firm's asset inventory and overall prevention, detection and response controls is based on both effectiveness and efficiency grounds. First from an effectiveness standpoint, it ensures that no matter where assets are developed, added and managed—such as in the CIO organization or in an individual business unit—there is one central group charged with ensuring standards are met. This reduces the occurrence of unauthorized assets and enables an empowered group to measure and hold accountable the entire enterprise to the good hygiene only achieved through adherence to high cybersecurity defense standards. Second, from an efficiency standpoint, the central, independent technical security operations team is then able to enjoy economies of scale in the management of the many controls and programs that make up the defense-in-depth strategy enterprise-wide.

There has never been a time when this is needed more with the volume, velocity and impact of change on the security posture of organizations in all industries and fields. According to a CompTIA report in December 2019, the top driver for increased focus on security is a change to IT operations. The survey also shows that 86% of the respondents stated that there has been a change to their technology approach within the past two years.[4]

As firms take on the digital transformation journey, new methodologies and processes are introduced to increase the efficiency and effectives of technology projects and their deliverables, such as cloud-based computing. However, as these new methodologies and technologies are introduced, firms must identify and address the security risk that will accompany the changes. To fully undertake the impact of digital transformation, security requirements need to be properly addressed up front so that they can be built and supported.

The IT vs. OT Security Issue

The biblical story of the divergent life experiences of twins Esau and Jacob has been told for millennia. Today a parallel tale has become the most pressing structural challenge enterprises face in cyber security. Operating Technology (OT) is information technology's (IT) essential twin; computers that run infrastructure such as ovens, air conditioning and fire alarm systems, production conveyor lines, test stations, calibration equipment and other industrial control systems. OT is dubbed "IT in non-carpeted areas" and represents about 35% of the total population of computers in most large organizations. Structural management challenges often lead to OT being managed differently than IT yet deployed on the same network and domain. This is the opposite of a secure model. These assets become the weak link to an otherwise secure organization and must be managed with secure IT policies and standards, while segmenting such machines onto separate network segments or enclaves. This problem is trending worse, due to technological, organizational, and financial reasons, and increasing home-working arrangements heightened during the COVID-19 pandemic.

The world's OT fleet is aging, poorly protected, and responsible for a large and growing fraction of headline cyber breaches. IT staff are frequently unaware of individual OT systems until a problem becomes manifest in the IT network, and its root-cause is traced back to a lab, production floor, or facilities office. Ensuring these assets are registered in the formal asset inventory and covered by prevent, detect and respond programs highlighted in this chapter is necessary to avoid these assets being the patient zero of a breach.

Breaches traced to OT include those at Honda, Norsk Hydro, Maersk, Boeing, Target, the UK's National Health Service, European Hospital Operator Fresenius, and DHL among many others—including the famous crippling attack on Iran's nuclear program known as Stuxnet. IT and OT may deploy identical machines, yet they quickly diverge. Operational and financial lifespans for OT are several times longer; patching and end point protections are sparser. OT machines, lacking a single human owner, are favorite targets for bad actors. The likelihood of compromise for OT machines on average is an order of magnitude higher. Mingling these twins on the same digital networks, without the same level of controls, erodes the defense posture benefits enterprises would otherwise enjoy through the increased adoption of Enterprise Risk Management (ERM) and strong cyber security standards.

SOURCE  Dr. Corey Hirsch, CISO at Teledyne Technologies

A defense-in-depth strategy must incorporate programs made up of control processes designed to prevent, detect, and respond to cyber-attacks.

The following defense-in-depth summary highlights the breadth of responsibilities cybersecurity technical operation teams must cover to deliver on a fit-for-purpose program needed to defend today's complex technology against the latest cyber threats. The prevent portion of the program is, by design, the most comprehensive of all areas of focus and covers all layers of the technology estate including network, host, application, and data layers. Detect covers security monitoring in all its forms and response must be coordinated to effectively manage containment of and recovery from incidents of all types.

## Prevention—Technical Operations

Prevention begins, as previously mentioned, with proper asset management.

### Asset Inventory Management

IT assets include all elements of software and hardware and network addresses in the business environment. IT asset management is the set of business practices that join financial, contractual and inventory functions to support lifecycle and strategic decision making for the IT environment and includes policy, management, governance, monitoring, reporting and control testing for hardware and software assets as well as the management of all company IP addresses and URLs. To maintain solid hardware asset management, firms need to maintain server and network asset lifecycle programs, govern and oversee asset onboarding, maintenance, end-of-life management and disposal. Software asset management includes the management of global software licenses and the monitoring and auditing of utilization and license requirements.

Closely interrelated to enterprise asset management is the first of the network domain areas under prevention: segmentation of assets. Segmentation is identifying and domiciling assets based on their risk through a well-designed container strategy that limits access to each environment to prevent unnecessary access and separates the assets to reduce the impact of unauthorized access should it occur.

Management of these two foundational, preventive, elements of security operations enables the measurement and management of all other programs

FIGURE 9.2  Hardware and software asset management lifecycle.

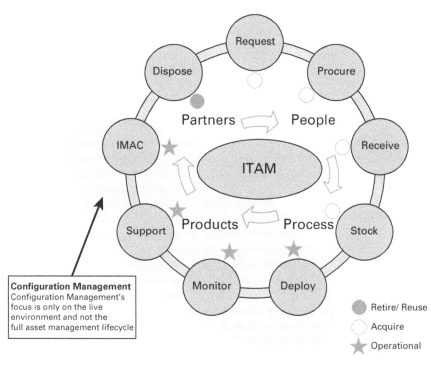

Hardware and Software Asset
Management Lifecycle

and controls to reduce risk exposure. Like physical security efforts to manage and measure programs and controls by location and owner, cyber-security prevention starts with maintaining an inventory of the assets to be protected with assigned asset owners so that controls not directly managed by the security group can be monitored and measured. The owners of the assets can then be held accountable to meet a firm's security standards.

Just like a physical security team tests adherence to access standards and security procedures at a bank branch such as dual access to a bank vault, the security operations team can test via penetration testing and ongoing monitoring and reporting the organization's adherence to all of the controls in the defense-in-depth strategy. Wherever possible, the security operations team should manage the controls centrally for efficiency and effectiveness purposes and build expertise and depth to ensure all applicable controls are implemented across all assets and domains consistently.

Although not comprehensive, key elements of a strong technical operations team prevention program are provided in the following subsections.

### Prevention (Network Layer)—Segmentation and Containers

Network segmentation segregates production networks from non-production networks. A container model for segmenting network environments from each other is a key cybersecurity prevention strategy. Each container should provide a separate set of security zones (e.g., DMZ, Application, and Data) so that all aspects of the container are separate from each other. Containers can be created for various applications and systems by business unit, process, function, financial risk and/or by client.

### Prevention (Network Layer)—Firewall Controls

Firewalls are used to define what communication is allowed or blocked to assist in controlling access to company or client data. Firms should block all communication by default, and then only allow communication (network traffic) that is needed between environments. Responsible leaders should perform periodic rule-recertification to identify unused or permissive rules that are no longer required for refinement or remediation purposes. This approach ensures implementation of least privileged network access with appropriate reviews for oversight and governance.

### Prevention (Network Layer)—Bastion Controls

Bastions configured with multi-factor authentication can be used to support the various segmented network environments (sometimes referred to as "containers"). A bastion model is not only used for support purposes but also for management and monitoring of privileged access to systems residing within the segmented environments. Bastion access should be provisioned on the principle of least privilege in that only appropriate personnel are author-ized to authenticate and utilize bastions to access any given segmented network. This model ensures a secure access method to support our various customers' production environments by eliminating the risk of direct access from our internal corporate network.

## Prevention (Network Layer)—Security Controls

There are a variety of network controls available to cybersecurity defense teams. They include Intrusion Detection and Prevention Systems (IDS/IPS), IP reputation, Network Access Control (NAC), incident response, behavior analysis, as well as forward and reverse proxies just to name a few. In addition to the network segmentation and firewall controls, these tools combined provide additional defense-in-depth to policing the network transport layer for inappropriate or malicious traffic. In addition to the above, firms can monitor and defend against known malicious IPs/address ranges, using security industry sources. These IP ranges can be blocked by an IPS and at the network perimeter firewalls as an added security measure.

## Prevention (Network Layer)—Vulnerability Management

Vulnerability management should be focused on identifying and remediating insecure system configurations, missing security patches and the use of outdated software on internal or external hosts. Scanning should consist of automated testing targeting internal and external hosts. Host scanning can be completed on a schedule; for example: external hosts weekly, internal hosts monthly, upon server build request, and ad-hoc to support remediation processes.

## Prevention (Network/Application Layers)—Security Test Team (STT)

A firm can deploy an internal, external or a combination Security Test Team (STT) with responsibilities ranging from functional program management to advanced penetration testing. The Security Test Team can be made responsible for testing the enterprise-wide deployment of network and application environments to identify current and emerging vulnerabilities. Prioritization can start with a risked-based approach, for example internet-facing assets that are used for electronic delivery of sensitive information and/or are used to process payment transactions. Examples of STT responsibilities are shown in Figure 9.3.

Security testing teams should be continually trained and educated in the latest techniques and technologies. For example, they should receive and maintain industry certifications such as Certified Information System Security Professional, Certified Ethical Hacker, Certified Information Security Auditor, Global Information Assurance Certification Penetration Tester, etc.

FIGURE 9.3 Examples of Security Test Team (STT) responsibilities

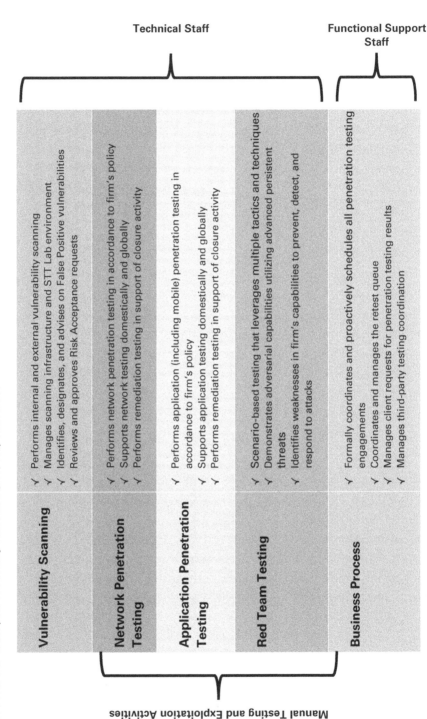

**Technical Staff**

**Functional Support Staff**

**Vulnerability Scanning**
- ✔ Performs internal and external vulnerability scanning
- ✔ Manages scanning infrastructure and STT Lab environment
- ✔ Identifies, designates, and advises on False Positive vulnerabilities
- ✔ Reviews and approves Risk Acceptance requests

**Network Penetration Testing**
- ✔ Performs network penetration testing in accordance to firm's policy
- ✔ Supports network testing domestically and globally
- ✔ Performs remediation testing in support of closure activity

**Application Penetration Testing**
- ✔ Performs application (including mobile) penetration testing in accordance to firm's policy
- ✔ Supports application testing domestically and globally
- ✔ Performs remediation testing in support of closure activity

**Red Team Testing**
- ✔ Scenario-based testing that leverages multiple tactics and techniques
- ✔ Demonstrates adversarial capabilities utilizing advanced persistent threats
- ✔ Identifies weaknesses in firm's capabilities to prevent, detect, and respond to attacks

**Business Process**
- ✔ Formally coordinates and proactively schedules all penetration testing engagements
- ✔ Coordinates and manages the retest queue
- ✔ Manages client requests for penetration testing results
- ✔ Manages third-party testing coordination

**Manual Testing and Exploitation Activities**

## Prevention (Network/Application Layer)—Network/App Penetration Testing

Penetration testing is designed to demonstrate risk realization of security vulnerabilities by attempting to exploit them from the perspective of a malicious attacker. Penetration testing includes leveraging automated and manual tools to attempt to find complex and obscure vulnerabilities. This activity allows firms to proactively respond to web application, network, and system level threats by identifying how vulnerabilities can be leveraged for further exploitation.

Network penetration testing should be conducted at least annually, cover internal and external assets and include methodologies based on industry standards and guidelines such as NIST and SANS.

Application penetration testing should be performed at least annually and cover all web-based, public internet, internal facing, firm hosted, and third-party hosted applications. The application penetration testing program should be developed in accordance with industry wide best practices, such as those detailed by National Institute of Standards and Technology (NIST), the Open Web Application Security Project (OWASP), and the Payment Card Industry (PCI) Security Standards Council.

## Prevention (Network Layer)—Distributed Denial of Service (DDoS) Protection

It is widely known that all internet-facing infrastructures are under a constant onslaught of attack from a variety of automated tools, as well as from targeted attacks. Where possible, DDoS protection should be "always on" so that the controls are applied automatically as often as possible. However, even if the threat is mitigated by automated controls, when a real and credible alert is received, it should be evaluated, and the appropriate response teams assembled. During this phase, technical and communication bridge lines are initiated to identify additional mitigation and communication steps that may be needed, such as:

- identify intended targets;
- notify intended targets;
- block traffic;
- initiate mitigation steps;
- monitor and adjust.

Mitigation steps may include engaging appropriate Internet Service Providers (ISPs) and, third party DDoS service providers, adjusting intrusion prevention systems (IPS) and contacting law enforcement. Firms should work with their ISPs to ensure border gateway protocol (BGP) peer addresses are not accessible on the public internet to prohibit distributed denial of service attacks against its peering routers.

## Prevention (Host Layer)—Change Management

Firms should employ a systematic approach to implementing system software, infrastructure and application changes. This also includes changes to the logical and physical security components of a company's environment. There is value in establishing a standard change process that includes key control points to help ensure changes are controlled and managed in a consistent manner. A change management system of record and an independent change management team should be created to oversee and enforce the change management process as well as apply final approval of changes. Change management processes and tools should support and enforce segregation of roles in the implementation of a change.

## Prevention (Host Layer)—Data Loss Prevention (DLP)

A Data Loss Prevention (DLP) tool can prevent the writing out to external media. Firms can achieve DLP through multiple controls employed in differing combinations across the enterprise. Individual controls are designed to address specific areas of security. Examples of these controls include, but are not limited to, end-user DLP policies that protect against unauthorized data transfers initiated from end user workstations, restrict the use of removable media (for those allowed to use removable media, content policies can block writing of sensitive data to removable media, i.e., non-public information, personal health information, and payment card industry information), and controls around email services to secure and encrypt data. Additional controls include full disk encryption and strict access controls in multiple forms to prevent unauthorized access to data.

## Prevention (Host Layer)—Workstation Prevention

Workstations and desktops should be protected by multiple agents. A firm's workstations can be protected by various PC-based agents that monitor for zero-day attacks and encryption, prevent installation of malicious software, prevent data exfiltration, and create forensic images. Employee internet access can—where allowed by law—be monitored even when off the company network. Workstation security controls include disk encryption, patch management, antivirus, DLP, application white listing, forensics and digital investigations among others.

## Prevention (Host Layer)—Email Security

Email security has multiple layer. Firms should utilize multiple means to send secure email. A standard email solution should be managed centrally using multi-factor authentication tools. Based on risk, TLS server-to-server session encryption should also be utilized. Finally, phishing campaigns should be managed centrally by the security operations team and results used for recognition, training and improvement.

## Prevention (Host Layer)—Security Culture Mgmt. and Employee Training

Security training should occur at relevant touch points. Security communication campaigns should be regularly promoted to set the tone and expectations regarding enforcement of compliance with security standards. Best practices include baseline security activities that are part of the everyday lives of employees. Employees should be presented with training at relevant touch points throughout the year including online training, phishing exercises, just-in-time training, table-top exercises and printed material.

## Prevention (Host Layer)—Application Whitelisting

Orgainzatiins should ensure only approved applications can be installed. Application Whitelisting can be instituted on Windows servers and desktops. The tool blocks unapproved software from executing on workstations and servers.

## Prevention (Application Layer)—Static Application Security Testing (SAST)

Application security controls can be tested through a variety of means. Software code should be scanned as part of the secure code development process with a static scanning tool that supports industry standard rules such as Open Web Application Security Project's (OWASP) Top 10

Vulnerabilities and/or SANS Institute/Common Weakness Enumeration (CWE) Top 25 Vulnerabilities, among others. Vulnerabilities identified via scanning should be prioritized for remediation based on criticality. Critical and high-risk vulnerabilities in new code should be corrected prior to deployment of the code to production.

---

### DEVSECOPS FOR ENHANCED SECURITY AND EFFICIENCY

In addition to implementing a defense-in-depth strategy, an organization must focus on establishing the right infrastructure and procedures to enhance cybersecurity throughout the application life cycle. Chapter 3 notes a variety of structures that are evolving based on unique corporate needs and regulatory mandates. A Deloitte survey in 2019 illustrates that the greatest challenge to managing application security risks is the lack of appropriate organizational structure to enable the integration of security into the application development life cycle, accounting for 48% of the respondents.[5] As firms take on new models and methodologies, business operations will become more complex and accompanied by new risks and security concerns. One of the ways in which security can be embedded throughout an application lifecycle is through the usage of DevSecOps.

DevSecOps is the infusion of security, policy and controls into DevOps culture, processes and tools. Through this methodology, enterprises can identify risks and security issues from the initiation stage to the final stage of the development lifecycle. The resulting benefits include reduced time and cost for application delivery as the process minimizes the redundant process of addressing security issues because they are managed from the start of the lifecycle. Also, DevSecOps addresses security as a joint effort between IT operations, development, and security teams, requiring collaborative effort by everyone involved in the process.[6] As stated in the Deloitte survey, "DevSecOps fundamentally transforms cyber and risk management from being compliance based activities—typically undertaken late in the development life cycle—into essential framing mindsets across the product journey".[7] This ties with our claim on internal audit's role in technology projects—as mentioned in Chapter 7—that participation of internal audit from the initial phase of technology projects will benefit the project by identifying any missing or overlapping gaps in risks or controls. Going forward, a proactive approach to security across the organization will be vital in managing cyber risk.

Interoperability engineering between several key enterprise functions surrounding the management of a hardened device should be considered. Asset management, endpoint controls, the product, application, and services inventory, vulnerability management, and change and incident management can all be integrated to provide a 360-degree view throughout the life of an asset. With this approach management and reporting for all business units can centralized, facilitating the use of common processes and best practices across the enterprise.

A firm's build standards and procedures should be based on an industry standard, for example, the Center for Internet Security (CIS) benchmark standards. Content surrounding configuration and build practices should be treated as confidential to protect against exploitation.

## Prevention (Data Layer)—Logical Access/Authentication Management

Logical access management is a key role for any firm. Access to data and information technology resources should be restricted through the assignment of user credentials to employees based on the individual's job responsibilities. Accounts and their associated rights should be created, managed, disabled, and deleted as determined by the principle of least privilege. Password change frequency should be maintained and governed according to a communicated password management standard. An account's lifecycle should be closely monitored as it advances through many stages from provisioning to authentication, authorization, verification, and de-provisioning. Firms should maintain oversight of all user's access through quarterly access reviews. These entitlement reviews should be designed to ensure that a user's access to systems is still necessary based on the user's role and responsibilities. These access reviews can be conducted by management and/or resource owners, then tested periodically by an independent assurance or audit function. Privileged access should be logged and alerted on for all infrastructure using a Security Incident and Event Management (SIEM) system.

## Detection—Technical Operations

Detection is a key domain generally owned by the cybersecurity technical operations team. Intrusion detection and prevention systems, security incident and event monitoring and egress monitoring are well established central functions for organizations to manage through their cybersecurity technical operations teams. Like prevention programs, keys to success include the need to manage these efforts centrally and holistically—with the joint goals of both capability and coverage as key success factors.

### Detection—Intrusion Detection / Prevention

Firms can deploy network intrusion prevention and detection systems (IPS/IDS) across their network to monitor network and system activities for malicious activity. The IPS/IDS systems provide a key control layer at the network perimeter and between data centers to identify malicious activity, log information about this activity, attempt to block or stop the activity, and report on it.

### Detection—Egress Monitoring

Firms can subscribe to a service for internet egress network traffic analysis which helps identify potential intruders' activities in near real-time. The service also provides additional capabilities to detect high-fidelity events or actionable items that may not be detected by other standard security tools including discovering exfiltrated data attempts and command and control attempts.

### Detection—Security Information Event Monitoring

Firms should collect and store their systems and network device logs within a Security Information and Event Management (SIEM) solution. These solutions provide correlation and cross reporting capabilities, effectively providing a better means of seeing a holistic picture of security activity. The SIEM enables a firm to proactively investigate security anomalies, malicious and/or out-of-policy activity and identify potential threats for necessary triage. The SIEM team should be a 24x7x365 operation.

---

### ADVANCED TECHNOLOGIES—HOW TO MANAGE RISKS EFFECTIVELY

While advanced technologies are introduced as part of the risk management plan, an enterprise must put in the effort to analyze and prepare for how these new technologies will impact the organization. As mentioned in a report by McKinsey & Company:

> Leaders hoping to avoid, or at least mitigate, unintended consequences need both to build their pattern-recognition skills with respect to AI risks and to engage the entire organization so that it is ready to embrace the power and the responsibility associated with AI.[8]

Proper identification and prioritization of the risks needs to be followed by adequate level of controls to effectively manage risks surrounding the innovate technology. What is also important is that risk assessment and management should be a continuous process throughout an on-going life cycle—from its idealization to is maintenance phase. Iterative risk management processes with collaborative efforts from different perspectives within the organization will allow revelations of new countermeasures and controls, reducing the possibility of security incidents. The McKinsey report states:

> As the costs of risks associated with AI rise, the ability both to assess those risks and to engage workers at all levels in defining and implementing controls will become a new source of competitive advantage.[9]

This approach to risk can be expanded to address other existing or new technologies that introduce additional risks or security concerns to organizations. This resonates with the general theme portrayed throughout this text; cybersecurity needs to be a continuous process that requires the support and cooperation from all staff throughout the enterprise.

## Detection—Threat Intelligence Internal and External

Every firm's threat intelligence unit should be the conduit for any internal self-identified security threats such as pen test results, phishing reporting and insider threats. Threat intelligence should also maintain established relationships with their sector partners, law enforcement, and various intelligence and information security communities, such as the FBI, US Secret Service, the Department of Homeland Security National Cybersecurity and Communications Integration Center, Interpol, the United Kingdom's National Crime Agency, the US State Department's International Law Enforcement Academies, the Overseas Security Advisory Council, and the Domestic Security Alliance Council. An internal and/or external threat intelligence team provides operational, strategic and actionable intelligence to multiple groups within a company which enables it to prepare for potential future events. Threats and related vulnerabilities should be reported to management and appropriate internal and external parties as necessary.

## Response—Technical Operations

Traditionally, security operations have been a reactive function, equated with a Security Operations Center, or SOC, where technical security teams detect, investigate, and respond to cyber-attacks. With the role of operations expanding to establish effective enterprise-level cybersecurity, the Security Operations Centers are taking on more responsibilities. In addition to their traditional role, SOCs are beginning to act as fusion centers, providing service data and analytic requirements for other risk management functions within the enterprise. These areas include fraud detection, physical security, compliance and more.[10] To adapt to its growing needs, SOCs are implementing advanced technology such as Machine Learning (ML) and Artificial Intelligence (AI) to enhance and optimize their function of preventing, detecting, and responding to risks and cyber-attacks.

The importance of a SOC for identifying and defending against attacks cannot be understated. However, the SOC itself is just one link in a chain of security operations that firms must establish, manage, and coordinate at an enterprise level to ensure a robust and resilient cyber-security program.

It is incumbent upon all organizations to identify and federate key areas of technical operations that must work together to manage cybersecurity risk. Common policies must be applied across the areas with performance measured against those policies regardless of where the control activities sit in the organization.

### Response—Incident Response

A Security Incident Response Team (SIRT) is a specialized group that investigates, contains, prioritizes, mitigates and resolves potential and actual security incidents. Each firm should have an incident response team, with the mission to proactively manage cyber threats and incidents to improve a firm's security posture. Firm employees should be encouraged to report all potential security and privacy incidents to the SIRT. These incidents include policy violations, imminent threats to data security/privacy as well as indications of inappropriate access or exploitation. Security tools should also deliver automated notifications to the SIRT. SIRT team members should have specialized investigation and response skills and tools to carry out computer forensics, malware analysis, code development and data mining. SIRT findings should be reported to management and appropriate internal parties as necessary. Management should then deliver required communications to additional internal and external parties such as the CEO, board of directors, regulators, employees and clients. Incident Response and Crisis Management—which are discussed in depth in Chapter 10—should be practiced through regular table-top exercises.

## Response—Business Continuity and Disaster Recovery

A Continuity Program Office should be established within the Security Operations Team and oversee a continuous cycle of evaluations, reviews, and exercises designed to manage risk to an acceptable level. After a Business Impact Assessment (BIA) is performed, a gap analysis should be conducted to determine risk acceptance or if mitigation efforts are needed. A threat assessment should be reviewed to determine alternatives for continuity risk mitigation, and strategies to mitigate these risks that are identified, including plan development. Recovery plans are exercised and assessed for effectiveness and adjustments are made to the BIA and plan at least annually. Plans are developed and written for a worst-case scenario and may be adapted to any situation in which operations are disrupted. Plans provide for the return to normal functions and processing as soon as possible following a disaster.

FIGURE 9.4  Business Continuity and Recovery Resources

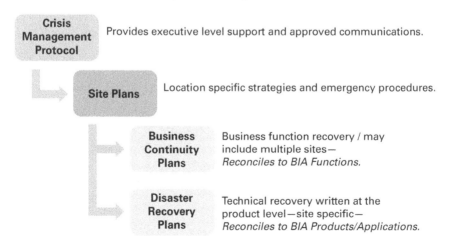

**Crisis Management Protocol** — Provides executive level support and approved communications.

**Site Plans** — Location specific strategies and emergency procedures.

**Business Continuity Plans** — Business function recovery / may include multiple sites— *Reconciles to BIA Functions.*

**Disaster Recovery Plans** — Technical recovery written at the product level—site specific— *Reconciles to BIA Products/Applications.*

Formal management, monitoring, and reporting protocols should be developed to drive recovery planning and testing initiatives.

While the defense-in-depth strategy includes a number of effective controls and techniques used to combat cyber-attacks, it is important to note that the strategy is most effective when the entire organization supports it. Leading firms take a "security is everyone's responsibility" approach. As mentioned in the Three Lines model in Chapters 3 and 7, collaborative work among different parts of the organization is crucial for effective governance as communication enhances the activities of risk functions by aligning them with the general objectives and the needs of the organization. Nowhere is this more important than in detection so that employees feel empowered to say something if they see something. Training and rewarding staff for identifying security risks, such as phishing attempts, is both detective and preventive in its nature. Security culture management and employee training requires cooperation across multiple departments including human resources, compliance, and legal to facilitate effective communication, develop tailored training program for employees, and align the business operation with compliance and security standards. The role of the CISO and the security team, which will be addressed in Chapter 12, is also vital in creating an effective cybersecurity culture. For secure technical operations to be embedded throughout an organization, there must be a coherent understanding of the needs of security.

## Conclusion

Technical operations security needs constant evaluation and evolution to safeguard enterprise assets in a digitalized era with increasing cybersecurity risks. Going forward, adoption of new technology and innovation will be crucial both in terms of promoting competitiveness of the business and to achieve more effective cyber risk management and mitigation. As stated in a PWC survey, the benefits of innovation are evident, closing the wide lead that attackers have held for a long time.[11] The shift of operations and security tools to cloud infrastructure, switching to advanced technologies, and restructuring operations through automation and rationalization are improving the cost efficiency and effectiveness of cyber operations throughout the enterprise.[12] However, there will also be risks associating new innovation, which may be detrimental if not accounted for properly. As organizations go through modernization processes and are subject to increasingly sophisticated attacks, such as SolarWinds, they need to incorporate strategies such as the defense-in-depth for proper management of the security programs and controls to not only enhance operational effectiveness, but also enhance operational security.

Maintaining and investing in a centralized and robust technical security operations team focused on defense-in-depth will best position an organization to meet and address these accelerating threats. Having the program elements in place is the first step, equally important is maintaining vigilance to keep coverage of all the program elements at the highest percentage possible. This coverage is key as threat actors will exploit gaps wherever they exist, regardless if they expose high risk assets or not.

With ownership of an organization's assets and defense-in-depth program elements defined, measurement of and adherence to the highest standards within those elements can be best effectuated. With this in place, cybersecurity roles and responsibilities for all other functions and staff come into focus and can enable requirements for collective efforts from participants across the entire organization.

To continue learning about the concepts in this chapter the following sources are recommended:

1  Center for Internet Security. The 20 CIS Controls & Resources, n.d. www.cisecurity.org/controls/cis-controls-list/

2  Control Objectives for Information and Related Technologies Framework.

3  What is COBIT? Framework, Components, and Benefits, November 17, 2020  www.simplilearn.com/what-is-cobit-significance-and-framework-rar309-article

4  L Barnaby. ISO/IEC 27000 – Key International Standard for Information Security Revised [blog] ISO, March 1, 2018. www.iso.org/news/ref2266.html

5  National Institute of Standards and Security. NIST Releases Version 1.1 of Its Popular Cybersecurity Framework [blog] *NIST,* April 16, 2018. www.nist.gov/news-events/news/2018/04/nist-releases-version-11-its-popular-cybersecurity-framework

6  National Institute of Standards and Security. SP 800-53 Revision 5. Computer Security Division, Information Technology Laboratory. SP 800-53 Revision 5Published. *CSRC. NIST,* September 23, 2020, csrc.nist.gov/Projects/risk-management/sp800-53-controls/release-search#!/800-53

7  Payment Card Industry (PCI) Security Standards Council. Official PCI Security Standards Council Site, PCI Security Standards Council®, n.d. www.pcisecuritystandards.org/

**8** SANS Institute. CIS Critical Security Controls, April 21, 2021. www.sans.
org/critical-security-controls/?msc=main-nav

## Endnotes

**1** Ellen Cranley. Cybercrime Against Healthcare Groups 'Worldwide' Is on the
Rise during Coronavirus Pandemic, Top UN Official Warns, Business Insider,
May 23, 2020, www.businessinsider.com/top-un-official-warned-of-
cybercrime-spike-during-pandemic-2020-5 (archived at https://perma.cc/
66ZB-YVTG)

**2** Louis Columbus. Dissecting The SolarWinds Hack For Greater Insights With
A Cybersecurity Evangelist, Forbes Magazine, December 27, 2020, www.
forbes.com/sites/louiscolumbus/2021/12/27/dissecting-the-solarwinds-hack-
for-greater-insights-with-a-cybersecurity-evangelist/?sh=4e39d48d23ec
(archived at https://perma.cc/W3ZL-ED6A)

**3** Ibid.

**4** CompTIA. Cybersecurity for Digital Operations, September 2019. https://
comptiacdn.azureedge.net/webcontent/docs/default-source/research-reports/
cybersecurity-for-digital-operations.pdf?sfvrsn=43ae3c1d_0 (archived at
https://perma.cc/747P-GHL4)

**5** Deloitte & Touche LLP. The Future of Cyber Survey 2019, 2019. www2.
deloitte.com/za/en/pages/risk/articles/2019-future-of-cyber-survey.html
(archived at https://perma.cc/NKN2-UTHR)

**6** IBM Cloud Education. What Is DevSecOps? [blog] IBM, July 30, 2020. www.
ibm.com/cloud/learn/devsecops (archived at https://perma.cc/ZG37-MPDW)

**7** Deloitte & Touche LLP. The Future of Cyber Survey 2019, 2019. www2.
deloitte.com/za/en/pages/risk/articles/2019-future-of-cyber-survey.html
(archived at https://perma.cc/NKN2-UTHR)

**8** B Cheatham, K Javanmardian, and H Samandari. Confronting the Risks of
Artificial Intelligence [blog] McKinsey & Company, April 26, 2019. www.
mckinsey.com/business-functions/mckinsey-analytics/our-insights/confronting-
the-risks-of-artificial-intelligence (archived at https://perma.cc/MA7Q-FUS2)

**9** Ibid.

**10** Deloitte & Touche LLP. The Future of Cyber Survey 2019, 2019. www2.
deloitte.com/za/en/pages/risk/articles/2019-future-of-cyber-survey.html
(archived at https://perma.cc/NKN2-UTHR)

**11** PwC. Global Digital Trust Insight Survey 2021, October 2020. www.pwc.com/
us/en/services/consulting/cybersecurity/library/global-digital-trust-insights.html
(archived at https://perma.cc/M45F-GB4U)

**12** Ibid.

# 10

# Crisis Management

BY GARY MCALUM, CHIEF SECURITY OFFICER, USAA, AND BEN PEIFER,
ISA RESEARCH ASSOCIATE

## Five Key Ideas to Take Away from This Chapter

1 Having an incident response plan will allow an organization to respond more quickly and more efficiently to a cyber crisis.

2 Periodically rehearsing and pressure testing the incident response plan will increase response efficiency and reduce cost.

3 Establish relationships with law enforcement agencies, external subject matter experts in forensics and crisis communications, and regulatory organizations early and work to maintain those relationships so that they can be effectively utilized in a crisis.

4 Track and document actions taken during a crisis in order to be able to conduct an After-Action Review to enhance continuous improvement.

5 The faster an organization can detect and respond to a crisis the better off it will be.

## Introduction

Although strategies described in other chapters of this book will significantly mitigate the risks of facing cybersecurity incidents, they do not eliminate the possibility of incidents from ever occurring. The cyber threat landscape continues to swiftly grow as the sophistication and number of attacks increases. No business is immune from a potential attack. Therefore, businesses should prepare for the virtually inevitable attack. Knowing that they will be breached, businesses should prepare their responses before-hand.[1] Since not all incidents can be prevented, response is a critical component of a cybersecurity program. Incident response capability is necessary for assessing incidents, minimizing loss and destruction, mitigat-ing exploited weaknesses and restoring businesses. This chapter outlines the steps that organizations should take to ensure that they have an effective incident response program.

Former FBI Director Robert Mueller once said, "There are only two types of companies: those that have been hacked, and those that will be".[2] To make matters worse, those of us protecting cyber systems must be right 100% of the time while the attackers only have to get lucky once. This real-ity speaks to the complexity of an organization's IT environment and the challenges of keeping it updated, such as configured correctly with security patches applied and so on. On the other hand, the bad guys operate anony-mously in cyber space, using a variety of tools and information sources to target vulnerabilities that an organization may not even know exist, and they have the luxury of choosing when to strike. Maybe it will happen during the middle of the week, during normal work hours, or maybe it happens at midnight on a holiday weekend, but it happens! It's a daunting challenge.

KNOW WHEN YOU FAIL

This applies to both the activities of attackers and the activities of employees. Attackers will get into your network. It is inevitable. What counts is how fast you detect them, which places a high premium on monitoring and keeping the number of one-off systems to a minimum. It means your network architecture must have choke points to provide visibility for monitoring more efficiently. And it means a company must capture and store data or metadata about system and network activities. Employees will also disable, bypass, or ignore policies and controls. This, too, is inevitable, so you must also have the technical or manual means to audit an employee's assets (how a desktop computer or server is configured or used) and what they do with data (data leak protection).

The need for cyber incident response capabilities became glaringly obvious as the SolarWinds incident emerged into global view in December 2020.[3] This cyber incident affecting over 18,000 companies and government agencies and could take years to fully understand and respond to. Based on what is known—and details will continue to evolve in the months and years ahead—the level of compromise for some organizations could be significant, requiring total rebuild of corporate networks.[4] As word of the SolarWinds compromise emerged and the magnitude became clearer, many companies activated incident response plans just to start the process for assessing impact. For companies without a plan, the response was more chaotic and, ultimately, less effective. There is no more obvious case for needing to have a well thought-out response plan than the SolarWinds compromise.

---

### KNOW WHAT TO DO WHEN YOU FAIL

This seems like a simple principle, but it has broad implications. At the technical level, it is about a security organization's incident response capabilities. Can they not only detect attackers, but do they also have (or contract for) the processes and skills to track the attacker's activities, find all of the backdoors, and cleanse the network? More than a few major attacks have reappeared a few months later because a company missed one computer with a backdoor. But this principle also has policy implications. A security organization must have the leadership's backing to make hard decisions in a crisis, and—more importantly—the difficult or unpopular decisions before a crisis. The senior leadership itself must understand and be able to perform its role in a cyber crisis that has become public or has regulatory implications.

---

As a result, it's imperative that an organization prepare for the worst-case scenario. The age-old military training motto absolutely applies here, "the harder we train in peacetime, the less we bleed in battle".

The NIST Cybersecurity Framework (NIST CSF) is comprised of five Functions: Identify, Protect, Detect, Respond, and Recover. The activities required to fulfill these functions are best articulated in a written Incident Response Plan (IRP).

## What is an Incident Response Plan (IRP)?

An IRP is an organization's formal approach to addressing and managing the aftermath of a security breach or cyber-attack. Most importantly, an IRP is an approach that is thought through and published, with responsible parties made aware preemptively. In many ways a good crisis response plan is a lot like life insurance, "it's too late to get it when you really need it, if you don't already have it".

Moreover, an IRP is orderly and systematic, like a drill that employees can follow through as if via muscle memory. When a breach occurs, a company may go into panic mode and be too overwhelmed to respond appropriately, unless they are well prepared. An inadequately prepared company may go directly into damage control and chaos may occur. The purpose of an IRP is to combat these kinds of impulsive reactions. Well-designed IRPs tackle breaches in a cost and time effective manner. An IRP is not just a broad framework of values to remember during an incident. It is a written document with step-by-step instructions on exactly how to proceed and who to contact. Ultimately, the goals of IRPS are to restore operations, minimize losses, fix vulnerabilities quickly and thoroughly and strengthen security to avoid future incidents.[5]

## Why do you Need a Plan?

As we documented in Chapter 1, cyberattacks have dramatically increased and are likely to continue to increase due to the advantages and benefits enjoyed by the attacker community. Organizations across all industry verticals are dealing with a massive number and variety of cyberattacks. Attacks may start with targeted email phishing campaigns but end up in a ransomware situation where the organization has been totally compromised and now is at the mercy of an unknown cyber-criminal entity. Some organizations have also been threatened with denial of service attacks that promise to knock an organization's e-commerce capabilities offline. Finally, the threat of an old-fashioned smash-and-grab data breach where anything from consumer personal data to corporate business plans may be stolen is always lurking as a distinct possibility.

Unfortunately, despite years of publicity regarding the cyber threat, still too many companies fail to adequately plan for the inevitable attacks. According to a 2019 survey conducted by CS&A International and PR News and reported in Forbes,[6] only about 62% of companies had crisis plans, and it was uncertain how many updated them on a regular basis. Almost 60% of the middle and senior managers surveyed said they have never conducted a crisis exercise or were not sure how often their companies held exercises. It's also important to realize the process of building the plan is perhaps more important than the actual plan itself.

As WWII general and former President Dwight Eisenhower once said, "Plans are useless, but planning is indispensable". Working through the details and questions that need to be answered in the comfort of a non-crisis environment can be invaluable to all stakeholders involved.

## Business Capabilities and Function Required to Support Incident Response

Cybersecurity incident response, like other aspects of cybersecurity, is an enterprise-wide issue which transcends the information technology department. A variety of teams across the organization must be engaged in the incident response for the response to be an effective one: governance, protective capabilities, detection, response and recovery.

### Governance

Governance describes the policies and processes which determine how organizations detect, prevent, and respond to cyber incidents. The International Standards Organization (ISO) and International Electrotechnical Commission (IEC) define IT governance as:

> The system by which an organization directs and controls security governance, specifies the accountability framework and provides oversight to ensure that risks are adequately mitigated, while management ensures that controls are implemented to mitigate risks.[7]

Governance and management are not synonymous. As outlined in Chapter 2, the board is broadly responsible for cyber risk oversight including a focus on strategic planning, however, it is the management team that is responsible for implementing plans and operations to secure the organization's information.[8]

### Protective Capabilities

An effective cyber-IRP will have clearly defined layers of protection spread across computers, networks, programs, devices, and data. These different capabilities all are working in coordination to ensure the safety of the systems they are protecting. Across the business, the people, technology, and infrastructure must all communicate with one another to guarantee a strong defense against possible attacks.[9]

## Detection

Threat detection involves monitoring and analyzing the organization's security ecosystem to identify any malicious activity that could compromise the network. This includes not only analyzing the business itself, but also other parties, such as suppliers, whose systems are linked to the organization and would allow a breach in one system to affect another. Chapter 8 provides a detailed analysis of these third-party risks and responsibilities. If a threat is detected, then mitigation efforts must be deployed effectively to terminate the threat before it can exploit any present vulnerabilities. Moreover, the concept of threat detection is multifaceted and multidisciplinary within a business's cybersecurity plan.

## Response

The IRP covers the methods that an organization uses to respond to and manage a cyberattack. The purpose of an IRP is to reduce the financial, legal and reputational damages of a cyber incident and recover as quickly as possible to ensure business continuation. Investigation is also a key component in order to learn from the attack and better prepare for the future. A strong response plan is essential because as cyberattacks increase in frequency and gravity, incident response plans become more vital to an organization's cyber risk management strategy. A poor incident response can decrease customers' trust and increase government regulation.[10]

## Recover

The NIST CSF defines "Recover" as the need to "develop and implement the appropriate activities to maintain plans for resilience and to restore any capabilities or services that were impaired due to a cyber security event". It is an umbrella term which covers recover planning, improvement, and communication.[11]

# Questions Senior Management Should Consider in Developing an IRP

As discussed previously, this book builds on the NACD-ISA Cyber Risk Oversight 2020 Handbook. That handbook outlines principles board of directors should follow in fulfilling their cyber risk oversight responsibilities. The current volume is designed as a guide for how management can meet the expectations boards will develop following the NACD-ISA Principles. This chapter specifically builds on Toolkit E, in that document, Incident Response. That section highlights the importance of how a company responds to attacks and notes the direct correlation with impacts to its brand reputation and stock valuation.

The board's expectations of management are encapsulated in a series of questions as a starting point to assess their organization's a crisis response plan.

## Incident Playbook and Overall Strategy

*Is there an incident playbook with clear definitions of incidents, roles and responsibilities, and escalation processes? Are core business functions such as IT, business, legal, and communication integrated into the response plan? How does it fit into the company's overall crisis and business recovery plan?*

An Incident Response Playbook is designed to provide a step-by-step walk-through for most probable and impactful cyber threats to your organization. The playbook will ensure that certain steps of the IRP are followed appropriately and serve as a reminder if certain steps in the plans are not in place.[12] As discussed in Chapter 3, cybersecurity management is an enterprise-wide issue, and therefore major components of a strong Incident Response Playbook include integration of core business functions and multiple departments into the response plan. Another component is an analysis of how the response to the cyber incident will fit into the company's overall crisis and business recovery plan.

Some people may confuse the term "playbook" with "checklist". These are two different, but related concepts. The overall playbook is really the framework on how a crisis, or incident, will be handled as it evolves. There may be several checklists within the playbook for particular functional areas or topics. For example, Corporate Communications might have a checklist that lists several actions such as developing an internal message for the CEO to send to all employees, developing and pre-staging basic talking points for call center representatives if customers call, developing public message for corporate website posting, monitoring social media trends and developing responses to expected questions for use by social media team, preparing a media statement, identifying spokespersons for any media interview requests, etc.

As will be discussed in more detail in this chapter, it is absolutely critical that an organization has an IRP already developed, coordinated, and periodically pressure-tested through tabletop exercises. These exercises, and other simulations, help taking the overall strategy and clarify how it will be operationalized in a variety of different instances and addressing multiple vexing questions that may come up in a crisis situation.

### THE PLAYBOOK DEFINES SOME KEY ELEMENTS

**Who are the stakeholders?** There typically will be a standard group that needs to be involved early on in any non-trivial incident. This standard group will typically be comprised of the Information Security team (the CIO/IT organization if they are separate), General Counsel, business representatives, and definitely the Corporate Communications team or whatever function is designated focal point for handling internal and external communications. However, there are other entities that may need be involved depending on the industry vertical and it is important that organizations identify their unique stakeholders early. For example, in a highly regulatory industry like financial services, it will be critical to have someone from regulatory relations to help coordinate specific updates to the appropriate regulatory agencies. Other potential stakeholders include outside consultants. Additionally, many organizations have crisis management specialists on retainers, and it will be important to bring them in quickly.

**Who's in charge?** The playbook should clearly identify who's in charge of guiding the overall process for however long it takes. One model is for companies to establish an Incident Management Team (IMT) based on the government's National Incident Management System.[13] The Incident Commander should be someone who is of sufficient enough level within the organization to be able to address lower-level issues while understanding when to escalate.

**What's the decision-making process?** It's one thing to get a group of people together to work through a high-pressure situation, but it's another thing to do it effectively. To do so the playbook ought to identify the key stakeholders and define operational roles and responsibilities.

For example, one company established a role within the Business Continuation area that is responsible for helping guide the process to get decisions made. There was also a facilitator, who is responsible for helping formulate the agenda, the meeting cadence, orchestrating the audio-visual systems, getting meeting invites out, tracking action items, and coordinating a myriad of actions that will go on for an indefinite period. This centralized facilitation function is critical to ensure the decision-making process can work effectively during the crisis, especially as new developments emerge. Responsibility for tracking action items also needs to be clearly assigned. This is no small task and ensuring closure can become a major administrative effort, but it must be done! Also, identifying the process to have a log or audit trail of all key decisions made will be critical as inevitably someone or some regulatory agency may want to know what key decisions were made, particularly if a risk acceptance component was part of it. Most major cyber crisis events will not be over quick so ensuring that audit trail of decisions is established is key to the overall process.

## Escalation Criteria and Final Decision-Making Authority

*What are the escalation criteria for notifying senior leadership and the board if necessary? Who has final decision-making authority?*

Incidents occur all the time. Often the cyber risk management team will be capable of managing the issue fully and appropriately thanks to adequate planning and training. However, there is also the question of when the issues transcend the decision-making authority and ability of the cyber risk management team. As such, organizations should have clear criteria for when the cyber teams should escalate concerns to notify senior leadership outside of their department, as well as the board. Moreover, once these outside individuals are notified, the organization should have criteria for additional roles and responsibilities including which organizational leader will be granted final decision-making authority.

### What's the Framework for Escalating Decisions?

During a crisis, it's important to not only have a process to follow for making initial decisions, but more importantly to know how to escalate decisions and to whom. This is where there needs to be clarity between the role of the initial cyber risk team, senior management and in truly significant cases, the board. Since incidents may present situations that do not clearly follow pre-existing structures or protocols table-top exercises can be extremely helpful in walking through an artificial crisis and having the opportunity to sort through the nuances of how and when to escalate. For example, an early decision that will undoubtedly happen will be if/when to invoke attorney-client privilege on all communications surrounding the event. There will be pros and cons to this decision and, if implemented, will have ramifications on other decisions such as if/when to involve law enforcement. The tabletop exercise can help clarify some of the gray area decisions or at least help define how these decisions will be achieved best in real-time actual events.

It's worth pointing out that the process and criteria for when a decision goes to the board is not always so simple. Sometimes it depends on the personality of the board and how the relationship between board and senior management has worked in the past. Some CEOs may be very controlling and want to limit board involvement until absolutely necessary. Other CEOs may be more collaborative and have an almost continuous dialogue. The culture of the organization can have a strong impact on decisions in a crisis situation and hence working things out in advance and achieving functional clarity is imperative.

In a serious breach, it's likely that the board will be actively and heavily engaged. That will generate an entire schedule of meetings, updates, board communications and potentially a new set of players brought into the mix such as shareholders. Information overload can quickly kick in so it's imperative to have all elements of the IRP decision-making process, information management, action item tracking, working together. Tabletop exercises can validate processes and pressure-test a variety of use cases to highlight who has final authority for a particular level of decision. According to a 2019 McKinsey report for the National Association of Corporate Directors (NACD):

> Relationships between managers and those who oversee them become frayed; information flows are found wanting; existing tensions and dysfunctions within the board and the C-suite—problems that may have seemed tolerable in normal times—become inflamed; and relationships break down. In the worst cases, a vicious cycle of blame and mistrust establishes itself at the highest level of the company, causing it to make serious missteps or to become paralyzed.[14]

The consequence of not having clear lines of responsibility, such as between board and senior management can lead to dysfunction and paralysis in a real crisis.

## Organizational Resiliency Testing and Simulation

*Is the organizational resiliency tested around large risk scenarios and exercised through tabletops and common threat simulation?*

Organizational resilience is "the ability of an organization to anticipate, prepare for, respond and adapt to incremental change and sudden disruptions in order to survive and prosper".[15] Like many aspects of cyber risk management, organizational resiliency is an issue that reaches beyond traditional understanding of risk management towards a more holistic view of business health and success. Just as important as the need to have a strategy is to have the ability to implement these strategies.

As highlighted above, tabletop discussions and full-blown simulation exercises are extremely helpful in preparing for an incident. Many companies, particularly in regulated industry verticals, already conduct exercises throughout the year for a variety of scenarios typically led by the Business Continuation team. These exercises are formalized affairs and typically involved an after-action review (AAR) and a final report documenting issues, opportunities, and lessons learned. The beauty of a robust exercise program is that some of the worst, most difficult situations can be considered before the stress of a real crisis.

A great example is around ransomware payments. The scourge of ransomware attacks has plagued companies and agencies across the world as cyber criminals have figured out how to monetize fear of an entity being shut down. One board asked a CISO, "would we ever pay a ransom?". It's a simple question without a simple answer. In this case, an exercise had coincidentally been conducted that year and the CISO was able to answer confidently, "Maybe, but only as a last resort. Let me walk you through our recent exercise how we arrived at that answer".

Another great benefit of exercises focuses on corporate communications. Every crisis will involve media relations. Exercises can help drive the development of pre-developed media statements. A recent article in *Info Security* highlights the importance and role of corporate communications in a ransomware crisis (but it applies to any major event): 'When dealing with a volatile and sophisticated cyber threat actor that yields public relations capabilities, controlling the narrative to mitigate business impact is paramount'.[16]

You don't want to have to figure out what to say and how to say it in the midst of a crisis.

## Outside Public and Private Relationships

*Are there established relationships with the government agencies and key regulators? Have information-sharing relationships been established through Information Sharing and Analysis Centers and consortiums and with other companies?*

Just as a cybersecurity team does not exist in silo, an organization exists in an ecosystem with the public sector, including the intelligence community and key regulators. An organization should have, even before a crisis, a solid relationship with law enforcement officials, such as the FBI and DHS, and regulatory bodies such as the SEC and the FTC or sector specific regulatory bodies. These relationships may also include establishing an information sharing relationship through nonprofit organizations such as an Information Sharing and Analysis Center, (ISAC) that provides a central resource for gathering information on cyber threats to critical infrastructure and providing two-way sharing of information between the private and public entities. The ecosystem also includes other companies in the sector. Many industry verticals are closely associated with Information Sharing and Analysis Centers. These organizations can be a great source of information and collaboration. For example, the Financial Services Information Sharing and Analysis Center (FS-ISAC) is extremely active in sharing threat information and driving collaboration. For example, between 2012 and 2013, a nation-state proxy was conducting target denial of service attacks against many US-based financial institutions. The FS-ISAC was instrumental in sharing near-real time threat and attack information.[17]

When you are the one going through a crisis, the sense of aloneness can seem overwhelming. Many sophisticated companies have the "standard 3" retainers in place with outside parties that will be needed in a crisis situation.

First, the cybersecurity team will likely have a forensics company on retainer ready to jump in and help, once they are notified. This, hopefully, pre-existing relationship is the cyber team's 9-1-1 call in a major cyber event. These companies specialize in rapid response. They are the cyber equivalent of "smoke jumpers" when called in to assist. Second, another key established relationship is with a crisis communication company who will likely be linked up tightly with the corporate communications team. Last, the general counsel will most certainly have outside legal advice on a short tether to be called.

In addition to the "standard 3", other relationships may include law enforcement (local and national) and cyber threat intelligence vendors that you have on contract. Any of these relationships can provide additional perspective and advice regarding your particular situation. Finally, as discussed in more detail next, if the company is in a highly regulated vertical like financial services or energy, it will certainly be expected (if not required) to inform the appropriate regulatory agencies of your situation. It's better for regulators to get a phone call informing them of an issue versus having them read about it in the news. Working closely with your regulatory affairs team can keep the right information flowing.

A more extensive list of possible entities who may be appropriate to notify depending on the unique variables of the company, its location, its business plan and other variables unique to each entity are outlined in the next section.

## Mandatory Reporting and other Regulatory Disclosure

*Does the organization have notification and mandatory reporting obligations (e.g., regarding regulations of the US Securities and Exchange Commission, the General Data Protection Regulation, the Department of Defense and Defense Security Service for cleared contractors, and the federal government)? What are they?*

Laws, both on the federal and state level, require that companies disclose this information and mandate how they disclose it, when they disclose it, what information they disclose, what they do for those affected, and to whom it must be disclosed.[18] As discussed in Chapters 2 and 6, regular coordination with the legal team and in significant cases with the board is an ongoing responsibility.

In addition to these general principles, depending on the industry sector there will also be a range of regulatory and legal implications for reporting and notification. Notable examples are (HIPAA) in the healthcare industry and Gramm-Leach-Bliley Act (GLBA) in financial services. If personal or customer data is involved, there would be many state privacies laws, like the California Consumer Privacy Act and the New York State Department of Financial Services, 23 NYCRR 500, that have to be addressed in a timely fashion. Also, international laws like the EU's General Directive on Privacy Regulation (GDPR) may also be relevant to your situation. As discussed in Chapter 2 and Chapter 6, enterprises need to keep abreast of these regularly changing requirements based on the industry sector, location and business plan.

## Investor Disclosure

*What are the criteria and what is the process for disclosing incidents to investors?*

Although breaches in themselves do not deflate stock prices (as it may be inconsequential or discreetly addressed) for those breaches that generate significant impact on an organization, there is a question of when a cyber breach is so consequential that investors should be made aware of the incident. Managers and corporate boards must follow the SEC mandate for corporations to disclose around material cybersecurity risks and incidents to their investors. Understanding heightened expectations regarding investor disclosure is vital for organizations as cybersecurity threats and incidents continue to grow more frequent and consequential for the overall performance of the organization, increasing investor's needs and desire to know.[19]

## Mitigating Losses After an Incident

As discussed in Chapter 4, organizations should develop a sophisticated cyber risk assessment that clearly, and empirically, identifies the organization's risk appetite in economic terms and identifies methods to mitigate or transfer risk from cyber incidents consistent with business plan.

The immediate aftermath of a breach is a critical time for the hacked organization. If leaders don't learn quickly what went wrong and act swiftly—in the right ways—to fix the problem, they risk exacerbating the damage in terms of financial and reputational harm.[20]

The costs of a major cyber incident depend on many factors including scope, scale, and nature of the event. Ultimately there are many cost drivers involved in a major incident. These include: the costs involved in detecting a breach, including investigation and forensics activities, assessment and audit; notification costs; lost business from system downtime and disruption and legal fees and costs related to activities like providing help desk services, credit monitoring, and ID protection for victims. Models that can assist organizations in computing the expected loss impacts of cyber events are referenced in Chapter 4. However, according to the Ponemon Institute's research for IBM in this area, a data breach on average cost companies $3.86 million per incident. The average breach cost in the US as usual was more than twice that, at $8.64 million on average.[21] As documented in Chapter 1, these costs continue to rise dramatically. Some costs, such as notification compliance, providing consumer credit monitoring, setting up call centers can be reliably predicted, and these harms can be transferred through cyber insurance. There are other costs such as loss of intellectual property and resulting negative competitive impacts and indirect costs such as impact to the company's brand that could lead to bottom line impact on customer growth and retention.

The IBM/Ponemon study showed that total data breach costs for organizations that reported having a complex security system environment was nearly $292,000 higher on average than companies that did not have the same issue. Other factors that substantially amplified the average cost of a breach included cloud migration, security skills shortages, and compliance failures.[22]

At the same time the study highlighted several other factors that can help mitigate breach costs for organizations. For instance, organizations that regularly tested their incident response plans ended up spending some $295,000 less than the global average on breach-related costs while those with a business continuity plan spent about $279,000 less. Other cost mitigating factors included red-team testing, AI-enabled response, and employee training.[23]

## Measuring Incident Response with Key Performance Indicators

Key performance indicators (KPIs) refer to a set of quantifiable measurements used to gauge a company's overall long-term performance. KPIs specifically help determine a company's strategic, financial, and operational achievements, especially compared to those of other businesses within the same sector, in specific activities.[24]

As we have repeated throughout this book, boards should identify and quantify financial exposures to cyber risks and which risks accepting, mitigate or transfer, because it is difficult to improve upon what one cannot clearly measure. KPIs provide a way to measure cybersecurity management success.

There's no murkiness when it comes to this question. The critical measurements revolve around detection and response. The average time-to-detect (or identify) refers to how long it takes to discover that an incident has occurred. Time-to-respond (or mitigate) describes how long it takes for an organization to contain the situation. These are common metrics used benchmark to assess the effectiveness of a company's incident response and containment processes. The faster incidents can be spotted and contained, the lower the costs. According to the IBM/Ponemon study, it takes an organization, on average, 280 days to spot and contain a breach. This timeframe varies among industry verticals and even within companies based on a variety of factors. However, the most important variable in the cost mitigation equation is detection. The faster the incident is discovered, the sooner that containment and mitigation can occur the lower the final costs will be.[25] When a victim was able to detect and shut down a breach in less than 200 days, total breach costs went down some $1.1 million on average.[26]

## Post-Incident

*What key steps do you follow after a critical incident? What steps do you follow to ensure this type of incident doesn't occur again?*

The steps that an organization takes after an incident are extremely crucial. These steps include those that address stakeholders in the short term and as well as to ensure that this type of incident will not occur again.

During a critical or high severity security event, the immediate focus will be on triage and containment. It may not be clear for some time how the event occurred. Was it an unpatched server? An open port? A rogue system administrator? Or did an unwitting employee click on a malware-laden attachment in a seemingly innocent email? In the short term there will always be more questions than answers. According to a recent Wall Street Journal article, many breached companies jump into action by adding controls or software that defends against the type of attack they just suffered. However, they don't address the underlying vulnerabilities. "The immediate aftermath is a time to focus on the fundamentals", says Jamil Farshchi, Chief Information Security Officer at Equifax Inc., who joined the company five months after the company's 2017 data breach. Mr. Farshchi had previously led a rehabilitation effort at Home Depot Inc. after a 2014 breach.[27]

To help answer the right questions, most companies will bring in a cyber forensics company that has the expertise and tools necessary to conduct the post-mortem analysis. This analysis may go on for weeks and even months depending on scope and scale of the event. Also, in the short term, they may need to focus on regaining control of the network, ensuring the bad guys are completely out of the system, and then helping rebuild critical services in a secure manner. Once the forensics analysis begins, it will be critical to let them focus on that tedious and significant work effort. There will certainly be a steady drumbeat of questions from all levels of leadership and outside entities, but this work is vitally important as it will become foundational for addressing many stakeholders and ultimately determining what level of liability could be ascribed to the company. In many cases, this work will be covered by attorney-client privilege and tightly controlled for obvious reasons. A great example of post-mortem analysis was in the case of the infamous Equifax data breach of 2017. In its report on the data breach, the United States Government Accountability Office (GAO) confirmed that, in July 2017, Equifax system administrators discovered that attackers had gained unauthorized access via the internet to the online dispute portal that maintained documents used to resolve consumer disputes. The Equifax breach resulted in the attackers accessing personal information of at least 145.5 million individuals. Equifax's investigation of the breach identified four major factors including identification, detection, segmenting of access to databases, and data governance that allowed the attacker to successfully gain access to its network and extract information from databases containing personally identifiable information. Equifax reported that it took steps to mitigate these factors and attempted to identify and notify individuals whose information was accessed.[28]

## Third Parties to Notify

In addition to external counsel, boards and management teams should consider when to notify independent forensic investigators, the company's insurance provider, and the company's external auditors, as well as others.

### Crisis Communications Advisors

Crisis communication advisors, who often work in a subsect of strategy consulting firms, can advise clients on how to align their actions with what they say, as well as on how to effectively convey their messages and evaluate the messages from the public's perspective.[29]

### Law Enforcement Agencies

Organization should have established relationships with law enforcements prior to incidents, including the following agencies:

- The FBI: the lead federal agency for investigating cyberattacks and intrusions.
- The Department of Homeland Security: an organization which builds the national capacity to defend against cyberattacks and works with the federal government to provide cybersecurity tools, incident response services and assessment capabilities to safeguard government networks.
- The Secret Service Cyber Fraud Task Force: a task force which facilitates coordination, sharing of expertise and resources, and dissemination of best practices for all its core investigations of financially motivated cybercrime.

## Regulatory agencies

There are various federal cybersecurity regulations which mandate how healthcare organizations, financial institutions, and federal agencies should protect their systems and information.

## Independent Forensic Investigators

Organizations can hire outside and neutral experts, such as consulting firms, to reconstruct and analyze digital information to aid in investigations and solve computer-related crimes. These independent forensic investigators look into incidents of hacking, trace sources of computer attacks, and recover lost or stolen data. Their job includes recovering data from damaged or erased hard drive, tracing hacks, gathering and maintaining evidence.[30]

## Company's insurance provider

Some insurance companies provide cyber liability insurance which covers financial losses that result from data breaches and other cyber events.

## Company's external auditor

Auditing standards require that organizations hire an outside auditor who must obtain an understanding of how the company uses information technology (IT) and the impact of IT on the financial statements. The outside auditor must understand the extent of the company's automated controls as they relate to financial reporting, including the IT general controls that are important to the effective operation of automated controls, and the reliability of data and reports produced by the company and used in the financial reporting process. In assessing the risks of material misstatement to the financial statements—including IT risks resulting from unauthorized access—financial statement auditors must consider the organization's IT systems and controls.[31]

# Conclusion

As we've seen repeatedly, and even more glaringly in light of recent events, every company needs to plan for how they would respond to a major cyber event. No matter how strong your defensive posture is, any company targeted by a sophisticated and patient attacker can be compromised. A robust response capability is essential to containing the damage and ensuring business disruption is minimized. The key to response is having a real plan that is exercised, tested, refined, and kept current. The time for developing the plan is not when the crisis hits! This chapter outlined nine key questions that companies should consider in formulating their plan on how to respond to a significant cyber crisis. There are key elements: clear delineation of responsibilities, a decision-making process, escalation framework, and crisis communications. Ultimately, the old saying is true—prior preparation prevents poor performance!

To continue learning about the concepts in this chapter the following sources are recommended:

1 Royal Bank of Canada. Cyber Security Crisis Management Template, Octobeer 21, 2019. www.rbc.com/cyber-security/_assets-custom/pdf/rbc-cyber-security-crisis-management-template-for-smbs_final_en.pdf

2 Thomas J Parenty, and Jack J. Domet. The CEO's Role In Preventing A Cyber Crisis [blog] Chief Executive, December 18, 2019. chiefexecutive.net/the-ceos-role-in-preventing-a-cyber-crisis/

3 J W Pfeifer. Preparing for Cyber Incidents with Physical Effects, *The Cyber Defense Review,* Vol. 3 Number 1. (Spring 2018). www.hks.harvard.edu/sites/default/files/centers/research-initiatives/crisisleadership/files/Pfeifer_Cyber_CDR_V3N1_SPRG2018.pdf

4 N Galletto. Focus on: The board's-eye view of cyber crisis management *Deloitte,* 2015. www2.deloitte.com/global/en/pages/risk/articles/boards-view-cyber-crisis-management.html

5 G Angafor, I Yevseyeva and Y He. Game-based learning: A review of tabletop exercises for cybersecurity incident response training *Security and Privacy,* Nov 2020. Vol. 3 (6). onlinelibrary.wiley.com/doi/full/10.1002/spy2.126

## Endnotes

1 Deloitte. Cyber Incident Response, 2017. www2.deloitte.com/content/dam/Deloitte/za/Documents/za_Cyber_Crisis_Response.pdf (archived at https://perma.cc/5YK3-7CEZ)

2  R Mueller. RSA Cyber Security Conference (Speech, San Francisco, CA, March 1, 2010). archives.fbi.gov/archives/news/speeches/combating-threats-in-the-cyber-world-outsmarting-terrorists-hackers-and-spies (archived at https://perma.cc/TJ59-CFB2)

3  Isabella Jibilian and Katie Canales. Here's a Simple Explanation of How the Massive SolarWinds Hack Happened and Why It's Such a Big Deal, *Business Insider,* December 24, 2020. www.businessinsider.com/solarwinds-hack-explained-government-agencies-cyber-security-2020-12 (archived at https://perma.cc/QCH7-85EU)

4  M J Schwartz. CISA Warns SolarWinds Incident Response May Be Substantial [blog] *Bank Information Security,* December 24, 2020. www.bankinfosecurity.com/solarwinds-cisa-warns-incident-response-may-be-substantial-a-15661 (archived at https://perma.cc/KF9K-BMDL)

5  RSI Security. The Importance of An Incident Response Plan, [blog] RSI Security, December 26, 2019. blog.rsisecurity.com/the-importance-of-an-incident-response-plan/ (archived at https://perma.cc/7HAQ-38ZC)

6  Edward Segal. 3 Ways to Ensure Your Crisis Management and Communication Plans Will Work, *Forbes Magazine,* October 18, 2020. www.forbes.com/sites/edwardsegal/2020/10/12/3-ways-to-ensure-your-crisis-management-and-communication-plans-will-work/?ss=leadership-strategy (archived at https://perma.cc/JX74-S3HV)

7  S Hedges and S Swinton. Cybersecurity Governance, Part 1: 5 Fundamental Challenges [blog] *Carnegie Mellon University: Software Engineering Institute,* July 25, 2019. insights.sei.cmu.edu/insider-threat/2019/07/cybersecurity-governance-part-1-5-fundamental-challenges.html (archived at https://perma.cc/4E77-FYSG)

8  S Atkinson. Breaking the divide Between Governance and Operational Cybersecurity [blog] *Center for Internet Security, n.d.* www.cisecurity.org/blog/breaking-the-divide-between-governance-and-operational-cybersecurity/ (archived at https://perma.cc/3QNN-KECW)

9  Barracuda. Glossary-What is Cybersecurity? [blog] *Barracuda, n.d.* www.barracuda.com/glossary/cyber-security (archived at https://perma.cc/K9RK-A2T6)

10  RSI Security. The Importance of An Incident Response Plan, [blog] RSI Security, December 26, 2019. blog.rsisecurity.com/the-importance-of-an-incident-response-plan/ (archived at https://perma.cc/7HAQ-38ZC)

11  National Institute of Standards and Technology. Framework for Improving Critical Infrastructure Cybersecurity, 12 February 2014. www.nist.gov/system/files/documents/cyberframework/cybersecurity-framework-021214.pdf (archived at https://perma.cc/PFL7-X6HK)

**12**  SBS Cyber Security. 7 Steps to Building an Incident Response Playbook [blog] sbscyber, February 6, 2020. https://sbscyber.com/resources/7-steps-to-building-an-incident-response-playbook (archived at https://perma.cc/XZ5X-BH3Y)

**13**  Department of Homeland Security. National Incident Management System: Third Edition, October 2017. www.fema.gov/sites/default/files/2020-07/fema_nims_doctrine-2017.pdf (archived at https://perma.cc/RGB7-ZWH8)

**14**  R Bew, F Van der Oord and L Liu. Building Board-Management Dynamics to Withstand a Crisis: Addressing the fault lines, September 2019. www.mckinsey.com/~/media/McKinsey/Business%20Functions/Risk/Our%20Insights/Building%20board%20management%20dynamics%20to%20withstand%20a%20crisis%20Addressing%20the%20fault%20lines/Building-board-management-dynamics-to-withstand-a-crisis-Addressing-the-fault-lines.pdf (archived at https://perma.cc/LQR5-AMYB)

**15**  D Denyer. Organizational Resilience: A Summary of Academic Evidence, Business Insights and New Thinking, 2017. cranfieldsombrochures.cld.bz/Organisational-Report (archived at https://perma.cc/WJ6W-22Q6)

**16**  M Griffanti and E Roberts. The Convergence of Ransomware and Public Relations, *Infosecurity Magazine,* November 16, 2020. www.infosecurity-magazine.com/opinions/convergence-ransomware-pr/ (archived at https://perma.cc/HSV2-8PDT)

**17**  Council on Foreign Relations. *Denial of service attacks against U.S. banks in 2012–2013,* September 2012. www.cfr.org/cyber-operations/denial-service-attacks-against-us-banks-2012-2013 (archived at https://perma.cc/QUB2-USYW)

**18**  S E Tuma. Guide to Responding to Data Breaches and Reporting Cybersecurity Incidents to Law Enforcement and Governmental Agencies [blog] *Business Cyber Risk,* October 1, 2020. shawnetuma.com/cyber-law-resources/guide-reporting-cybersecurity-incidents-law-enforcement-governmental-regulatory-agencies/ (archived at https://perma.cc/AJL9-PXFP)

**19**  PWC. Rethinking Cybersecurity Disclosures to Investors, June 2018. www.pwc.com/us/en/cybersecurity/assets/pwc-rethinking-cybersecurity-disclosures-to-investors.pdf (archived at https://perma.cc/P3W5-GKNJ)

**20**  Rob Sloan. What to Do-and What Not to Do-in the Aftermath of a Cybersecurity Attack, *The Wall Street Journal.*, December 8, 2020, www.wsj.com/articles/what-to-doand-not-doin-the-aftermath-of-a-cybersecurity-attack-11607461064 (archived at https://perma.cc/889M-MLT5)

**21**  IBM Security, Ponemon Institute. Cost of Data Breach Report:2020, 2020. www.ibm.com/security/digital-assets/cost-data-breach-report/#/pdf (archived at https://perma.cc/E4GZ-FLRZ)

**22**  IBM Security, Ponemon Institute. Cost of Data Breach Report:2020, 2020. www.ibm.com/security/digital-assets/cost-data-breach-report/#/pdf (archived at https://perma.cc/E4GZ-FLRZ)

**23**  IBM Security, Ponemon Institute. Cost of Data Breach Report:2020, 2020. www.ibm.com/security/digital-assets/cost-data-breach-report/#/pdf (archived at https://perma.cc/E4GZ-FLRZ)

**24**  A Twin. Understanding Key Performance Indicators (KPIs) [blog] *Investopedia,* August 28, 2020. www.investopedia.com/terms/k/kpi.asp (archived at https://perma.cc/FAQ2-DFGZ)

**25**  Ponemon Institute. 2017 Cost of Data Breach Study, June 2017. www.ponemon.org/research/ponemon-library/security/2017-cost-of-data-breach-study-united-states.html (archived at https://perma.cc/8QDR-J3KP)

**26**  IBM Security, Ponemon Institute. Cost of Data Breach Report:2020, 2020. www.ibm.com/security/digital-assets/cost-data-breach-report/#/pdf (archived at https://perma.cc/E4GZ-FLRZ)

**27**  Rob Sloan. What to Do-and What Not to Do-in the Aftermath of a Cybersecurity Attack, *The Wall Street Journal,* December 8, 2020, www.wsj.com/articles/what-to-doand-not-doin-the-aftermath-of-a-cybersecurity-attack-11607461064 (archived at https://perma.cc/889M-MLT5)

**28**  U.S. Government Accountability Office. *Data Protection: Actions Taken by Equifax and Federal Agencies in Response to the 2017 Breach*, August 2018. www.gao.gov/assets/700/694158.pdf (archived at https://perma.cc/S6YU-DQ4G)

**29**  Center for Audit Quality. Understanding Cybersecurity and the External Audit in the COVID-19 Environment, July 24, 2020. www.thecaq.org/understanding-cybersecurity-and-the-external-audit-in-the-covid-19-environment/ (archived at https://perma.cc/JUA3-E2CK)

**30**  T Roufa. Forensic Computer and Digital Forensics: Salary, Work Environment, and Education [blog] *the balance careers,* November 27, 2019. www.thebalancecareers.com/digital-forensics-job-and-salary-information-974469 (archived at https://perma.cc/YMB9-3VN7)

**31**  Center for Audit Quality. Understanding Cybersecurity and the External Audit in the COVID-19 Environment, July 24, 2020. www.thecaq.org/understanding-cybersecurity-and-the-external-audit-in-the-covid-19-environment/ (archived at https://perma.cc/JUA3-E2CK)

# 11

# Cybersecurity Considerations During M and A Phases

BY ANDREW COTTON, PARTNER, EY, AND CARTER ZHENG,
ISA RESEARCH ASSOCIATE

## Five Key Ideas to Take Away from This Chapter

1 In the current landscape, cybersecurity due diligence often receives limited focus under tight time constraints.

2 Acquirers need to conduct cyber risk assessments as early as possible in the process.

3 During the identification phase, acquirers need to identify the cybersecurity risks before engagement with the target, model the financial impact, and understand the regulatory environment.

4 During the due diligence phase, acquirers need to estimate the cost of cyber risk remediation in order to meet defined standards under transitional services arrangements.

5 During the integration phase, acquirers need a plan to remediate compliance concerns, address risk exposure, and integrate security operations—wherever appropriate.

## Introduction

Over the past few years, numerous high-profile cybersecurity incidents have emerged during or after large Mergers and Acquisitions (M and A) deals. These incidents have raised concerns among corporate executives, investors, and regulators. For example, in 2017, a large internet company disclosed three consecutive data breaches between the initial announcement and closing of its acquisition. The acquirer ultimately reduced its initial offer by $350 million, a 7% price cut, with the acquiree also guaranteeing 50% of liabilities caused by future data breaches.[1]

Corporate executives and M and A professionals will point to improved processes and outsourced services to identify and prevent security issues. However, despite heightened awareness and the existence of various vendors who can assist in the cybersecurity elements of the M and A process, many believe the cyber risks for a potential acquirer in M and A transactions are increasing.

The dynamics of the M and A market can make identification of risk difficult. Investment banks frequently engage in an auction process to foster competitive dynamics between interested bidders. Under tight time constraints, when a delay could create significant financial and opportunity cost, acquirers may be inclined to rush the due diligence in a deal process.

In a typical deal process, acquirers need to balance internal resources to evaluate a target while quickening the process to remain competitive. Simultaneously, the decision makers in an M and A transaction will tend to approach the strategy, finance, legal, or operational risks before accounting for cyber risks. As noted by Rob Gurzeev of TechCrunch:

> With limited time and less priority on cybersecurity, M and A teams are inclined to focus on more "urgent" transactional areas of the deal process, including negotiating key business terms, business and market trend analysis, accounting, debt financing, and internal approvals. With an average of only 2–3 months to evaluate a transaction before signing, cybersecurity typically only receives a limited amount of focus.[2] It is probably not a coincidence that a recent poll of IT professionals by Forescout showed that 65% of respondents expressed buyer's remorse due to cybersecurity issues. Only 36% of those polled felt that they had adequate time to evaluate cybersecurity threats.[3]

As the cost of breaches climbs, companies are taking a fresh look at the role of security reviews in the due diligence process. While an acquirer may be loath to reject a deal solely for the sake of identified or suspected cyber risks, companies want as much certainty and quantification as possible about the scale of their inherited risks and are negotiating deal terms that either build the cost of any needed remediation into the arrangement or offer insurance or other means of claw-back if the identified vulnerability becomes an incident.

Timely identification of cyber risks allows appropriate quantification of the valuation considerations, including estimated one-time and recurring costs to remediate cyber vulnerabilities or gaps in regulatory compliance. An acquirer that follows those principles can demonstrate to its board, shareholders, and regulators that they are proactively mitigating cyber risk—while protecting the deal value and strategic drivers.

## When is the Best Time to Conduct the Risk Assessment in M and A? The Earlier, the Better

Because the cyber threat landscape has changed quite dramatically and will continue to evolve, companies need to assess cyber threats and calculate cyber risks proactively. Early investigation and identification of the target company's cyber posture and risks are critical during the M and A process. Surprisingly, a 2020 report by IBM shows more than half of surveyed companies do not perform their cybersecurity assessments until after the completion of due diligence.[4] Forescout similarly indicates that only 38% of their surveyed acquirers started the evaluation at the point at which the strategy determinations were being conducted.[5] In fact, the earlier cybersecurity assessment takes place during the M and A process, the more resilient will be the remediation opportunities available to the acquirer. Therefore, acquirers need to start risk assessment from the very beginning of the M and A process and continue through integration and post-integration

When companies conduct a risk assessment, they should be aware that:

- A cyberattack may have already resulted in the loss of the target company's intellectual property, thus reducing the value of the company.
- A cyberattack that occurred prior to closing, regardless of when it was detected, could expose the parent company to investigation costs, financial liability, regulatory penalties, or reputational damage.
- Attackers might still be in the acquired company's network, creating a risk of the attacker migrating into the parent company's network.
- The acquired company may be targeted immediately after the announcement, because the presumably less cybersecurity-mature, smaller acquisition target could become a backdoor into the larger company when their networks are connected. Additionally, the subsequent integration of the acquiree's legacy systems or applications (such as ERP) may introduce

malware and or other vulnerabilities to the acquirer through the third parties hired to build and deploy the integrated solution.

In fact, the risk of attack may start even before an official offer or merger announcement is made. Sophisticated attackers look for hints that a company is considering a merger, acquisition, or divestiture. They may be tipped off by industry chatter, a slowdown in a company's release cycle, staff reductions, or data leakage through social media channels. According to published reports, hackers have in the past targeted law firms, signaling that thieves are scouring the digital landscape for more sophisticated types of information than credit card accounts. Law firms, financial advisers, and other associated firms are attractive to hackers not only because they hold trade secrets and other sensitive information about corporate clients but also because they are privy to details about early-stage deal exploration that could be stolen to inform insider trading or to gain a competitive advantage in deal negotiations.

Accordingly, management should start to conduct a cyber risk assessment for each phase of the transaction life cycle. Chapter 4 suggests assessment tools that can quantify cyber risks that may impact the company before, during, and after the deal process.

## Strategy and Target Identification Phase

Effective security governance is integral to a high-functioning cybersecurity strategy. Perhaps the most important aspect of effective governance is ongoing review and renewal, since best practices evolve quickly as technology changes and hackers seek to exploit open loopholes. In an interview for an article with West Monroe, Paul Cotter states "when scrutinizing a potential M and A target's security governance, several questions are important to answer:

- Does the company have appropriate policies and procedures in place for its risk profile?
- How well are those policies documented?
- Does the company actively review and manage its policies for changes in business or outside threats?"[6]

The fact gathering in the earliest stages of the transaction should be multi-discipline, at a minimum involving legal, corporate development and security specialists, to identify and evaluate all relevant publicly available information on the target's cyber "history" including any disclosed or rumored undisclosed breaches. By using analytics to monitor social media, the acquiror can also access real-time information on how a target's cyber reputation is perceived by customers and its marketplace.

During the strategy and target identification phase, management should therefore gain an understanding of cyber risks associated with the target company and model the impact of those risks to compliance posture, financial forecasts, reputation, and potential impacts on the valuation. premium.

Management can perform the following analyses even before direct engagement with the target company:

**Modeling the financial impact of identified cyber risks:** Risk factors, vulnerabilities, and consequences need to be analyzed and quantified. This should include cyber risk models that can reflect not only the impact on a company's return on invested capital, but also the results of loss of competitive advantages, costly remediation, fines, and possibly years of litigation, depending on what was stolen. An initial estimate of the impact may be material enough to encourage strategy teams to alter a deal trajectory. The estimate can be refined as the transaction process continues and as risks are mitigated.

**Understanding the cybersecurity regulatory environment of the target company:** Cybersecurity regulations at the state level in the United States vary widely, and each industry faces an increasing number of US federal regulators. Outside of the United States, other countries are increasingly implementing their own cybersecurity laws and regulations, which at times can be at odds with the regulations with which the acquiring company has experience. Of particular note, the implementation of the European Union's Global Data Protection Rule (GDPR) which can lead to potentially massive penalties (up to 4% of a company's revenues) represents a significant acquisition risk that boards should understand before moving forward with any acquisition involving the data of European individuals.

The most fundamental step for managing information and privacy risks related to the transaction is understanding what types of data the target organization creates, receives and collects as part of its business processes. Only by understanding what data they have will the acquiror be able to determine the legal and regulatory requirements with which they must comply post combination. Privacy compliance in particular is impossible without knowing the types of personal data that are being collected by the target and from whom.

As a starting point, companies should consider requesting the target's data inventory that identifies the types of data that are most critical to the target organization (e.g., intellectual property, financial documents), require special handling or protection (e.g., personal data), or are required by law or regulation (e.g., records). Inventories can then be used by the acquiror to develop classification frameworks to identify these key data types across the target enterprise. Organizations are increasingly using advanced text analytics and various artificial intelligence (AI) technologies to inventory and classify data. Search criteria and predictive analytics are established to explicitly identify types of data and where the data is stored.

Knowing what data the target organization holds is of limited use unless you also know where it is. Organizations that cannot efficiently locate personal data will be hard-pressed to demonstrate compliance with privacy regulations, including responding to data subject access requests (DSARs) within prescribed timelines, implementing proper controls for protecting personal data in systems and repositories, and implementing appropriate transfer tools and safeguards when transferring data across jurisdictions and to third parties.

Protecting the privacy of customer and employee data is impossible without appropriate technical and organizational security measures. The target should have controls in place to ensure that personal data is safeguarded from unauthorized access, processing, destruction and damage.

Finally, the acquiror should understand the target's controls over disposition of data once it exceeds retention requirements and need not be preserved under any legal hold. A sound information governance strategy is preemptively disposing of data before it exceeds retention requirements and propagates across systems. Deletion requests from data subjects pose a growing privacy risk as they must be handled in compliance with relevant regulations, under strict deadlines. Under both the GDPR and the California Consumer Privacy Act (CCPA), it is not enough for an organization to dispose of personal data upon request—its processors and service providers must delete that information as well.

## Due Diligence and Deal Execution Phases

During these phases, cybersecurity due diligence is critical. Significant identified problems would call for negotiation of a reduction in purchase price to cover costs of necessary remediation. Depending on the risks identified, the board may want to manage identified matters through a transitional services arrangement with each party's responsibilities clearly identified, may defer approving the transaction until remediation is complete, or may decide to back out of a transaction if the identified risks are too great to scope/assume. Due diligence teams can identify cyber risks by conducting a tailored cybersecurity assessment designed to:

- identify insufficient investments in cybersecurity infrastructure, as well as deficiencies in staff resources, policies, etc.;
- identify lax cultural attitudes toward cyber risk;
- determine cybersecurity-related terms and conditions (or the lack thereof) in customer and supplier contracts that have a potential financial impact or result in litigation for noncompliance;
- discover noncompliance with cybersecurity-related data privacy laws or other applicable regulations and requirements;
- identify recent data breaches or other cybersecurity incidents.

Ideally, the acquiring company would assess these risks through an on-site assessment, especially when the target is a small company where under-spending on IT and cybersecurity is more likely. Such an assessment would review the security architecture, conduct forensic analysis on key network devices, and review logs looking for any indication the target might already be compromised. It should also include a review of recent or ongoing breach responses, tools, policies, and regulatory positions to identify security gaps, risks, and potential liabilities.

The output of the assessment would be a very rough estimate of the cost of bringing the target up to the acquirer's defined standards (which might affect the business case) and an assessment of whether or not elements of the target's intellectual property is already publicly available or in the hands of competitors. Acquirers may consider establishing a contingency fund to be held in escrow for potential exposures that may occur after closing. Where there has been a recent breach, the assessment should also reveal if the target has made sufficient improvement to prevent a recurrence. Boards should not, however, assume that on-site assessments are guaranteed to identify all deficiencies. The nature of due diligence means the assessment team may not be given access to interview key security personnel who are not aware of the potential acquisition.

Prioritization will certainly be a necessary key judgment. Some issues may need to be addressed immediately if the acquired company is going to be integrated within the short term. If the entity is to be run as a separate, wholly owned subsidiary, however, the target's risks may be "quarantined", although the risk of a known vulnerability impacting the acquiring company's reputation should always get a high level of attention in the due diligence evaluation, regardless of the integration plan.

Acquirers should fully understand the target company's requirement for domestic and global compliance and reporting. Depending on the industry and the target company locations, the regulatory environment of the target company could be very different than that of the acquirer. The acquirer must not only understand any new regulatory requirements, but must also demand information on any recent, current, or anticipated engagements with regulators due to cyber incidents. It should be noted that the Federal Trade Commission (FTC) views statements made by companies in their privacy policies as "promises" that should be kept even when the company that made them has been acquired by another.

Acquirers should consider conducting "dark web" (anonymously run and difficult-to-access websites favored by hackers) searches about the target, their systems, data, and intellectual property. This helps identify whether the company is already on attackers' radar, whether its systems or credentials are already compromised, or whether its sensitive data is for sale or being solicited.

Acquirers should also consider engaging vendors specializing in researching malware infections to look for infections in the target company and for any holes in their defenses that are visible from the outside. This cybersecurity hygiene-related information is publicly available and can be used to compare one company to another, allowing management to save time and energy by not pursuing companies whose risk profile is unacceptably high.

Effective due diligence on cybersecurity issues demonstrates to investors, regulators, and other stakeholders that management is actively seeking to protect the value and strategic drivers of the transaction, and that they are aiming to lower the risk of a cyberattack before integration. These risks can then be factored into the initial price paid and into performance improvement investments, enabling a robust transaction proposal to be presented to shareholders for approval.

Evolution in the legal landscape must be taken into account for effective due diligence. For example, the US Securities and Exchange Commission's 2018 Cybersecurity Guidance states that companies should consider disclosing risks arising from acquisitions in the Risk Factors section of their periodic filings. Moreover, global requirements should also be considered during the acquisition process. Requirements in the European Union's General Data Protection Regulation, as described above, might affect what sensitive information can be shared between potential buyers and the seller company.

After the public deal announcement and before close and subsequent integration, new threats may emerge. Malicious actors know that there will be security audits in this period and granting of temporary network access to outsiders, so they may look to take advantage of the situation to penetrate networks in this period.[7]

## Integration Phase

Once the organization has made the decision to acquire or divest, it needs a plan to remediate compliance concerns, address risk exposure, and integrate security operations—where appropriate. This starts with a consolidated technology, security, and operations roadmap.

Acquirers should consider the merits of maintaining discrete operations with separate business and operating models. If the assets of the target will merge with core business operations, then integration is called for.

Aside from traditional post-deal integration challenges related to people, processes, systems, and culture, an additional cyber risk accrues to both companies on the day the deal is announced. On day one, they become a target for social engineering attacks by those seeking to use the small company as a back door into the parent. Attackers will also seek to take advantage of the inconsistencies that exist between the platforms and technology operations of the two companies. Thus, the sooner the parent company can integrate the target company into their security environment, the better.

Many of these integration activities are complex and could take a year or more to complete. Integration teams need to have the cyber expertise to address the smallest of details to identify and mitigate cyber risks, including:

- security gaps identified during preceding phases;
- prioritization of remediation activities based on potential impact of identified gaps;
- prioritization of integration activities;
- employee training on newly integrated systems.

Approvals from regulators across a number of jurisdictions might be required before a deal can close, although levels of pre-closing integration are permitted. Integration leaders should work closely with the legal team to understand these risks and requirements and to establish action plans for various situations, mitigating the risk of any additional cyber incidents occurring in the period before closing. Prior to the transaction close, careful consideration should be given to prevent the sharing of competitive information and asserting influence on the target, also known as "gun-jumping", to avoid violating antitrust laws.

Over the first six months post-integration, boards should pay particular attention to integration projects slipping to the right due to lack of funding, which is often a result of overly optimistic cost estimates. Such underestimation is common when estimates are created from incomplete knowledge inherent in a closely-held due diligence process.

However, there must also be a day one integration plan to extend as much of the parent company's cyber protections as possible to the target company immediately. At a minimum, the plan should include the following:

- An exchange of threat information to include internet domains to be blocked.

- Employee awareness training emphasizing the risk of phishing attacks mimicking emails from the new parent company and other new risks. As companies combine their IT departments, hackers may use this time to impersonate administrators.

- A much deeper on-site assessment to further refine risks and integration costs.

- Re-engagement with the open-source research vendors recommended during due diligence to identify spikes in indicators of cyber risk—a sudden increase in hygiene-related traffic after an announcement could be an indirect measure of other malicious activity.

- Ideally, routing the target company's email through the parent company's email screening process if that capability exists.

During this phase, it is also important to perform an operation-focused gap analysis to determine if one company has certain cyber capabilities or processes that the other does not have or that the combined organization could benefit from long term. If this is the case, the transaction is an ideal time for business changes or transformational activities to add value to the combined organization. While this phase will take time and has a cost to execute, it will highlight the differences and raise questions on what the best long-term approach will be.

Acquirors should consider the benefits of leveraging cloud services to integrate the combined companies' applications and data faster. This can result in faster realization of synergies, less reliance upon third party services and potentially a reduction in overall risk through hosting your own data applications.

Boards should also note the special case where only a portion of a company is being acquired. In this case, the target's parent company will certainly be less willing to accept what they see as intrusive assessments, either pre- or post-closing. Furthermore, the need to decouple the target from the parent company's infrastructure could delay the target's integration into the acquirer's security infrastructure by a year or more. Together, these two factors mean that the acquiring company's ability to detect and mitigate cyber risk is greatly reduced.

## Conclusion

Cybersecurity diligence during M and A calls for a two-pronged approach. Companies must conduct rigorous due diligence on the target company's cyber risks and assess their related business impact throughout the deal cycle to protect the transaction's return on investment and the entity's value post-transaction. In addition, all parties involved in the deal process need to be aware of the increased potential for a cyberattack during the transaction process itself, and should vigilantly maintain their cybersecurity efforts. Applying this two-pronged approach during M and A will serve to ultimately protect stakeholder value.

To continue learning about the concepts in this chapter the following sources are recommended:

1 FRSecure. Mergers and Acquisitions Cybersecurity Checklist. frsecure. com/mergers-and-acquisitions-cybersecurity-checklist
2 S Davis and M Polunic. The Critical Role of Cybersecurity in M&A: Part 1, Due Diligence [blog] Crowdstrike, October 20, 2020. www. crowdstrike.com/blog/role-of-cybersecurity-in-mergers-and-acquisitions-part-1

**3** S Davis and M Polunic. The Critical Role of Cybersecurity in M&A: Part 2, Pre-Close [blog] Crowdstrike, November 4, 2020. www.crowdstrike.com/blog/the-critical-role-of-cybersecurity-in-ma-part-2-pre-close

**4** S Davis and M Polunic. The Critical Role of Cybersecurity in M&A: Part 3, Post-Close [blog] Crowdstrike, November 12, 2020. www.crowdstrike.com/blog/role-of-cybersecurity-in-mergers-and-acquisitions-part-3

## Endnotes

**1** R Gurzeev. It's Time to Better Identify the Cost of Cybersecurity Risks in M&A Deals [blog] TechCrunch, September 10, 2020. techcrunch.com/2020/09/10/its-time-to-better-identify-the-cost-of-cybersecurity-risks-in-ma-deals/ (archived at https://perma.cc/2XXA-VMG7)

**2** Gartner Press Release. Gartner Says the Average Time to Close an M&A Deal Has Risen More Than 30 Percent in the Last Decade [blog] Gartner, October 15, 2019. www.gartner.com/en/newsroom/press-releases/2018-10-15-gartner-says-the-average-time-to-close-an-manda-deal-has-risen- more-than-30-percent-in-the-last-decade (archived at https://perma.cc/6ELD-V9K6)

**3** Forescout Technologies. The Role of Cybersecurity in Mergers and Acquisitions Diligence, June 2019. www.forescout.com/company/resources/cybersecurity-in-merger-and-acquisition-report/ (archived at https://perma.cc/S5GA-EXZB)

**4** J Meyrick, J Gomes, N Coleman, and S Getty. Assessing Cyber Risk in M&A: Unearth Hidden Cost Before You Pay Them, September 2020. www.ibm.com/downloads/cas/RJX5MXJD (archived at https://perma.cc/C8LN-7SPP)

**5** Forescout Technologies. The Role of Cybersecurity in Mergers and Acquisitions Diligence, June 2019. www.forescout.com/company/resources/cybersecurity-in-merger-and-acquisition-report/ (archived at https://perma.cc/S5GA-EXZB)

**6** West Monroe. Cybersecurity Due Diligence in M&A, July 2016. www.westmonroe.com/perspectives/signature-research/cybersecurity-due-diligence-in-manda (archived at https://perma.cc/JZB3-RH8H)

**7** H Taylor. The Role of Cybersecurity in M&A [blog] Journal of Cyber Policy, July 29, 2019. journalofcyberpolicy.com/2019/07/29/role-cybersecurity-ma/ (archived at https://perma.cc/7CZT-Q7LZ)

# 12

# Developing Relationships with the Cybersecurity Team

BY JR WILLIAMSON, CHIEF INFORMATION SECURITY OFFICER,
LEIDOS, AND BEN PEIFER, ISA RESEARCH ASSOCIATE

## Five Key Ideas to Take Away from This Chapter

1 Relationships are essential for all successful organizations and tend to flourish within a healthy culture where personnel wellness, morale, inclusion, and mutual respect exists. This is particularly true for the cybersecurity team.

2 There is no one right way to build relationships and culture; different organizations and different business processes require different strategies and assessment depending on inputs like size, industry, and value.

3 Organizations are in the cybersecurity fight together and should be establishing relationships with each other to generate cohesiveness and build a collective consciousness of new and emerging threats.

4 A cybersecurity professional with empathy and emotional intelligence will be far more effective at building the necessary relationships inside and outside their organization then one without.

5 The Chief Information Security Officer (CISO) of an organization should have clear and consistent communication with the board in order to convey the health and maturity of the cybersecurity team in addition to operational performance and risk management.

# Introduction

Previous chapters have analyzed cybersecurity in organizations through the lenses of departments such as human resources, general counsel, and operations. They've also analyzed the best structure for organizations in the digital world, the economic cost, the role of the board, and more. Here we will look at the relationships in the cybersecurity team, including the CISO's governance and trusted advisor role in relationship to other senior functional executives; how cybersecurity teams communicate both inside the company; with other departments; and outside the company with customers, partners, suppliers, and industry competitors; and finally, how organizations can assess performance relating to cybersecurity to ensure strong partnerships and shared outcomes. Relationships with the cybersecurity team goes hand-in-hand with establishing a strong culture of cybersecurity throughout the company. We cannot presume that just because we do some annual training of our employees and contractors on our networks, that we have instilled a culture of safety from a cyber perspective. It requires a focused and continuous effort to constantly evaluate an individual's performance and behavior as it relates to making the right decisions when faced with cybersecurity-related threats. According to Gallup, drivers for a high performance culture in an organization includes traits such as leadership that communicates effectively, values and rituals that fit with both their employees and their customers, instinctive work structures, human capital that focus on individual growth, and caring about cultivating strong performance.[1] High performing organizations demonstrate competency in many critical functional areas including program management, financial management, engineering, service/capability delivery, and cybersecurity.

We also cannot assume that high performing organizations only do it one way, or that the measure of a mature cybersecurity program occurs by simply counting all the tools that they have deployed, or how many people that they have on their team. Maturing cybersecurity programs focus not only defensive technology, alerting, and incident response, they also focus on improving processes that help to incorporate standard cybersecurity practices throughout all of the critical business workflows and activities. Augmenting the DNA of those workflows helps with educating the functional consumers of those workflows about cybersecurity risks, but it also serves to force the functional teams to work together with the cybersecurity team to establish the security controls for the business processes that are appropriate for the company's cybersecurity risk tolerance. Not all business processes pose the same risk profile and therefore each should be evaluated to determine how much rigor (as expressed by the controls placed on those activities) is required based on the risks identified in the risk assessment process discussed in Chapter 4. Placing too much rigor onto a low-risk business process will likely create too much friction with the consumers, cost more than needed, take too long to achieve, and potentially stifle innovation. Similarly, not placing enough rigor on a high-risk business process will likely lead to low quality of execution, loss of sensitive data, and/or compromise of critical systems thereby negatively disrupting the business process and potentially leading to company brand erosion and reputational harm. As such, each process should be reviewed with the business functional owners *and* the cybersecurity team to determine, document, and measure the appropriate controls for that business process. Higher risk should lead to higher rigor, but lower risk should lead to lower rigor. The concept of a sliding scale of the elasticity of rigor based on risk is sometimes referred to as "risktascity". Risktascity is both a risk management principle and a strategy by which the CISO and the cybersecurity risk management team builds relationships with and partners with the functional leaders in the company to arrive at an agreed-upon level of measurable safety of their business processes and strives to consistently apply information security risk management and governance across the company.

## A Healthy Culture

CISOs and their security teams occupy one of the most high-stress positions in an organization. In many companies, the threat never really stops so there is an expectation of being available 24-7. Too often, these cybersecurity teams do not receive adequate internal support and are blamed when there are system failures or performance issues that they did not cause. Low morale not only leads to high turnover, frequently it also leads to lower efficiency and increased risk. Increasing qualified personnel can begin to address this issue. According to PwC:

> More than half (51%) of executives in our Global DTI 2021 survey say they plan to add full-time cybersecurity personnel over the next year. More than one-fifth (22%) will increase their staffing by 5% or more.[2]

The personal wellness of the security team should also be top of mind. Adequate staffing, consistent schedules, training and development, time away from the mission, and performance recognition all contribute significantly to maintaining their wellbeing.

Cybersecurity team members being respected by their peers and their customers also goes a long way to creating a healthy work environment where cybersecurity personnel feel comfortable bringing their "whole selves" to work and engaging fully in achieving the mission. A key challenge with many in this field relates to the fatigue that comes from the perception that they are constantly battling with the other functional teams or employees of the company related to cybersecurity policies and procedures. The age-old tension between doing something safely and doing it fast and easy is extremely high among cybersecurity teams as they see safety as a critical success element of their roles. A company culture that considers cybersecurity as the lowest factor to consider for a business decision will likely lead to a disillusioned team and a low morale/high turnover outcome that will erode effectiveness and stall any aspirational growth in maturity.

## Empathy: Understanding Others' Feelings is Part of Cybersecurity

Working with others in an organization can always be stressful. Technology can compound tensions especially if the technology does not function as anticipated or becomes part of a potentially serious security incident. In such circumstances individuals can feel defensive, be reluctant to communicate, and can even become aggressive. Empathy means attempting to feel as another feels—not just to think as they think or "should" think. Creating a functional culture of security involves more than simple technical training. Encouraging empathy in cybersecurity can be a crucial element in creating a positive culture. Alex Stamos, former CSO of Facebook and professor at Stanford University Center for International Security and Cooperation, discussed the concept in his speech at the 2017 Black Hat Security Conference saying, "We have a real inability to put ourselves in the shoes of the people we are trying to protect".[3] Security staff would do well to try to put themselves in the place of others in the organization who may not be as tech-savvy as they are, just as non-security staff can be trained to understand that technical breakdowns are rarely the fault of the security staff. Such sensitivity can enhance communication and facilitate problem solving especially in times of high stress or crisis.

The volume, veracity, and the continuously changing threat levels adds significant stress to cybersecurity teams—a sort of battle fatigue in defending the company where just one mistake can lead to a disastrous incident and harm the company's reputation and/or put it into a contract performance dispute. Even well-funded cybersecurity programs have difficultly hiring qualified personnel to join their teams. According to *Cyber Crime Magazine,* "There will be 3.5 million unfilled cybersecurity jobs globally by 2021, up from one million positions in 2014".[4] Not an easy gap to fill in a demanding high-turnover field, but the solution should not be to sacrifice current employees' personal wellness. All companies are advised to commit to a cybersecurity workforce strategy that focuses on wellbeing, talent retention, development, and acquisition that will balance out the natural challenges of the role with a culture of commitment to career satisfaction and growth.

## The CISO's Role

Conversations about relationships in cybersecurity should include the CISO. Tasked with leading an organization's information security program they will set the tone of the conversation and play a pivotal role in establishing an effective culture of cybersecurity. The CISO's role is not to prevent every cyberattack an organization sustains—such an expectation is impossible and applying that level of pressure to the CISO and their team would likely create the low morale and the unhealthy cybersecurity culture previously discussed—but rather their role is to establish the appropriate level of governance and operational policies and procedures that are essential to enabling the company's performance objectives while ensuring that the company's brand and reputation are not negatively impaired. Companies establish the upper and lower control limits by determining what they perceive to be "acceptable risk tolerance" for their customers, shareholders, and employees in the markets that they serve. In some markets, that risk tolerance may be significantly affected by regulatory compliance requirements (such as the health care, defense, and critical infrastructure providers) where others perhaps to a lesser degree. Company chief executives and board members should be able to describe to the CISO what that risk tolerance is for their company and provide a clear understanding of the CISO's role in influencing business planning and critical decisions that teeter on the edge of effective cybersecurity risk management.

To effectively manage cybersecurity risk, the CISO should have a level of consistent access to the rest of the C-suite and the board. Whether that access is direct or indirect through an intermediary that the CISO reports to such as the CIO, CTO, or COO the CISO's cybersecurity risk management voice needs to be heard by the CEO and CFO. Cybersecurity is a constantly evolving field with dramatic changes taking place nearly every day. The board needs to not only have access to a subject matter expert in the cybersecurity space, but consistently utilizing the CISO's experience and expertise is critical to effective risk management and governance.

Unfortunately, this is not the case in many organizations today. According to a study by Deloitte in which they surveyed 500 C-level executives of companies with at least $500 million in annual revenue, "only 4% of respondents say cybersecurity is on the [board's] agenda once a month".[5] Additionally, Deloitte highlights another significant discrepancy in their survey that further demonstrates a problem with current relationships between boards and their CISOs. A large majority of CISOs, 77%, reported cyber being on the board's agenda quarterly, whereas other executive management personnel reported it to be much lower. Deloitte's hypothesis is that "this data supports the fact that the CISO may not actually have line of sight to executive management and the board, whereas most of the other functional executive roles do".[6] Boards cannot expect to expand their understanding of the rapidly developing cyber landscape at a rate of less than quarterly engagements. Some forward-leaning boards have developed a subcommittee of the full board that focuses on cybersecurity; sometimes in combination with other risk management topics, and sometimes as part of a technology and product delivery focus (incorporating the concept of embedded cybersecurity into the product portfolio).

The relationship between the board and the CISO should be persistent and ongoing, and built on both informal and formal engagements to build trust. The communication should not be just reactionary, such as in crisis management, but also preventative as well (such as preparing for high-business impacts such as a ransomware and critical data loss or destruction use cases). Historically, awareness of cyber threats may have only come into the boardroom in times of crisis, after the incident has occurred and the risk has been realized, which typically puts the CISO into the crosshairs of the litany of "how did *you* let this happen"—questions that can erode trust. This type of relationship is neither efficient nor effective and should be altered in favor of a partnership between the board and the CISO that encourages cyber threats and opportunities to be proactively evaluated in the context of traditional business risk management on a recurring basis. The NACD/ISA cyber risk handbook, *Cyber Risk Oversight 2020* provides a series of questions the board can incorporate into their communications with cybersecurity staff such as:[7]

- Do we thoroughly understand the most significant cyber threats to this business and what impacts they could have on the company's strategy and ultimately on its long-term growth?
- Can all directors effectively contribute to a robust conversation with management about the current state of the company's cybersecurity?
- In which areas does our lack of knowledge/understanding of cyber-matters prevent effective oversight?
- Are we able to effectively interpret/assess management's presentations and their answers to our questions?
- Is the organization adequately monitoring current and potential cybersecurity-related legislation and regulation?

One of the end goals of asking these sorts of question at the board level is that cybersecurity should be seen as an enterprise-wide strategy and risk-management issue that should be addressed holistically and proactively.

## Relationships with the Cybersecurity Team

The CISO is accountable but is not solely responsible for cybersecurity in an organization. This text has demonstrated that in high-performing enterprises all members of an organization—regardless of their department—are responsible for cybersecurity; but the CISO should have a team dedicated to cybersecurity to operate effectively and rapidly in the organization.

The typical makeup of a cybersecurity team was already discussed in Chapter 3, therefore it is the intent of this chapter to describe the essential relationships that the cybersecurity team must build and sustain to be effective. As was also discussed in Chapter 3, the siloed organizational structure is not conducive to the digital age. While there are a variety of potential structures available, a common trait among them is the encouragement of interdepartmental communication. Unfortunately, IT departments—which currently and not correctly often include cybersecurity responsibilities—have not been generally known for their exemplary communication skills.

Just as the relationship the CISO has with the board should extend beyond crisis situations, so too should the relationships between functional groups like sales, HR, and audit, as well as other groups also not be confined to crises. Teams should also be partnering on present and future potential risks and opportunities that could negatively or positively affect the corporate objectives. These relationships must be built and sustained with all of the functional and lines of business executive leaders. The old adage that you cannot build a relationship when you need it has never been truer than with the dynamic and constantly shifting threats in the cybersecurity world.

The board should also be spending time with the cybersecurity team outside the boardroom. This is an excellent opportunity to become more familiar with the operational capabilities as well as personally assess the maturity and health of the cybersecurity team. Board members should arrange to visit the cybersecurity team and receive briefings and demonstrations firsthand from personnel situated at the front lines. These meetings will provide valuable insights and learning opportunities for board members far beyond what they could obtain from highly scripted presentations from just the CISO and/or CIO. These engagements should be situational and oriented to agreed-upon critical risk scenarios and use cases so that confidence in the team's ability to manage through those scenarios can be achieved. Additionally, the board's engagement with the cybersecurity teams will likely increase its visibility, raise morale, and reinforce their role in defending the enterprise and will further contribute towards creating that healthy culture among the cybersecurity team discussed earlier in the chapter.

## Relationships Inside the Organization

This text has highlighted several different departments' roles in cybersecurity and how they can increase their effectiveness. Be it internal audit, human resources, legal, or supply chain, all departments have important roles to play in maintaining an enterprise-wide effective cybersecurity defensive and risk-managed posture. The CISO and the information security team, however, should not only be fulfilling their obligation to stay informed and up to date on emerging cyberthreats and defense, but should also be coordinating and collaborating with these other departments so that they apply context to these threats to their functional business processes without having to spend valuable time researching the threats or trying to become cybersecurity experts themselves.

In 2018 the city of Atlanta fell victim to a severe ransomware attack that left their municipality crippled with their services being held in an online hostage situation. The cost of the attack was significant. The city anticipated spending $17 million to recover. Critical services such as court schedules, police dashcam footage, and legal files were destroyed or locked away for days to months. Atlanta was aware of their vulnerabilities as an audit conducted several months prior to the attack had pointed out a complacent culture and extensive vulnerabilities. Unfortunately, without the necessary prioritization and strong internal relationships, the required action to remedy these issues was not taken and attackers were able to successfully exploit the known vulnerabilities.

The CISO and their team should be able to articulate their cybersecurity strategy and how they are implementing it on behalf of the known business risks clearly and effectively to the CEO, the CIO—and all other senior executive management—as well as to more operational level roles throughout the company. In an interview conducted by Security InfoWatch, Kevin Walker (former CISO for Walmart.com) says he also puts some of the onus on his colleagues in the information security space, many of whom are still "pounding desks" and pushing for "strong passwords" rather than creating outreach programs and teaching others within the organization about what's really needed, which would go a lot further in solving the problem. He also advises security executives to set goals that are appropriate for their respective organizations, adjust them as needed on an ongoing basis and to be an advocate for security, not just a "traffic cop".[8]

As Mr. Walker correctly highlights, "pounding desks" is not an effective method of developing strong relationships in cyber operations. Strong passwords play an important role in cybersecurity and should be kept in mind, however, they are not the be-all of an effective cybersecurity program. Programs where the CISO and information security team can enhance the cybersecurity maturity and culture of an organization and develop the necessary horizontal relationships are far more valuable. Cybersecurity subject matter experts who rely only on being right or correct are often marginalized in the eyes of the business who sees them as security zealots that are not interested in helping the business be successful by managing risk, but rather always arguing to try to eliminate risk. A successful cybersecurity team understands that it is not enough to be right, you must also be appropriate and demonstrate empathy with those that you serve and support. You must educate the customer so that they can understand the *why* and be able to answer the question of "so what?". Knowing what you are talking about is a good start but requires more than just understanding the technical risk elements, you must also learn how to apply context of the risk to the business process, and then partner as Mr. Walker advises with the business to develop countermeasures to those risks that are aligned to the needs of the expected business outcomes, the company's risk tolerance, and the principles of risktascity.

The top of the organization can set the tone for internal relationships throughout itself. As CompTIA summarizes in their white paper *Building a Culture of Cybersecurity*:

> Senior leaders are uniquely situated to lead the kind of coordinated response that cybersecurity requires. Because they sit at the top of the organization, they can see across departments, which gives them a more comprehensive view than business unit managers have. They are also bestowed with the authority to ensure that groups work together—even those that do not always see eye-to-eye or share the same objectives.[9]

Setting that tone from the top is not about being dictatorial or an authoritarian bully. Even a benevolent dictator who is admired for their subject matter expertise and competency can fail to establish trust with their functional peers in the organization. Those behaviors are more likely to create more of a culture based on fear rather than one of mutual respect that leads to inclusion and active engagement to solve particularly challenging business issues. Executive leadership is an excellent starting point for the internal relationships needed and as discussed in the CISO's role above, there are clear improvements in communication that can be made. Executive leadership is not end of the line. All levels and members of an organization play a key role in cybersecurity and a culture that excludes departments—or levels—because they may not have a traditional role in cybersecurity will not be as successful. A mature cybersecurity program will have at its core an educational function that seeks to continuously improve the cybersecurity team, but also strives to continuously improve the understanding of the other employees of the company so that they can effectively practice strong cybersecurity practices in their daily routines and activities.

The importance of these internal relationships will only grow as the digital landscape expands and technology becomes more and more ingrained into organizations at all levels. An emerging technology that highlights this development and the importance of strong internal relationships is Artificial

Intelligence (AI). AI has become increasingly used in organizations for a variety of functions across fields such as banking, medical, automotive, and defense. Its implementation demonstrates the need for companywide communication and integration to ensure effective and safe use. As McKinsey points out in their discussion on risk management of AI: "Making real progress demands a multidisciplinary approach involving leaders in the C-suite and across the company; experts in areas ranging from legal and risk to IT, security, and analytics; and managers who can ensure vigilance at the front lines".[10] Cyber operations and technology are only going to increase as tools like AI are developed and integrated in organizations. Developing the necessary internal relationships between departments like Legal and IT should be prioritized not just at the top of the organization but down through and across the management levels as well to ensure safe, effective, and profitable use of new tools and processes.

## Relationships Outside the Organization

Relationships in cybersecurity teams should not just be developed and sustained internally. Currently, smaller organizations are often using part-time external employees to fill their staffing gaps, "The majority of CISOs (81%) and CIOs (56%) indicated that full-time employees made up less than 20% of their cyber teams".[11] As such, the security team itself will need to extend its own culture of security to assure it matches that of the contractors who are assisting in the overall cybersecurity effort. Consistency of approach for the entire team—full and part-time—is necessary to have a coherent approach to security.

In addition, there are new cyber threats developing everyday across the world and organizations are struggling to keep up. The famous quote "It takes a village to raise a child" is an African proverb that means that an entire community of people need to come together with like-minded purpose to give its children the safe and supporting environment they need to thrive. Similarly, it takes an entire village (or industry) to come together to defend against a common enemy that would otherwise attack each family (or company) individually and succeed. By working together across industries and communicating effective strategies, these threats can be more appropriately mitigated, and all of the companies will thrive instead of just the ones that spend the most money or focus the most on technology. Just as departments inside an organization need to break down the walls of their silos and communicate with other departments, organizations as a whole should be doing the same with other organizations. The CISO and the information security team should be participating in cybersecurity information-sharing initiatives to stay up do date on the latest strategies and lessons-learned by those who may be ahead of them on their maturity growth curve. Additionally, relationships with law enforcement agencies such as the FBI, DHS, INTERPOL, the US Secret Service, the Department of Defense, NSA, and with regulatory agencies' divisions will be hugely beneficial. Building a strong relationship with critical members of your supply chain will also help with situational awareness and supply chain risk management.

## Assess Performance

Cultures and relationships should be evaluated to determine effectiveness. Establishing milestones and performance measures allows for indications of effectiveness. Using frameworks from the National Institute of Standards and Technology (NIST), and the International Organization for Standardization (ISO) will help assess cybersecurity hygiene from an organization-wide perspective but are not the final step or sole assessment measure that should be taken. ESI points out in their study that:

> While NIST provides a solid foundation for cybersecurity planning, communication, and regulatory compliance, it is not enough to ensure the effectiveness of companies' cybersecurity programs. Rather than applying the NIST framework as a box-ticking exercise, the most cyber-mature companies adapt this and other frameworks to their business goals, strategies, and individual risk profiles. Cybersecurity leaders also combine analysis from advanced quantitative tools and input from internal business partners and third-party experts to make the best decisions.[12]

Check-the-box evaluations of an organization's cybersecurity will not provide an adequate assessment of the cybersecurity posture. Frameworks may help but they should not be the stopping point of assessment. As in budgeting and meetings, there should be a continual evaluation to allow for flexibility. Don't fall into the false conclusion that achieving all of the compliance checklists means that you have an effective and maturing cyber-security program. Being compliant doesn't mean you are safe or that you are capable of defending against a new attack vector or in handling an unex-pected and significant incident response activity. It simply means that you have implemented all of the compliance requirements at a point in time when they were assessed. Compliance doesn't equal security and does nothing to describe a cybersecurity team's effectiveness, potential to rapidly adapt to change, or wellbeing.

Assessing an organization's cybersecurity team's performance should not be limited only to the team itself but should also extend to members of the rest of the company as cybersecurity is an enterprise-wide risk and business issue. CompTIA suggests that one simple method of assessing the cybersecurity awareness and readiness of an organization that has truly implemented a strong cybersecurity culture would be a phishing test:

> Regular "phishing tests" are relatively inexpensive but can substantially increase security awareness. In these simulations, individual employees receive e-mails that prompt them to engage in risky behaviors, like clicking an unverified link. Individuals who are tricked by these fake e-mails are then informed that this was not a real attack and are taught how to avoid similar traps in the future. Often, very inexpensive tests like these can significantly decrease the likelihood of a very costly attack.[13]

A key point to highlight in that recommendation from CompTIA is that the recommendation is not to terminate employees who "fail" a phishing test. These are training exercises that are designed to improve your ability to detect a phish and prevent a user from clicking a malicious link. They are not meant to be punitive. A very experienced cybersecurity professional can fall prey to a well-crafted phish. Train the employee or employees about what they missed and the danger it represents to the organization to improve their individual confidence and performance and promote that healthy culture of cybersecurity.

Similarly, running tabletop exercises as discussed in Chapter 10, for significant threats such as ransomware attacks, destructive malware, protection of crown jewels, supply chain integrity, insider threat, and use of privileged accounts can be extremely effective in improving process maturity, communications, and common understanding that can lead to operational resiliency.

In the NACD/ISA Cybersecurity Handbook, Principle Five focuses on cybersecurity measurement and reporting. The approaches highlighted in the handbook seek to establish both a baseline for cybersecurity performance for an organization as well as expressing those factors an organization should consider in determining what makes the most sense for that organization based on their risk tolerance.[14] Measuring cybersecurity performance in relation to company strategic outcomes has been a best practice for a number of years and is increasingly occurring in more mature companies; however, measuring the culture of cybersecurity in even those higher maturing companies is still quite nascent. Tool F in the handbook provides board-level cybersecurity metric examples broken into four categories of strategic metrics, operational metrics, economic metrics, and business program/project metrics.[15]

Similar to the CompTIA article referenced above regarding the steps of building a culture of cybersecurity, Uniting Digital published a complementary article on their five steps for establishing a culture of cybersecurity.[16] But how do you know when you've achieved it and are reaping the benefits of a strong cybersecurity culture? Just like the recommended metrics listed previously from the NACD/ISA Cybersecurity Handbook for performance, it is important to not just aspire to improve a culture, but to actually construct change-oriented initiatives and then meaningful measures to determine if you are making progress towards achieving those expected outcomes. Some ongoing work via a partnership among ISA, NACD, and the WEF has proven fruitful in this regard and they have produced a list of proposed measures focusing on analyzing training effectiveness, risk management adoption in the lines of business, security-related incidents, employee sentiment analysis, and the contribution of enterprise risk management initiatives on critical performance-based business outcomes. These measures can be instrumented and shared with the company's senior executives as well as the board to demonstrate both the commitment and the progress the company is making towards establishing a culture of cybersecurity.

## Conclusion

In this chapter, we've described how information security teams need to work with their customers and stakeholders to establish a risk management framework based on the company's defined risk profile by implementing the strategic risk concepts of risktascity. Furthermore, we have discussed that although managing risk is a critical element of all cybersecurity programs, there are other factors which are equally essential to increasing maturity. The other factors include building and sustaining the right relationships, both inside and outside of the company; establishing a culture of cybersecurity—a mental model of safety for all members of the company, not just the information security team; focusing on performance measures that both demonstrate the contribution that the information security team has to achieving strategic business outcomes as well as ensuring that the information security team is invested in personal growth and wellbeing; and the role of the CISO in cementing the tone from the top related to customer intimacy, empathy, respect, engagement, inclusion, development, and continuous improvement. An information security team will be constrained in its effectiveness if it focuses only on securing the enterprise at the expense of important business outcomes and experiences. In this context, developing emotional intelligence and empathy in our cyber warriors will exponentially improve cohesion and continuity and significantly reduce derision, distrust, distain, and cultural declination.

To continue learning about the concepts in this chapter the following sources are recommended:

1   A Moneer. Developing Cybersecurity Culture to Influence Employee Behavior: A Practice Perspective, *Computers & Security* 2020, Vol. 98 (ISSN 0167-4048), doi.org/10.1016/j.cose.2020.102003

2   K Bissell, P D Cin and R M. Lasalle. Innovate For Cyber Resilience, 2020. www.accenture.com/_acnmedia/PDF-116/Accenture-Cybersecurity-Report-2020.pdf#zoom=40

3   ISACA/CMMI Institute. Narrowing the Culture Gap for Better Business Results, 2018. cmmiinstitute.com/getattachment/c335c66a-7000-48b4-b953-acbf395c5832/attachment.aspx

4   T Robinson. CISOs should be ready to confront the psychology of cybersecurity in 2021, December 16, 2020. www.scmagazine.com/home/security-news/insider-threats/cisos-should-be-ready-to-confront-the-psychology-of-cybersecurity-in-2021

5   Flashpoint. Interview with Runa Sandvik (podcast) August 7, 2018. www.flashpoint-intel.com/blog/podcasts/runa-sandvik-on-a-culture-of-security-at-the-new-york-times

## Endnotes

1   S M O'Keefe and V Ratanjee. Cultivate 5 Drivers for a High-Performance Culture [blog] Gallup, September 25, 2020. www.gallup.com/workplace/320960/cultivate-drivers-high-performance-culture.aspx (archived at https://perma.cc/5UQZ-5LYW)

2   PwC. Global Digital Trust Insights Survey 2022, 2021. www.pwc.com/us/en/
    services/consulting/cybersecurity/library/global-digital-trust-insights.html
    (archived at https://perma.cc/PSW2-26JB)

3   M Orcutt. Facebook Security Chief: Cybersecurity Pros Need More Empathy
    to Protect Us [blog] *MIT Technology Review,* July 26, 2017. www.
    technologyreview.com/2017/07/26/150319/facebook-security-chief-
    cybersecurity-pros-need-more-empathy-to-protect-us (archived at https://
    perma.cc/K8SA-43Y8)

4   Steve Morgan. Cybersecurity Talent Crunch to Create 3.5 Million Unfilled
    Jobs Globally by 2021, *Cybercrime Magazine,* November 9, 2021,
    cybersecurityventures.com/jobs (archived at https://perma.cc/A8WG-QJD8)

5   Deloitte. The Future of Cyber Survey 2019, 2019. www2.deloitte.com/za/en/
    pages/risk/articles/2019-future-of-cyber-survey.html# (archived at https://
    perma.cc/LMF4-47B8)

6   Deloitte. The Future of Cyber Survey 2019, 2019. www2.deloitte.com/za/en/
    pages/risk/articles/2019-future-of-cyber-survey.html# (archived at https://
    perma.cc/LMF4-47B8)

7   National Association of Corporate Directors and Internet Security Alliance.
    NACD Director's Handbook on Cyber-Risk Oversight 2020, February 25,
    2020. isalliance.org/isa-publications/cyber-risk-oversight-handbook/ (archived
    at https://perma.cc/NS7D-W6LF)

8   J Griffin. How to Build a More Effective Cybersecurity Culture [blog] *Security
    Info Watch* Feb 24, 2017. www.securityinfowatch.com/security-executives/
    article/12309174/how-to-build-a-more-effective-cybersecurity-culture.
    (archived at https://perma.cc/2KPD-TUZW)

9   CompTIA. Building a Culture of Cybersecurity, 2018. connect.comptia.org/
    content/whitepapers/building-a- culture-of-cybersecurity-a-guide-for-
    corporate-executives-and-board-members (archived at https://perma.cc/
    UK9T-9HS5)

10  B Cheatham, K Javanmardian and H Samandari. Confronting the Risks of
    Artificial Intelligence [blog] McKinsey, April 26, 2019. www.mckinsey.com/
    business-functions/mckinsey-analytics/our-insights/confronting-the-risks-of-
    artificial-intelligence (archived at https://perma.cc/5F73-HYVA)

11  Deloitte. The Future of Cyber Survey 2019, 2019. www2.deloitte.com/za/en/
    pages/risk/articles/2019-future-of-cyber-survey.html# (archived at https://
    perma.cc/LMF4-47B8)

12  ESIThougtlab. Driving Cybersecurity Performance, 2020. www.
    econsultsolutions.com/esi-thoughtlab/driving-cybersecurity-performance/
    (archived at https://perma.cc/6GVY-35KE)

13  CompTIA. Building a Culture of Cybersecurity, 2018. connect.comptia.org/
    content/whitepapers/building-a-culture-of-cybersecurity-a-guide-for-corporate-
    executives-and-board-members (archived at https://perma.cc/PUF2-FS6P)

**14**  National Association of Corporate Directors and Internet Security Alliance. NACD Director's Handbook on Cyber-Risk Oversight 2020, February 25, 2020. isalliance.org/isa-publications/cyber-risk-oversight-handbook/ (archived at https://perma.cc/NS7D-W6LF)

**15**  National Association of Corporate Directors and Internet Security Alliance. NACD Director's Handbook on Cyber-Risk Oversight 2020, February 25, 2020. isalliance.org/isa-publications/cyber-risk-oversight-handbook/ (archived at https://perma.cc/NS7D-W6LF)

**16**  A Wang. Time to Strengthen Your Cybersecurity Culture and How to Measure Its Effectiveness [blog] *Uniting Digital,* June 30, 2020. www.unitingdigital.com/articles/2020/6/30/time-to-strengthen-your-cybersecurity-culture-and-how-to-measure-its-effectiveness (archived at https://perma.cc/66VZ-3UV7)

# INDEX

Note: Page numbers in *italics* indicate figures

Advanced Persistent Threats (APT)  19–20
after-action review (AAR)  191
AICPA  132–33
AIG  34
American National Standards Institute
    (ANSI)  57
American's with Disability Act
    (ADA)  154–55
Anderson, R  15–16
application penetration testing program  169
Applied Cyber Economics for Cyber Risk  76
Applied Intelligence and Cybersecurity Risk
    Management  96
Argentina  5
Artificial Intelligence (AI)  86, 121, 208
    bias  134
    compliance and audit, role in  133–35,
        136
    enabled attacks  6–8
    integration into business processes  6, 7
    internal relationships  223–24
    risk management, role in  159, 174–75
    weaponization of  6–7
Association of India Communications and
    Multimedia and Infrastructure  35
Atlanta city ransomware attack (2018)  223
attackers
    APT-style attacks  19–20
    attackers-defenders economic balance  22
    cyberspace economic balance
        favors  17–18
    digital transformation and  51
    insider threat  87–89, 97–98, 99
    Know when you fail  182
    M and A phases, taking advantage
        during  211
    as nation-states  15
attorney-client privilege  118, 189–90, 196
auction process  204
audit and compliance. *See* cybersecurity
    audit and compliance
    considerations
auditing  89
    "check-the-box" approach  21–22, 70,
        71, 75, 80, 121, 226

IT general controls, focused on  131–32
auditors  128–30
    and board members  129
    external  131–33, 197, 198
Austin  149
automation  133–35, 136
    *see also* Artificial Intelligence (AI)

bias  131, 134
Big Data analytics  6
Black Hat Security Conference (2017)  218
blockchain  121, 134–35
Boards of Directors
    board thinking, evolution in  33–34
    cyber risk, understanding of  42–43
    cybersecurity ecosystem, role in  33, 40
    and cybersecurity team relationship  222
    pyramid structure integration  51, 52
    as responsible for cyber risk
        oversight  33, 36, 40, 44–45,
        46, 185
    risk tolerance  69, 72, 219, 224
    on technology disruption  7
    *see also* Incident Response Plan (IRP):
        questions
Boards of Directors: cybersecurity
        principles  32–47
    culture of security, creating  32,
        35–37, 41
    cyber risk quantification,
        understanding  39, 44–45
    cybersecurity as technical/IT problem,
        misunderstanding of  1, 2, 3–4,
        40–41, 52
    developing and validating  35–37
    five consensus principles  38–40
        principle I  40–41
        principle II  41–42, 123
        principle III  42–43
        principle IV  44
        principle V  44–46
    integrating cyber into ESG
        framework  36–37
    international principles process,
        developing  37–38

CPSIA information can be obtained
at www.ICGtesting.com
Printed in the USA
JSHW031727060322
23626JS00001B/1